Gothic death 1740–1914

Gothic death 1740–1914
A literary history

Andrew Smith

Manchester University Press

Copyright © Andrew Smith 2016

The right of Andrew Smith to be identified as the author of this work has been asserted by him in accordance with the Copyright, Designs and Patents Act 1988.

Published by Manchester University Press
Altrincham Street, Manchester M1 7JA
www.manchesteruniversitypress.co.uk

British Library Cataloguing-in-Publication Data
A catalogue record for this book is available from the British Library

Library of Congress Cataloging-in-Publication Data applied for

ISBN 978 0 7190 8841 4 hardback

First published 2016

ISBN 978 1 5261 3191 1 paperback

First published 2018

The publisher has no responsibility for the persistence or accuracy of URLs for any external or third-party internet websites referred to in this book, and does not guarantee that any content on such websites is, or will remain, accurate or appropriate.

Typeset by Out of House Publishing

For my parents
Anne Smith (née Jobson), 1919–86
Arthur Stanley Smith, 1920–2014

In memoriam

Contents

	Acknowledgements	*page* viii
	Introduction	1
1	Touched by the dead: eighteenth-century Gothic poetics	11
2	Mourning, memory and melancholy: constructing death in the 1790s–1820s	44
3	From writing to reading: Poe, Brontë and Eliot	75
4	Gothic death and Dickens: executions, graves and dreams	106
5	Loving the undead: Haggard, Stoker and Wilde	138
6	Decoding the dying: Machen and Stoker	164
	Conclusion	193
	Bibliography	197
	Index	207

Acknowledgements

I completed this book during a period of research leave from the University of Sheffield in the Spring term of 2015. I am deeply grateful for the support provided by colleagues on the School of English's Research Strategy Committee. I would also like to thank Mark Faulkner and Anna Barton who took on my administrative duties whilst I was on sabbatical. Thanks also go to my head of School, Susan Fitzmaurice, and the School's head of research, Cathy Shrank, for their support. The School of English at the University of Sheffield has provided a convivial and collegial environment in which to work, and I would like to acknowledge the encouragement provided by colleagues working across the eighteenth and nineteenth centuries, including Angela Wright, Madeleine Callaghan, Anna Barton, Amber Regis, John Miller, Hamish Mathison, Jane Hodson, Joe Bray and Helena Ifill. I would also like to thank Jerrold E. Hogle, Helena Ifill, Ben Fisher and Carol Margaret Davison who commented on parts of this project as it developed.

Various parts of this book have been delivered as keynote addresses at the Universities of Ghent (2012), Hull (2012) and Falmouth (2015) and as a conference paper at the American Literature Association conference in Washington, DC (2014). I also delivered research seminar papers on the project in 2012 at the universities of Sheffield, Bristol and Sheffield Hallam. I owe a debt of gratitude to the conference delegates, and attendees at the seminars, for their helpful and supportive comments.

Writing a book about death is not without its morbid moments and I would like to thank my wife, Joanne Benson, for her love and tolerance throughout the writing of this book. Joanne knows just how much this book took out of me.

A section of Chapter 2 draws upon an article, '*Frankenstein*'s Melancholy', which was published in *English Language Notes*, 48.1 (Spring/Summer 2010). I gratefully acknowledge permission from the Regents of the University of Colorado to reproduce that material.

Introduction

As I rapidly made the mesmeric passes, amid ejaculations of 'dead! dead!' absolutely *bursting* from the tongue and not from the lips of the sufferer, his whole frame at once – within the space of a single minute, or even less, shrunk – crumbled – absolutely *rotted* away beneath my hands. Upon the bed, before that whole company, there lay a nearly liquid mass of loathsome – of detestable putridity.[1]

Poe's conclusion to 'The Facts in the Case of M. Valdemar' (1845) captures the moment of Valdemar's physical dissolution once he has been released from the coma-like state in which he had been mesmerically suspended for seven months. The later mesmeric passes are intended to awaken him, but with the disastrous consequences recorded above. This image of the rotting corpse might seem to be quintessentially Gothic, but the horror is augmented by the seemingly alive Valdemar who is trapped within this corpse, which had led him to plead with the mesmeric narrator, '"quick! – quick! – put me to sleep – or, quick! – waken me! – quick! – *I say to you that I am dead!*"' (p. 359, italics in original). The mesmeric trance has left him neither asleep nor awake, as he becomes suspended between life and death. There is thus a tension between the repulsive physicality of the corpse and the liminal metaphysical space inhabited by Valdemar. This liminality indicates how death can be used to explore wider ideas than death per se. A clue to this is suggested in the seemingly minor change to the end of 'The Facts in the Case of M. Valdemar' published in 1850, and Poe's preferred version, which is quoted above.[2] The 1850 edition gives the final line as 'of detestable putrescence' rather than 'of detestable putridity', where the use of 'putrescence' can only refer to physical rotting, whereas 'putridity' also permits an interpretation of moral corruption. Poe's preferred nuanced ending thus directs the reader towards looking beyond the corpse to also consider the '*bursting* ... tongue' that speaks. The inner world of the subject is thus juxtaposed with the physicality of the corpse as Poe indicates that it is the humanity of Valdemar that we should also contemplate. The dead can thus be used as a device to explore ideas about life. The superficial revulsion to the corpse in this instance might seem to be Gothic, but in reality, as this book will explore, the dead often fail to signify in any crudely Gothic way. Poe's preferred ending also implies that the Gothic is the space where metaphysical ideas can be explored. It is a highly self-conscious Gothic tradition that is explored here and it is argued that this capacity for self-reflection indicates the presence of a radical strand within the Gothic that is centred on ideas about death, art, creativity and modes of interpretation.

The focus in this book is on how the dead and dying were represented in Gothic texts between 1740 and 1914 – between Graveyard poetry and the mass death occasioned by the First World War. The corpse might seem to have an obvious place in the Gothic imaginary, but, as we shall see, the corpse often refuses to function as a formal Gothic prop, and in order to understand why this occurs we need to explore what the corpse figuratively represented in the Gothic during the long nineteenth century. Representations of death, as in the example of Poe above, often provide a vehicle for other contemplations than just death.

A central aim of this study is to explore how images of death and dying were closely linked to models of creativity, which argues for a new way of looking at aesthetics during the period. It is noteworthy, for example, that Edward Young's *Night Thoughts* (1742–45) celebrates our capacity to imaginatively perceive our place within a divine cosmos, where death constitutes the positive point of entry into a spiritual world. Young also maps a Gothic world characterised by a disordered and frightened imagination that conjures false fears about death as the end. For Young, the contemplative spiritual turn enables us to feel our place in a wider world, and Young promoted this positive attribute of the imagination in 'Conjectures on Original Composition' (1759) when claiming that the true imagination copies from nature, whereas the second-rate imagination copies from literature. For Young, the imagination that discerns our eternal life within death is the same imagination which is inspired by a divinely ordained nature. This implicit yoking of death and creativity would be revised later in the century by critics such as William Duff and Nathan Drake, who suggested that true literary originality was to be found within the Gothic, with Drake in 'On Gothic Superstition' (1798) going so far as to locate the inspirational presence of spectres within the natural world (spectres dismissed by Young as the product of a debased imagination in *Night Thoughts*). Death and the creative imagination were given a new affiliation in *Frankenstein* (1818, revised 1831), where Frankenstein can be likened to the creative Romantic poet. Crucially, such Romantic texts reflect on the manufacturing of emotional states. Frankenstein's creature is a physical (anatomical) assembly and he is mentally constructed through a reading of texts (Milton, Volney, Goethe, Plutarch and Gibbon). This self-consciousness of the Romantic Gothic undermines Young's position on original, natural, composition.

How to write the Gothic becomes subsumed by the problem of how to write about death, and this is the central paradox of the Romantic Gothic mapped here. Drake would claim that the Gothic imagination (post-Young) has a privileged access to a world of spirits, which provides true inspiration. However, there is another cultural impulse at work that rhetorically conjures emotions around death and so effectively renders such feeling inauthentic. Poe develops this strain further in his 'The Philosophy of Composition' (1846) where he discusses the writing of 'The Raven' (1845), explaining how he manufactured its melancholy mood (in which the repetition in the rhyme scheme suggests that the narrator is trapped by a sense of loss). This emphasis on self-conscious literary production indicates how writing about grief forms an essential part of how death in the Gothic was represented. Poe's position can be compared with George Eliot's 'The Lifted Veil' (1859), where Latimer's account of the events leading up to his death dwells upon his poetic ambitions, even whilst the narrative is about how to tell the story of his death. This emphasis on narrative construction shifts the focus away from writers towards readers, a move that is clear from the adult Heathcliff's complaint in *Wuthering Heights* (1847) that he is trapped by signs of Cathy's death because he sees traces of her everywhere. Death in the long nineteenth century, however, does not constitute a coherent narrative and the variety of contexts in which it can be discussed will be addressed in a chapter on Dickens, which explores his views on capital punishment and his claim that the presence of a death wish pushes the vulnerable to seek the centre-stage adoration of the scaffold. The move from writer to reader in accounts of death to some degree pivots on Dickens, whose *The Mystery of Edwin Drood* (1870) represents a blend of Gothic and detective fiction that emphasises the importance of reading as a form of detection. This shift from writers to readers will also be addressed in the two final chapters on the *fin de siècle* Gothic, which explore how romantic love was used by Rider Haggard and Bram Stoker as a way of keeping the dead alive, even whilst 'love' often obscured a reading of the seemingly dead love object. The final chapter examines how an emphasis on scientific method in religious and quasi-scientific texts can be applied to *Dracula* (1897) and the writings of Arthur Machen. Such *fin de siècle* engagements with death appear in self-consciously constructed Gothic texts that turn death into a problem of knowledge.[3]

The Gothic tradition examined here is a largely canonical one as this illustrates how a popular Gothic discourse engaged with a model of death that would have been widely understood at the time. This also enables us to critically rethink that canon because the focus on death and dying produces a radically different way of reading this Gothic history.

That the corpse fails to signify as a coherent Gothic trope is bound up with the movement from sentimentality to science during the period. It is possible to overemphasise this, and whilst there is an argument to be made about the emergence of a secular culture, that is not the focus of this study. Indeed, we will see how *fin de siècle* texts repeatedly wrestle with the idea of faith and the afterlife, even when locating these terms within putatively scientific contexts. Such a focus has implications for how we relate the Freudian uncanny to the Gothic.

Freud's 'The Uncanny' (1919) addresses images of hauntology that centre on the dead and the authority they seem to exercise over us. Freud's conceptualisation of the double also appears to helpfully capture this idea of a fractured, but haunted, version of the self that is reflected in the Gothic discourse of the period discussed here.[4] However, because the corpse fails to signify as a clear Gothic trope, a Freudian approach also becomes problematised. It has been argued by Terry Castle that a Gothic uncanniness emerges during this period that anticipates Freud.[5] Diane Long Hoeveler, however, has noted that any such uncanniness is edged by an ambiguous secularity that never quite casts off vestigial religious ideas.[6] This present study is not about the uncanny, although it will entertain Freudian ideas where relevant (as in the discussion of love, for example). Whilst a discourse of the uncanny can be seen in the period, an important factor to note is that this uncanniness often seems to be devoid of any form of uncanny affect, as Freud would have understood it. Freud's account of uncanny obscurity, in which we struggle to account for feelings of unease, is belied by the uncanny's self-conscious rhetorical production in the Gothic of the long nineteenth century. Poe's 'The Philosophy of Composition' provides just one example of how a self-conscious manufacturing of a discourse of uncanniness seems to evacuate the uncanny of any genuine terrors. The roots of this are to be found in the earlier Romantic Gothic because its self-conscious artistic reflections provide an alternative model of key Gothic concepts, including the uncanny.

This book is also about how Gothic aesthetics challenge certain interpretative strategies that have typically been employed when critically reading the Gothic. This is not to deny the significance of psychoanalytical readings, but to emphasise that an historical consideration of how death is figured in the Gothic produces a narrative that is persistently resistant to such an approach – and that this resistance cannot be simply attributed to the adoption of an historicist reading. The corpse might be represented as a tragic figure, or as an object of knowledge, but it is one that either elicits empathy or invites forms of scientific understanding; it is not an object of terror and therefore fails to generate the type of damaging emotions that suggest the foreshadowing of a Freudian model of subjectivity. Even when this Gothic narrative historically coincides with Freud this resistance can still be observed. F. W. H. Myers's *Human Personality and Its Survival of Bodily Death* (1903, revised 1907), which is discussed in Chapter 6, makes reference to Freud's work on hysteria but asserts the presence of an integrative subconscious subliminal realm, rather than a Freudian fragmentary and trauma-ridden subconscious.[7] Myers's subject is not defined by trauma and any emotional upset is attributed to a purely temporary problem that the subliminal realm will correct. His theory emphasises the relationship between the self and creativity in which the imagination operates at a subliminal level that enables the subject to converse with other spirits as it is also the place where our inner ghost resides. This version of the subject appears in texts like *Dracula* and Machen's *The Three Impostors* (1895), which evidence an ambition to decode death that moves these texts beyond any conventional Freudian account and anticipates Myers's way of reading death. Importantly, it also means that Freud should not be seen as unproblematically generated out of this Gothic tradition, especially when the focus is on death.[8]

This study aims to complicate our understanding of the Gothic by focusing on how death is used to configure ideas about creativity, the imagination, aesthetics and forms of interpretation. The movement from writers to readers echoes the transition from a Romantic culture, which emphasised the importance of the imagination, to a Victorian culture shaped by quasi-scientific interpretations of the subject. This is not, however, a progressively unfolding historical narrative, because issues about the relationships between writers and readers can be found at most stages within this history, although ultimately we will witness a shift from seeing death as a source of inspiration to an epistemology of death that, at the end of the nineteenth century, largely centres on matters of methodology.

The first chapter explores transformations between the elegy and a poetic discourse of the elegiac in the mid eighteenth century. The notion that the dead elicit our sympathy can be found in Adam Smith and Edmund Burke, and this empathetic reaching out to death underpins the elegy of the time. By examining Edward Young's *Night Thoughts*, Robert Blair's 'The Grave' (1743), James Hervey's 'Meditations among the Tombs' (1745–47), Thomas Warton's *The Pleasures of Melancholy* (1747) and Thomas Gray's 'Elegy Written in a Country Church-Yard' (1751), we can see how a discourse about death, dying and mourning was established. Repeated tensions between natural spirituality and processes of memorialisation appear across these quite diverse texts. How to produce an aesthetic that captures feelings of loss appears at different levels of self-consciousness in these writings, which all outline often competing artistic positions that the elegiac poet might occupy. Young would develop these ideas further in his account of original composition, and a debate emerges (in the writings of Duff and Drake referred to earlier) about whether the Gothic represents an illegitimate model of 'fancy', which is different from 'nature', or whether the fantastic indicates, in a positive way, the breadth of the imagination because of its capacity to engage with the dead.

This link between creativity and death is developed further in Chapter 2, which explores the Romantic Gothic and the construction of a culture of mourning. Ann Radcliffe's poem 'To Melancholy' in *The Mysteries of Udolpho* (1794) begins with an evocation to a Muse of melancholy. This emphasis on the literary construction of melancholy provides a starting point for a reconsideration of the inter-textual aspects of Charlotte Smith's *Elegiac Sonnets* (1784), which suggest that mourning should be seen as a textual production. Memory, as a form of mourning, and its links to creativity was addressed by Samuel Rogers in *The Pleasures of Memory* (1792). For Rogers, death becomes positive, because in imaginatively overcoming our anxieties about death we gain moral strength. For him the imagination is able to reason and so he comes to see 'fancy' in a positive light, even whilst he regards the imagination as acting upon the subject in a subconscious way, one that works to unite us with others (including the dead) through a magnetic affinity that implicates Franz Mesmer's idea of animal magnetism. Mesmer appears as a character in James Boaden's *The Man of Two Lives* (1828), which explores ideas about reincarnation. Boaden's novel will be read as a riposte to *Frankenstein*. The bleakness of Shelley's novel is reflected in the coarse physicality of the creature and in the battle between him and Frankenstein in the dead zone of the polar ice cap. Boaden, however, wants to make death meaningful by suggesting that a contemplation of a past life enables us to reflect upon, and so rectify, the harm that we have done to others. The implicit doubling between Frankenstein and his creature is reworked by Boaden through reincarnation as the subject attempts to make amends for the conduct of an earlier self. Boaden's narrator is a would-be artist and the texts discussed here all centre on ideas about death and creativity. Feelings of mourning are aesthetically constructed in increasingly self-conscious ways in the Romantic Gothic that emphasise the role of the writer, or artist, as a creator, and this provides a way of looking at the significance of death and the imagination within the wider Romantic culture.

Ideas about mesmerism were reworked by Poe in 'Mesmeric Revelation' (1844), 'The Facts in the Case of M. Valdemar' and 'A Tale of the Ragged Mountains' (1844), which are explored in Chapter 3. The near-dead subject becomes an object for quasi-scientific investigation in Poe, which can be related to his theory of the cosmos outlined in *Eureka* (1848), where he claims that God is now absent from the world, but will return at the end of time to guarantee that the universe has meaning. God is described as an author who has plotted the structure of the universe and Poe claims that literary plots represent an inadequate Neoplatonic echo of this creative power. Poe also suggests that at the end, at the moment of death, meaning will be produced, and this is a theme developed in the tales about mesmerism, and in others that centre on death and resurrection such as 'Morella' (1835) and 'Ligeia' (1838). The idea that meaning will appear at the end is also a theme in Poe's detective tales, and the account of Poe will emphasise how the problems of decoding are linked to interpretations of death and dying. An emphasis on readers can also be witnessed in *Wuthering Heights* and 'The Lifted Veil', which also centre on issues of interpretation that are bound up with models of writing and reading. The dead in the mid nineteenth century become objects of analysis, and how death might speak to us is explored further in the following chapter on Dickens.

Chapter 4 begins with a discussion of Dickens's views on capital punishment that were informed by his concern that popular media coverage of executions created a death wish in the most susceptible, who would relish the lead role provided by the drama of the scaffold. For Dickens, the presence of this death wish constituted an uncomfortable metaphysical truth. Dickens was also concerned that media interest in capital offences granted the condemned an undeserved post-mortem existence. These ideas were first explored in *Oliver Twist* (1837), which argues that the criminal dead should be forgotten (such as Sikes and Fagin), whereas the loving dead (such as Agnes) should be remembered. Dickens's solution to illegitimate criminal resurrections was set out in letters sent to *The Times* in 1849 in which he advocated that executions should no longer be held in public, and argued that the media should not be permitted to publish stories about the condemned. That Dickens's views were informed by religious ideas about resurrection is also clear from the self-sacrificing Sydney Carton, who at the end of *A Tale of Two Cities* (1859) recites the Order of the Dead from St John's Gospel, quoting, "'I am the Resurrection and the Life, saith the Lord'".[9] The emotional disruption caused by the execution can be compared with how Dickens writes about graves as the site where the family reconvenes (is resurrected) after death, which introduces a cultural narrative about the significance of burial practices during the period. These images of death constitute a pattern in Dickens, which also includes references to writing, reading and dreaming. In his various accounts of dreams, for example, Dickens explores whether dreams might reveal hidden criminal propensities, or memories that we have seemingly forgotten, or indeed if they are the place where artistic inspiration is generated. These seemingly disparate contexts coalesce in *The Mystery of Edwin Drood*, which links dreams, death and reading in a complex way that invites reconsideration for why a self-incriminating conscience emerges in Dickens's later writings.

The shift from writers to readers implicates a number of strategies through which one might understand the dead, and the *fin de siècle* was a period in which various epistemic engagements with dying reveal how death was constituted as a problem of knowledge, interpretation and understanding. This was not confined to quasi-scientific investigations (as conducted by those exploring spiritualism, for example), but also drew upon discourses of empathy that had been available from the mid eighteenth century. Chapter 5 explores how love provided one way of knowing the dead in Rider Haggard's *She* (1887), *Ayesha: The Return of She* (1905), Stoker's *The Jewel of Seven Stars* (1903, revised 1912) and *The Lady of the Shroud* (1909). A dialogue across these novels centres on loving the femme fatale, where love provides an ambivalent, and often partial, way of comprehending 'Otherness'. Such engagements should be seen as part of an Orientalist discourse concerning attitudes towards Egypt at the time due to tomb excavations and continuing British political interest in the area because of the Suez Canal. Understanding the dead 'Other' through love effectively resurrects ancient Egypt, but in troubled terms that reflect the political and theological instabilities that pertained in assessments of both modern and ancient Egypt. These heterosexual, although repeatedly homosocial, models of love can be contrasted with Wilde's *The Picture of Dorian Gray* (1891), which conceals same-sex love by displacing discussion about desire onto art. This helps to establish Wilde's text as a counterpoint to the masculine adventure story of Haggard and Stoker. The novel also introduces a discussion about science that appears in Lord Henry's explicit interest in social experiments and in Dorian's engagement with theories of evolution. Dorian also discusses atoms when searching for an explanation for the physical transformation occasioned by his Faustian pact. Science does not displace love, but provides a way of looking at how human relations are governed by forms of knowing that echo those found in love. Wilde's discussion of the soul, art, love and death also helps to establish how these terms appeared in a strand of the *fin de siècle* Gothic that explored science, which is discussed in the final chapter.

In Chapter 6, images of the dead and the dying are explored in quasi-scientific contexts in Arthur Machen's *The Great God Pan* (1894), *The Three Impostors* (1895) and Stoker's *Dracula*. Subjecting the dead and dying to scientific scrutiny is echoed within narratives that also emphasise the importance of generating evidence. Within these multi-vocal texts there is a clear emphasis on how readers produce forms of interpretation that need to be reconstituted as narrative. How to decode the dead also relies upon particular methodologies that shape how evidence generates epistemic certainty.

This book seeks to advance an understanding of the Gothic in the long nineteenth century by exploring how death and dying complicate our view of the Gothic during this period. Death might seem a self-evidently morbid topic but, as this study shows, ideas about death created new ways of looking at life, art and the imagination. Death is not quite the end in these narratives, but merely the prelude to a creative way of thinking about life.

Notes

1 Edgar Allan Poe, 'The Facts in the Case of M. Valdemar', in *Edgar Allan Poe: Selected Writing*, ed. and Introd. David Galloway (Harmondsworth: Penguin, 1982), pp. 350–9, p. 359, italics in original. All subsequent references are to this edition and are given in the text.

2 Rufus Griswold edited this edition. The 1845 edition had 'putridity', but there were other reprints that retained 'putrescence', which Poe had seemingly editorially changed to 'putridity' in a proof of the 1845 text. I am grateful to Ben Fisher for correspondence on this matter.

3 An important study in this regard is Garrett Stewart's *Death Sentences: Styles of Dying in British Fiction* (London: Harvard University Press, 1984), which also

explores the relationship between death, creativity and reading in the period. My approach is different in degree due to the focus on the Gothic and the space that I give to Graveyard poetry. Unlike Stewart, my focus is also not on the specifics of death scenes, as I engage more widely with the contextual discourses of empathy, sympathy and science. I also explore a more complex vestigial religious discourse that runs throughout the period, which Stewart does not allow for. Stewart's methodology is shaped by New Critical and Deconstructive criticism that addresses the specificity of language use, whereas my approach is more historicist. Overall, I also give much more weight to the presence of death in the late eighteenth and early nineteenth century prose than Stewart, but in the main that is due to my consideration of broad conceptions of death rather than a specific focus on the deathbed scene.

4 Sigmund Freud, 'The Uncanny', in *Art and Literature: Jensen's 'Gradiva', Leonardo da Vinci and Other Works*, The Penguin Freud Library, vol. XIV, ed. Albert Dickson (Harmondsworth: Penguin, 1990), pp. 335–76.

5 Terry Castle, 'The Spectralization of the Other in *The Mysteries of Udolpho*', in *The Female Thermometer: Eighteenth-Century Culture and the Invention of the Unconscious* (Oxford: Oxford University Press, 1995), pp. 120–39.

6 Diane Long Hoeveler, *Gothic Riffs: Secularizing the Uncanny in the European Imaginary, 1780–1820* (Columbus: Ohio State University Press, 2010).

7 Frederic W. H. Myers, *Human Personality and Its Survival of Bodily Death* (London: Longmans, 1907).

8 In my *Gothic Radicalism: Literature, Philosophy and Psychoanalysis in the Nineteenth Century* (Basingstoke: Macmillan, 2000), I charted a trajectory from Burke to Freud that was reworked in the Gothic of the period. The focus there was on ideas of subjectivity rather than death and therefore identified a more coherent trajectory of implicit influence than that mapped here, although one that emphasised that the Gothic of the time critically reads this dominant tradition of Idealism.

9 Charles Dickens, *A Tale of Two Cities*, ed. George Woodcock (Harmondsworth: Penguin, 1989), p. 403.

1

Touched by the dead: eighteenth-century Gothic poetics

Between 1740 and 1750 there were dramatic developments in a new type of writing centred on mourning. This can be mapped as a change within the history of the elegy as it moved away from the specific (an individual's death) to the general (death more abstractly considered, or the death of a community). The elegy became progressively culturally supplanted (but not eradicated) by the elegiac. This development was in part supported by a discourse of sensibility as new forms of emotional understanding came to provide both a support for models of mourning and new ways of understanding grief. Sensibility, as we shall see, provided a focus for personal grief *and* produced an epistemology about dying. A key issue concerns the status and function of melancholy. How to write about melancholy became a pressing concern for those poets (such as the Graveyard poets) who attempted to evoke feelings of melancholy by metaphorically resurrecting the dead. However, the gap between feeling and aesthetic reconstruction threatened to link sensibility to the literary imagination, which challenged models of genuine feeling. How to write about the emotions during the period thus posed a problem for those working within the evolving form of the elegy.[1] These implicit debates concerning the relationship between feeling and writing constitute the moment when a discourse of the Gothic emerged. Feelings and their potential invalidation threatened to compromise ideas of 'humanity', and, as we shall see in the following chapter on Charlotte Smith, Ann Radcliffe and Mary Shelley, the Gothic subjects the 'human' to close critical scrutiny. The Gothic, as it emerges in the 1740s-1750s in Graveyard poetry, is generated out of this metaphysical uncertainty even whilst it formally models images of the dead that will become one of its iconographical features. The Gothic, in other words, was born out of anxieties about death, but in order to explain this it is helpful to outline critical discussion that supports a Gothic reading of the elegy.

The elegy: critical overviews

Peter M. Sacks in *The English Elegy: Studies in the Genre from Spenser to Yeats* (1985) provides an historical overview of the elegy from ancient Greece and explores its origins as an extension of pastoral, in which erotic myths centring on vegetation gods (as images of death and fecund renewal) shaped ideas about how to commemorate the dead. Sacks notes that at these ceremonies elegiac couplets were read, accompanied by flute music. For Sacks, this identifies a recurring feature of the elegy: the tension between feeling and words, as he notes that 'One of the least well observed elements of the genre is [the] enforced accommodation between the mourning self on the one hand and the very words of grief and fictions of consolation on the other'.[2] His analysis of mourning argues that the grief-stricken become psychologically healthy when a process of symbolic substitution takes place. Sacks notes in the story of Apollo and Daphne that Apollo's acceptance of his loss of Daphne is demonstrated by his taking up of a laurel wreath that symbolises that loss. This leads Sacks to conclude that 'It is this substitutive turn or act of troping that any mourner must perform' (p. 5). The necessity for this act of substitution is because, following Freud's 'Mourning and Melancholia' (1917), it indicates that the mourner is healthily working their way through grief by substituting the lost loved one with a transitional symbolic object that moves them beyond the initially devastating feelings of loss. The words of the elegy thus effect the same transition, so that 'The dead ... must be separated from the poet, partly by the veil of words' (p. 9). For Sacks, the elegy thus functions as a psychological stage in a process of mourning. These associations with healthy development may appear to be anti-Gothic as they suggest a positive reaction to trauma. The type of symbolism read by a Freudian such as Sacks should not, however, be regarded as an endorsement of a Gothic trajectory that will lead to Freud. As we shall see, literary texts from the mid eighteenth century and the late nineteenth century repeatedly assert that decoding the symbol generates a positive epistemic exposure – and although we will be looking at often competing forms of epistemology, there is throughout the period a shared emphasis on the presence of an occluded knowledge that can be read. These issues are notably acute in the Gothic, and Jerrold E. Hogle has written an account of the elegy that explores these Gothic tendencies.

Hogle notes a similarity between the elegy and the early Gothic because both pivot on moments of death, with early Gothic narratives (Hogle cites Walpole's *The Castle of Otranto* (1764) as an example) typically focusing upon 'a mystery linked to sudden ... deaths, often of relatives or ancestors whose mode of destruction or burial harbours hidden truths'.[3] Hogle also acknowledges an important difference: the elegy tries to lay, no matter how problematically, the past to rest, whereas the Gothic is more interested in resurrecting the past because its unresolved dramas have a continuing presence (which need to be engaged with before that past can 'die'). Nevertheless there are also, for Hogle, telling symbolic (and structural) points of connection between the elegy and the Gothic. Hogle notes that Richard Bentley's illustration to Thomas Gray's 'Elegy Written in a Country Church-Yard' (1751) makes visible a number of issues in the poem that are also to be found in later Gothic narratives from the eighteenth century. These include an 'emptying out of the vestiges of the past' and an attempt to fill the past 'with alternative meanings provided in the present' and a final process of reorienting this reworked model of the past so that it speaks to, and in some sense for, the present. Hogle examines how this process is elaborated within the Gothic by a close reading of the two Prefaces of Walpole's *Otranto*, the first of which claimed that the text was a sixteenth-century narrative by a Catholic priest (and so is a possible counter-Reformation story), whereas in the second edition (1765) Walpole acknowledged authorship and claimed that the novel was a blend of ancient and modern romance (and so is about the 'real' world, although one transposed to the past).

Hogle notes that *Otranto* might have (in the first edition) passed as Catholic and then worked as Protestant (as Manfred wrestles with his disposition against the forces of fate), but that much of the elegiac content of Graveyard poetry feels strangely secular as its resolutions (via feelings of melancholy) are more psychological than theological – a position that also feeds into the Gothic of the time. It is, however, also important to acknowledge that Graveyard poetry centres on Protestant readings of Catholic memorials, and this cultural translation provides the space in which a critical reading takes place. Hogle's identification of a symbolic link between the Gothic and the elegy echoes Sacks's view that symbolism supports a psychological 'truth' that, paradoxically, depends on the literary object. For Hogle, this links to ideas of the pastoral, the elegiac challenge to which (as pastoral becomes a graveyard in Gray) renders nature unnatural. He notes that 'death is best "naturalized" by schemes that highlight the fundamental artificiality in the image of death' (p. 575). Death thus functions as a multivalent sign in elegies because it represents the projection of present-day concerns – just as the Gothic disguises its historical engagements by locating them in the past. The danger is that such projections simply highlight the presence of a symbolic mode that 'call[s] out for new cultural content to fill this symbolic void' (p. 577). In the elegy, as in the Gothic, death dies and becomes replaced by alternative symbolic discourses concerning history, politics and ideas about social power (Hogle notes the class divisions captured in Bentley's illustration of Gray's poem). 'Death', however, also becomes a vehicle through which other forms of death (especially of cultures and memories about them) are shown as being in conflict with emerging modes of power – which is also captured in the tensions between the 'ancient' and 'modern' romance in *Otranto*'s second Preface, which emphasises the importance of placing the text within a discourse about writing. This leads Hogle to conclude that 'the drive' that links the elegy with the Gothic is the urge 'to project newer complexes of meaning, including modern struggles between waning and rising beliefs about many areas, back into the spaces once occupied by the dying schemes of older systems that still haunt us with their images of cultural, as well as individual death' (p. 581). This tension between the past and the present has been given a systematic investigation by Thomas Pfau, who relates the elegy to models of history.

Pfau discusses the elegy within the context of the 1790s and addresses how the form should be read through the new aesthetic models developed by Kant, Schiller, Hölderlin and Novalis. The 1790s represent a sea change in the elegy because the implicit discussion of symbolism within the form is now given explicit aesthetic treatment. He also argues that by the 1790s a new model of time emerges that is secular and linear, and this contrasts with earlier (classical) models of time which had suggested that time was cyclical (as we are reborn).[4] However, 'Unlike mythical time, modern temporality and history not only can never recur but can only ever be experienced as "passing" into the past or as the anxious projection of an uncertain future' (p. 550). For this reason modern 'death' has become secular and devoid of meaning and this very absence conjures into being theories of aesthetics that attempt to put back the forms of meaning (about human value, agency and the creative imagination) which have been lost. The chief irony is that elegies are themselves, as we saw in both Sacks's and Hogle's account of the form, fundamentally aesthetic engagements that imply acts of creativity (or perhaps reconstruction would be closer to Hogle's terms) which indicate both the presence of a void, because they are unreal, and an overcoming of that void, because for Sacks, *pace* Freud, the symbol represents a moment of psychological transition. What we are witnessing in this historical moment is an acute metaphysical uncertainty. Ideas about post-mortem resurrection, for example, are transferred to texts and issues about representation, so that metaphysical hesitations are nervously manifested around models of textual interpretation and textual composition. Along the way a new type of metaphysics becomes 'performed' that both erases a Catholic past and moves beyond a completely committed Protestant way of reading, meaning that the idea of representation becomes addressed in predominantly abstract terms. New reflections upon reading and writing are generated by the rhetorical production of this emerging Gothic subject – a subject who also complicates the idea of resurrection and spiritual ascendency because they indicate the presence of absence, or the reality of the void.

Pfau's discussion of Schiller's distinction between the naive and the sentimental is central to this new understanding of a late-eighteenth-century aesthetic and it also has points of contact with Sacks's reading of Freud.[5] For Pfau, the naive represents a lost condition of childhood in which an innocent overwhelming by the world has been superseded by a self-conscious sentimentality that effectively creates the world as it engages with it. This leads him to the view that 'the rise of aesthetics and of comprehensive theories of "culture" must be understood as a symptom of an all-pervading malaise and loss for which art offers itself as a self-conscious supplement' (p. 555). For Pfau, this position supports De Man's view that the allegorical mode of romanticism indicates that literature self-consciously refers to itself rather than either a Kantian realm of noumenal ideas or phenomenal objects.[6] Considered in these terms, the emptiness of 'death' in the elegy is only provisionally compensated for by precarious acts of creativity that unconsciously point towards their own emptiness as forms of aesthetic reconstruction. We will pursue these ideas in the following chapter in a discussion of how *Frankenstein* (1818, revised 1831) engages with aesthetic discourse as a means of concealing death, in which new psychological versions of the subject are developed through a complex literary self-consciousness.

The readings of the elegy provided by Sacks, Hogle and Pfau helpfully identify the highly symbolic nature of the elegy. There are different resolutions to this issue of symbolism and Sacks's Freudian reading is certainly more optimistic than that of either Hogle or Pfau. However, the relationship between death and creativity is acknowledged at different levels of engagement by all three, and although Pfau observes this within a quite specific trend of the 1790s, its roots can be found earlier and in texts that explore the relationship between creativity and the Gothic, such as in Edward Young's 'Conjectures on Original Composition' (1759), William Duff's *An Essay on Original Genius* (1767), Nathan Drake's later

'On Gothic Superstition' (1798) and Radcliffe's 'On the Supernatural in Poetry' (1826).[7] However, before discussing these engagements it is necessary to consider how ideas about sensibility impacted on the elegy, as they appear, if only superficially, to provide an extra-textual model of the emotions that puts back what aesthetics had seemingly taken out.

Sensibility

Adam Smith in the *Theory of Moral Sentiments* (1759) views death through the prism of empathetic sensibility:

> We sympathize even with the dead, and overlooking what is of real importance in their situation, that awful futurity which awaits them, we are chiefly affected by those circumstances which strike our senses, but can have no influence upon their happiness. It is miserable, we think, to be deprived of the light of the sun; to be shut out from life and conversation; to be laid in the cold grave, a prey to corruption and the reptiles of the earth; to be no more thought of in this world, but to be obliterated, in a little time, from the affections, and almost the memory, of their dearest friends and relations. Surely, we imagine, we can never feel too much for those who have suffered so dreadful a calamity.[8]

Such a position radically complicates the idea of death as a coherent Gothic trope in the period. Feelings about death may provoke models of mourning and melancholy that are elegiacally generalised, but in this instance thoughts of death awaken our compassion, not our fear. As Esther Schor has noted, Smith uses a model of sensibility in order to imaginatively place himself in the grave.[9] Smith goes on to note that:

> The idea of that dreary and endless melancholy, which the fancy naturally ascribes to their condition, arises altogether from our joining to the change which has been produced upon them, our own consciousness of that change; from our putting ourselves in their situation, and from lodging, if I may be allowed to say so, our own living souls in their inanimated body and thence conceiving what would be our emotions in this case. (pp. 11-12)

As we shall see in Chapter 3, this is a view adopted by Poe, who, in the 1840s, reformalises this position into a quasi-scientific mode of investigation.

Schor argues that the movement between philosophical discourse and the literary narrative of the elegy creates a popular 'theory of moral circulation' (p. 39), in which the elegy elaborates a view of sentiment found not only in Smith but in Hume's 'Of the Passions', Book II of his *Treatise of Human Nature* (1742), where Hume explores how literary forms, most notably tragedy, provide 'a showcase for sympathy' (Schor, p. 31). Whilst Schor pursues a line concerning the popular circulation of sentiments that echoes Smith's account of the flow of paper money as a source of financial conversion in *The Wealth of Nations* (1776), it is the idea of death and sensibility and its anti-Gothic dimensions that will be explored here. Hume and Smith are not lone voices on sensibility, and their clear Gothic counterpart is Burke's *A Philosophical Enquiry into the Origins of Our Ideas of the Sublime and the Beautiful* (1757).

Burke's treatise is often regarded as providing a model of Terror that Gothic writers responded to, and there is a link between his model of the sublime (as sublime terror) and what is reconstituted in the Gothic. However, what is often overlooked is how Burke develops a view of sympathy that accords with the type of empathetic engagements elaborated by Hume and Smith. In Part I, Section XIV on 'The effects of SYMPATHY in the distress of others', Burke examines the feelings of pleasure to be derived from observing scenes of emotional distress, because they awaken our moral sensibility; he notes that 'The delight we have in such … scenes of misery; and the pain we feel, prompts us to relieve ourselves in relieving those who suffer'.[10] Death and suffering in these models of sensibility are thus devoid of any meaningful Gothic content; indeed, they function as a response that overcomes fear. For Burke, even the feelings of melancholy induced by grief become a source of pleasure. According to Burke, 'It is the nature of grief to keep its object perpetually in its eye, to present it in its most pleasurable views' (p. 34), so that 'in grief, the *pleasure* is still uppermost' (p. 35, italics in original), a view that Burke also extends to melancholy. Burke has two versions of death, one sublime and the other 'delightful' (p. 36), which appear in the crucial Section VII in Part I, 'Of the SUBLIME', where Burke claims that 'pain is stronger in its operation than pleasure, so death is in general a much more affecting idea than pain; because there are very few pains, however exquisite, which are not preferred to death' (p. 36). However, the key modifier concerns the violence and immediacy of that death, with Burke referencing the execution in France of the attempted regicide Robert-François Damiens, who had been quartered in a public execution in 1757. For Burke, 'When danger or pain press too nearly, they are incapable of giving any delight, and are simply terrible; but at certain distances, and with certain modifications, they are delightful' (pp. 36–7). Burke returned to this theme in Part IV, Section VII, 'EXERCISE necessary for the finer organs', where he claims that as long as 'terror is not conversant about the present destruction of the person', such intimations of fear 'are capable of producing delight; not pleasure, but a sort of delightful horror, a sort of tranquillity tinged with terror; which as it belongs to self-preservation is one of the strongest of all the passions. Its object is the sublime' (p. 123). Burke's use of 'object' is telling as it suggests that one is not subject to the sublime (which would involve an immediacy with death). Burke outlines a position that would be occupied by the Gothic reader who can safely experience the sublime in a distanced way, and the closing section of his thesis provides an examination of how art and poetry generate 'safe' models of sublimity that can be culturally admired.

Burke's closing Part V of his treatise addresses aesthetics in depth. At one level his analysis of literary language suggests that language is able to supplant nature, which potentially compromises his discussion of natural sympathies and the sublime. However, he attempts to recuperate this position by sketching a discourse of sensation that accounts for why we may be personally moved by different natural objects, which conditions how they might be written about. Burke is also, of course, emphasising the role of creativity in manufacturing a version of the sublime. The sublime is therefore not just found in nature, it is also a central feature of the artistic imagination. Burke's resolution, however, raises another problem for the discourse of sensibility, imitation: 'Certain it is, that the influence of most things on our passions is not so much from the things themselves, as from our opinions concerning them; and these again depend very much on the opinions of other men, conveyable for the most part by words only' (p. 158). In this scheme 'our passions' are someone else's, and this widens the discussion about aesthetics and feeling beyond the realm of art to include formal models of subjectivity. It is this debate that, as we shall see, the Gothic is focused upon as it works to elaborate a view of feeling that is transgressive, passionate and putatively subversive, within what are specifically literary versions of it. Death, as the site of absence, plays a crucial role in these discussions about representation.

Death, for Adam Smith, played a central part in his theory of sensibility, but Burke's idea of emotional inheritance is also to be found there. Adela Pinch has explored how during the eighteenth century feeling was subject to empirical enquiry (in Hume and Kames), which in turn led to an understanding of the limits of the human. Pinch notes that Hume's version of the subject (like that of Burke, above) depends on an idea of language, which leads him to conclude in *A Treatise on Human Nature* that 'nice and subtile questions concerning personal identity ... are to be regarded rather as grammatical than as philosophical difficulties'.[11] This view also suggests the possible personification of ideas (because the 'person' is made of words). This bringing to life of the inanimate will be discussed further in relation to poems that personify death published towards the end of the eighteenth century, which are discussed later in this chapter. However, Pinch also explores models that suggest that sensibility can be acquired, an idea that has been explored by Ildiko Csengei, who argues that Smith's view of empathetic engagement with the dead requires a necessary fictionalisation of what it might feel like to be dead, which in turn collapses Hume's idea of the grammatically defined self with the literariness of the literary text. In effect, we can catch sensibility through words (as Burke would have it) and this makes our engagement with sensibility narrative-driven, which implies a community of readers. This, for Csengei, reworks Hume's idea that sensibility is a transferable emotion the very inheritance of which suggests a social, rather than strictly personal, engagement. In Smith, the dead are thus transposed into narrative, which leads Csengei to conclude: 'As we animate the dead, so we turn away from the pain of the other ... or make real – and identify with – the characters in fiction.'[12] Death, in other words, is a matter of stylisation.

So far we have looked at a number of critical views on the elegy and sensibility. Hogle is the only explicitly Gothic critical voice here, although many of the others (notably Pinch, who discusses Radcliffe) also make engagements with the Gothic. It is the premise of this chapter that the Gothic is born out of this schism between feeling (as a mode of knowledge) and writing (a new Gothic aesthetic), as it is *the* form that is centred on issues of representability and explores emotional extremes (and how to modify or contain them). The tensions between the extra-textually authentic and literary conceptions of creativity were explored in relation to Pfau's idea of a compensatory aesthetic that attempts to overcome symbolic absence. The degree to which the self is fashioned within an aesthetic of absence identifies the elegy as the starting point for the Gothic tradition – it is one in which ideas about 'knowing' also indicate how closely death, writing and emotion form a complex trinity in an epistemology of the self.

The elegy

In Edward Young's *Night Thoughts* (1742–45), feelings about death are supplanted by embracing a spiritual world. A model of knowledge and reason shapes Young's argument and it is his ambition to align our capacity to reason with an apprehension of the divine. For Young, 'reason speaks in all:/From the soft whispers of that God in man'.[13] The point is to look within to discover this inner world in which 'The telescope is turn'd' on the self (II. l. 140). Young's account of natural science argues that we are part of a divine nature, so that the tools we have to examine nature (such as inverted telescopes) enable an appreciation of the God within. Feelings of melancholy are unnatural as they imply a lament for a finite life, rather than acknowledge the true life, which is everlasting. God in nature, God within and an appreciation of our place within an infinite timescale overcome feelings of self-indulgent melancholy that falsely implies that death is the end. Young's poem contains a literary device as it is expressed in the form of a monologue delivered by a nameless narrator to one Lorenzo, which we, as readers, overhear. Words are thus granted significance as the focus is in part on the telling of the tale. Young's narrator praises:

> Speech, thought's canal! Speech, thought's criterion too!
> Thought in the mine may come forth gold or dross;
> When coined in word, we know its real worth. (II. ll. 474–6)

For Young, the importance of ideas is their transferability, as in Smith ideas or feelings are only important to the degree that they can be circulated. However, this identifies a theme in *Night Thoughts* that concerns narrative inspiration which is discerned in the heavens, so that:

> Parts, like half-sentences, confound: the whole
> Conveys the sense, and God is understood;
> Who not in fragments writes to human race:
> Read his whole volume, Sceptic! then reply. (VII. ll. 1242–5)

Young's reading of the night applies an idea of God-given reason to it that stands in opposition to any potential Gothic content. He notes that without the application of reason all that we would see in the night would be 'Bulls, lions, scorpions, monsters' (IX. l. 656), which are the projected images of our fears, whilst what we need to see instead is 'a lecture to mankind' (IX. l. 658) that reveals divine, not Gothic, forms when we discern 'those other beings' who are 'Natives of ether! sons of higher climes!' (IX. l. 661). For Young, 'Eternity is written in the skies' (IX. l. 663); how to read that 'lecture' is not, however, straightforward because divine messages appear as analogies, leading Young to conclude that reason is manifested within 'analogy pronounced so true:/Analogy, man's surest guide below' (VI. ll. 749–50). The problem with reading is linked to the assembling of fragments, which also poses a problem for sight. Young claims that in heaven:

> There, not the moral world alone unfolds;
> The world material, lately seen in shades,
> And in those shades by fragments only seen. (VI. ll. 169–71)

These divine fragments need to be reassembled to reveal the whole, which includes all life forms from:

> Huge as Leviathan to that small race,
> Those twinkling multitudes of little life,
> As swallows unperceiv'd! (VI. ll. 186–8)

This is extended to include the microscopic elements of our frame that could only be discerned by turning the 'telescope' on ourselves so that we might see 'particles, as atoms ill-perceived:/As circulating globules in our veins' (VI. ll. 190–1). This discourse of natural science manifests itself through our capacity to apply reason to the world that enables us to understand that these forces represent the presence of the divine. Divine mysteries may appear through analogies to writing, but their realities are confirmed by quasi-scientific procedure – which echoes Henry Drummond's emphasis on scientific method in *Natural Law in the Spiritual World* (1883), which is discussed in relation to models of evolution in Chapter 6. As we shall also see, the issue of assembling fragmentary messages constitutes an issue throughout the Gothic of the period.

Young's celebration of reason exorcises the night of any Gothic content as its monsters are exposed as unreal projections because the real world is structured, sensible and designed. The night (and death, with which it is analogously associated by Young) becomes a place of certainty as we decode it for its hidden messages. However, whilst God might provide us with messages to read, death troublingly eludes coherent representation. For Young, to try to represent the dead leads to the false claims of a Gothic vision, in which:

> An artist at creating self-alarms,
> Rich in expedients for inquietude,
> Is prone to paint it dreadful. (VI. ll. 50–2)

Such portraits conceal the presence of the everlasting life as 'Fear shakes the pencil' (VI. l. 58). Central to Young's argument is a refutation of a Gothic world of superstitious horror: 'Dark demons I discharge' (V. l. 840) because 'By night an atheist half believes a God/Night is fair Virtue's immemorial friend' (V. ll. 177–8). Young's anti-Gothic night, however, rests upon a principle of exchange in which life (rather than death) now constitutes a source of woe. As he notes, 'Life is much flattered, death is much traduced' (III. l. 57) because 'Life makes the soul dependant on the dust;/Death gives her wings to mount above the spheres' (III. ll. 61-2) as 'Death but entombs the body, life the soul' (III. l. 470). Life is the problem, not death, and more specifically it is the tendency to imagine that is problematic for Young because it is rooted in 'fancy' rather than 'reason' – or in human rather than divine creation. When writing of the artist's attempt to represent death, he notes:

> Fancy loves excess;
> Dark ignorance is lavish of her shades;
> And these the formidable picture draw. (VI. ll. 58-60)

Fancy is not part of the natural world for Young, rather it is part of the human world and stands in opposition to reason. He begins Section III of the poem:

> From dreams, where thought in fancy mad,
> To reason, that heav'n-lighted lamp in man,
> Once more I wake. (III. ll. 1-3)

The onus shifts from the unconscious to the animated human mind – a psychological move that heralds the secularisation of the Gothic even whilst it appears within religious claims about the containment of death. However, this issue of secularisation should not be overstated. The emphasis here is on the imagination and creativity, and the poem illustrates the presence of a metaphysical uncertainty that is reflected in these issues about representation.

If death is an aspect of reason for Young, for Robert Blair in 'The Grave' (1743) death becomes returned to the human world of melancholy that Young had worked so hard to eradicate. Blair focuses not on death but on the psychological effects of the graveyard (the place that is oddly missing in Young's poem). The graveyard is a site of communality in Blair, but it also provokes fancy (in Young's terms):

> Strange things, the neighbours say, have happen'd here;
> Wild shrieks have issued from the hollow tombs;
> Dead men have come again, and walk'd about.[14]

Blair notes the 'school-boy, with his satchel in his hand' (l. 59):

> Sudden he starts! and hears, or thinks he hears,
> The sound of something purring at his heels.

> Full fast he flies, and dares not look behind him,
> Till, out of breath, he overtakes his fellows;
> Who gather round, and wonder at the tale
> Of horrid apparition, tall and ghastly,
> That walks at dead of night. (ll. 64–70)

The schoolboy's fear could become a symbol of youthful folly, but Blair also claims that at the prospect of death, 'Nature turns back and shudders at the sight' (l. 375). This view of death is far from the consolations of reason promoted by Young because Blair's anxiety is that 'body and soul must part' (l. 377), which is quite different from Young's celebration of the emancipated soul that is entombed by 'life'. Blair puts back the Gothic that Young deflects towards life because Blair refuses to resolve a body and soul dualism via a discourse of reason, as he asserts death as a source of rational, because understandable, fear. These divergent approaches indicate the hesitancy around metaphysical issues at the time. It is within this divergence that we start to see the formation of the Gothic.

Blair contemplates the various tombs and the passing lives that they register, and it is important to acknowledge that this should be read as a Protestant reflection on Catholic memorials. These various tombs lead him to one question:

> Tell us ye dead! will none of you, in pity
> To those you left behind, disclose the secret?
> O! that some courier's ghost would blab it out,
> What 'tis you are, and we must shortly be. (ll. 432–5)

This position reverses Adam Smith's empathetic engagement with the dead. The silence of the dead isolates the living. However, the antidote to such alienation is to be found in God, or more precisely in Christ, whose resurrection demonstrates a triumph over death. Blair's narrator confronts death with this fact:

> Him in thy power
> Thou couldst not hold; self-vigorous he rose,
> And, shaking off thy fetters, soon retook
> Those spoils his voluntary yielding left. (ll. 670–3)

The poem recuperates death as the means of taking us to God and so towards the everlasting life. In the end, the narrator's anxieties are settled by recourse to scripture and a positive image of the resurrection. However, this resolution does not explicitly disavow the legitimate claims of melancholy, and as Blair personifies death (as an interlocutor) he also personifies the resurrected self who is constructed out of dead body parts:

> Ask not, how this can be? sure the same pow'r
> That rear'd the piece at first, and took it down,
> Can re-assemble the loose scatter'd parts,
> And put them as they were. (ll. 744-7)

Such a resurrected body constitutes a new type of bodily perfection, 'With a new elegance of form, unknown/To its first state' (ll. 754-5). The, admittedly inverted, echoes with the later *Frankenstein* are implicit but clear, and this move towards Shelley's more secular sublime builds upon, as we shall see, this idea of life created out of death, but via a discourse of creativity that touches on Pfau's observation that death is paralleled by emerging languages of aesthetics, which are also (like Shelley's creature) constituted out of death. Young and Blair in their different ways are also interested in ideas about knowledge and implicitly elaborate an epistemology that attempts to give voice to death (a strategy of personification that is developed in *Frankenstein*). More widely, there are links between fragments and forms of knowing that will persist throughout the nineteenth century, which are addressed in Chapter 6 on the quasi-scientific contexts of the *fin de siècle* Gothic. How to gather fragments of knowledge into a coherent whole underpins the fragmented text so that writing (as a form of composition) and epistemological processes become elided (a feature that, in epistemic terms, suggests links between the epistolary *Frankenstein* and the multi-vocal structure of *Dracula* (1897)). These ideas about knowing were given a central space in James Hervey's 'Meditations among the Tombs' (1745-47).

Hervey's 'Meditations' provides, in an epistolary format, an exploration of what the dead mean to us and what occult knowledge they might possess, and argues that such knowledge cannot be separated from religious contemplations. Hervey begins his meditations within a church in an isolated part of Cornwall; he recalls that 'A sort of religious dread stole insensibly on my mind, while I advanced, all pensive and thoughtful, along the inmost isle. Such a dread, as hushed every ruder passion, and dissipated all the gay images of an alluring world.'[15] He notes on the church floor a tombstone that is covered in religious inscriptions. Hervey focuses on the phrase '*O! that they were wise*' (p. 6, italics in original), and contrasts this idea of wisdom with scholarly erudition and 'the noise of secular affairs' (p. 6), which drowns out the 'gentle whisper' (p. 6) that asks us to reflect upon our lives in a spirit of religious 'contemplation' (p. 6). In death, peace and democracy triumph because the dead 'were huddled, at least, they rested together, without any regard to rank and seniority' (p. 7). Whilst for Young it was life rather than death that was the problem, for Hervey life is imbued with death: he notes of our blood that 'The crimson fluid, which distributes health, is impregnated with the seeds of death' (p. 19). This is what we need to contemplate, and meditations on tombs have a similar effect as they enable thoughts about death to shape our moral, Protestant, vision. This leads Hervey to critique the idealised tombs that fail to recollect individuals because they have been turned into abstract ideals. He reads such tombs as analogies of the life they memorialise, so that in the instance of 'Sophronia's' tomb (p. 20), 'The Surface [is] smoothly polished, like her amiable temper, and engaging manners. The whole adorned, in a well-judged medium, between extravagant pomp, and sordid negligence; like her undissembled goodness, remote from the least ostentation, yet in all points exemplary' (p. 21). The tomb is thus a symbol of her goodness. However, Hervey regards all such celebrations as in vain, because they fail to reflect the complexity of a life and the often conflicted needs that shaped it. Hervey distrusts symbolism because it externalises idealised feelings that can only represent one aspect of a life. To that degree tombs, and their epitaphs, cannot be trusted and this raises an issue about writing and interpretation that we witnessed in Young.

For Hervey, outward-facing messages need to be replaced by introjected narratives drawn from the life of Christ, which are written in his blood (a substance that is both alive and dead for Hervey) and transfused into our own so that the message circulates through our system and so is written on, and in, our hearts. Hervey asks us to:

> Inscribe the memory of thy matchless beneficence, not with ink and pen; but with that precious blood, which gushed from thy wounded veins. Engrave it, not with the hammer and chizel; but with that sharpened spear, which pierced thy sacred side. Let it stand conspicuous and indelible, not on outward tables of stone; but on the very inmost tables of our hearts. (p. 37)

Increasingly, ideas about writing and reading dominate 'Meditations'. He attempts some verses in which he asks, 'In thy fair book of life divine,/My God, inscribe my name' (p. 40). He enters the gloomy crypt that is 'full of the remains of the rich and powerful' (p. 41) and notes on one monument, 'HERE LIES THE GREAT', to which he responds, 'False marble! where? Nothing but poor and sordid dust lies here' (p. 42). This view of writing conditions his sense of what he has learnt from looking at the tombs in the crypt:

> Ye have taught me more of the littleness of the world, than all the volumes of my library. Your nobility arrayed in a winding-sheet, your grandeur mouldering in an urn, are the most indisputable proofs of the nothingness of created things. Never surely did providence write this important point, in such legible characters, as in the ashes of my lord, or on the corpse of his grave. (p. 43)

Messages only have validity if they properly signify what they contain. The empty messages on tombs (which is also captured in their symbolism) represent a misuse of language – signifiers without their signifieds. Such a view conflicts with theories of creativity that explored how words function to evoke a legitimate emotional response (as in Burke), which implicitly challenge the idea of the scriptural truth asserted by Hervey. The power of words and the ability to generate the unreal was also, as we shall see, a central idea in Nathan Drake's model of aesthetics. If, for Pfau, theories of writing become empty at the end of the eighteenth century, during the 1740s Hervey identifies writing and emptiness with a need for communication that might overcome any potential alienation. Introjected scriptural messages crucially transform the subject who wishes to pass them on – 'Oh! that I might be enabled, in every public concourse, to lift up my voice like a trumpet' – and spread the divine word (p. 50), which is manifested to us in a 'sublime, and emphatical language' (p. 51). Hervey extends this model of writing to the resurrection and judgement day when 'Behold! the books are opened. The secrets of all hearts are disclosed. The hidden things of darkness are brought to light' (p. 60), at a moment when there will be 'the vast expanse of the sky wrapt up like a scroll' (p. 62). Writing accords with Young's view of reason; however, the Gothic returns in Hervey's 'Contemplations on the Night' (1747).

For Young, dreams produce fanciful images from which we need to awaken. For Hervey, the night is also the time of dreams, when 'Reason now resigns her sedate office; and fancy, extravagant fancy, leads the mind through a maze of vanity. The head is crowded with false images, and tantalized with the most ridiculous misapprehensions of things' (p. 192). He also notes of the night that 'This is the time in which ghosts are supposed to make their appearance' and that 'Now the timorous imagination teems with phantoms, and creates numberless terrors to itself' (p. 196). For Hervey, the Gothic imagination represents a failure of nerve; indeed, such imaginings indicate the presence of a 'Preposterous stupidity!' (p. 197), unless such apparitions can be brought within the purview of religious discourse as Hervey approvingly refers to the presence of a phantom in the book of Job, which was used to support moral instruction. All other phantoms are false – indeed they represent a form of day-dreaming in which fancy enters into the world. Such fancies constitute diversions from death even whilst they seem to embrace it. For Hervey there is irony here, because 'One cannot wonder, that people should suffer themselves to be affrighted at such fantastical [images] and yet be quite unaffected with real presages of their dissolution' (p. 201). Hervey, like Young and Blair before him, is at pains to separate the real from the unreal. Like Young he is keen to depopulate the night of its projected fancies and to exonerate thoughts of death because they take us towards the divine. However, this disavowal of the Gothic as unreal has important links to a later discourse of personification that humanises ideas of 'otherness'. It is also clear that writing about death is centred on models of aesthetics, rather than evolving ideas of sensibility. In these texts we do not identify with the dead because they are beyond our knowledge, whereas death, abstractly considered, takes us away from the empty rhetoric of the grave. The key question is, what role does melancholy have in such deliberations?

Thomas Warton's *The Pleasures of Melancholy* (1747) tellingly provides a literary rather than theological explanation for feeling. It enthusiastically embraces the type of fancy that has been denied elsewhere in Graveyard poetry. Warton's 'melancholy' is of the imagination; it is not the consequence of physical malady, which had long been regarded (since the fourth and fifth centuries BCE from Hippocrates) as the cause of negative feelings. Warton begins by evoking Cynthia, the Greek goddess of the moon, who is described as:

> Mother of musings, Contemplation sage,
> Whose grotto stands upon the topmost rock
> Of Teneriffe; 'mid the tempestuous night.[16]

The invocation of a pre-Christian deity is also a conjuring of a literary discourse rather than a scriptural one. Writing is now associated with imaginative inspiration, which encourages, rather than disavows, the claims of fancy. However, it also forges links between emotion and imaginative inspiration, which, paradoxically, ontologically redeems melancholy *and* threatens to turn melancholy into a literary trope that undermines claims for its authenticity. The Muse becomes a guide here, not the God of Young, Blair and Hervey:

> O, lead me, queen sublime, to solemn glooms
> Congenial with my soul; to cheerless shades,
> To ruin'd seats, to twilight cells and bowers,

> Where thoughtful Melancholy loves to muse
> Her favourite midnight haunts. (ll. 17–21)

Melancholy is not just a state of mind, it becomes a place to visit. This is different from the churchyards and churches found in Blair and Hervey and yet the intimation of a 'religious dread' finds an echo here:

> As on I pace, religious horror wraps
> My soul in dread repose. But when the world
> Is clad in Midnight's raven-colour'd robe,
> 'Mid hollow charnel let me watch the flame
> Of taper dim, shedding a livid glare
> O'er the wan heaps; while airy voices talk
> Along the glimm'ring walls; or ghostly shape
> At distance seen, invites with beck'ning hand
> My lonesome steps, thro' the far-winding vaults. (ll. 41–9)

Such imagery feels more familiarly Gothic than that which we have seen hitherto. In part this is because fancy is embraced rather than dismissed. Warton's heavily stylised quasi-Gothic imagery inherits an idea of unreality from the earlier poetry that sits outside a model of 'nature'. Warton's narrator notes of their night-time rambles that 'every beast in mute oblivion lie;/All nature's hush'd in silence and sleep' (ll. 54–5). Nature is metaphorically asleep as the narrator asserts the presence of an inspirational fancy that creates poetry:

> But let the sacred Genius of the night
> Such mystic visions send, as Spenser saw,
> When thro' bewildering Fancy's magic maze,
> To the fell house of Busyrane, he led
> Th' unshaken Britomart; or Milton knew. (ll. 62–6)

Reference to Spenser's *Faerie Queene* (1590–96) endorses a view of the apparently fantastical imagination that Hervey had mocked in 'Contemplations on the Night' when he claimed that in dreams fancy takes us to 'fairy fields, and gathering garlands of visionary bliss' (p. 192).[17] Warton makes reference to *Comus* (1634) but suggests that drinking his cup 'stamps the monster on the man' and that pleasure can be found in melancholy rather than through an artificial agent:

> Thus Eloise, whose mind
> Had languish'd to the pangs of melting love,
> More genuine transport found, as one some tomb
> Reclin'd, she watch'd the tapers of the dead. (ll. 96–9)

Melancholy has two sources, graves and a tradition of tragedy, which is invoked by reference to Melpomene, the Muse of tragedy, and by a theatrical tradition including Otway and Shakespeare, which culminates in a language of sympathy that anticipates Adam Smith, in which:

> By soft degrees the manly torrent steals
> From my swollen eyes; and at a brother's woe
> My big heart melts in sympathizing tears. (ll. 223–5)

A gendered narrative appears in which 'Eloise' mourns her lost lover, whereas 'manly' tears are shed for theatrical plights. Muses are female but the playwrights are male, and the poem as a whole seeks to bridge these worlds through an implicit narrative centred upon love – it is one that at the end gives birth to 'a smiling babe' who listens to 'the rapid roar/Of wood-hung Menai, stream of druids old' (ll. 313–15). The pre-Christian and the theatrical are thus finally united.

Warton's comparatively brief exploration of melancholy is revealing for its emphasis on narrative form. However, it also engages with a model of the pastoral that is understated in Young, Blair and Hervey, but which is later elaborated by Gray in 'Elegy Written in a Country Church-Yard'. Warton's poem, for all its references to the theatre, takes place within a recognisable landscape that initially appears as anti-pastoral. Warton's narrator notes:

> A mournful train: secure the village hind
> Hangs o'er the crackling blaze, nor tempts the storm;
> Fix'd in unfinish'd furrow rests the plough:
> Rings not the high wood with enliven'd shouts. (ll. 147–50)

This is an arrested pastoral that makes way for fancy and an alternative Gothic world that enables us to 'forget/The solemn dullness of the tedious world,/While fancy grasps the visionary fair' (ll. 176–8). These visions supplant, if only temporarily, the pastoral:

> The water's murmuring lapse, th' entranced eye
> Pierces no longer through th' extended rows
> Of thick-ranged trees; till haply from the depth
> The woodman's stroke, or distant tinkling team
> Or heifers rustling through the brake, alarms
> Th' illuded sense, and mars the golden dream. (ll. 180–5)

There is ambivalence here with an intervention that is both 'haply' accepted even whilst it 'mars' the visions of fancy. Warton's solution is to adjourn to a church, which is enjoyed for the melancholy gloom that it generates:

> let me sit
> Far in sequester'd aisles of the deep dome,
> There lonesome listen to the sacred sounds,
> Which, as they lengthen through the Gothic vaults,
> In hollow murmurs reach my ravish'd ear. (ll. 201–5)

Terry Gifford has claimed that 'Pastoral is essentially a discourse of retreat', but not one of escapism as pastoral provides a conceptual space in which ideas about social power (such as landownership, for example) can be discussed, albeit in a displaced way.[18] This famously led William Empson to conclude that pastorals should be read allegorically, a view that accords with Hogle's account of Gray.[19] If pastoral represents some form of critical retreat from pastoral in order to examine it the better, then it raises questions about how one returns to it. Gifford's reading of Keats's *Endymion* (1818) is instructive as it argues that the poet is required to return from their dreams, because 'To fail to return is to remain in high-flown madness, to have been self-indulgent and to have failed the tribe. Indeed, the whole purpose of negotiating the dream journey is to return, not with social solutions, but with strange stories that mysteriously have the power to heal' (pp. 93–4). This view is close to Warton's account of the transformative possibilities of fancy. Whilst Warton is not elaborating a version of the poet in the way that Keats is, nevertheless it indicates how imaginative visions are, in this instance, both the source of, and the antidote to, melancholy, because in their theatrical and poetic expressions they represent a safe (impersonal) and so healing engagement with negative feeling. Warton does not propose a theological solution that denies melancholy, nor identifies fancy as an exercise in stupidity (as Hervey does), but rather suggests, in the closing images of the 'babe', the possibility of a pre-Christian (druidic) new birth rather than the type of Christian resurrection that we have witnessed earlier.

The pastoral takes on a particular allegorical function, which Hogle has noted in Gray's 'Elegy'. Gifford also claims that in Gray's poem, 'pastoral celebrates the ultimate retreat. This is the defining poem of the discourse of retreat towards deathliness. It is set in the crepuscular borderland between the living and the dead, and sensuously displays the imagery of the Gothic' (p. 50).

Gray's poem begins with the disappearance of pastoral:

> The Curfew tolls the knell of parting day,
> The lowing herd wind slowly o'er the lea,

> The ploughman homeward plods his weary way,
> And leaves the world to darkness and to me.[20]

Gray repopulates this now dead community with various representative figures, but it is clear that it is the death of pastoral that is also being mourned:

> Oft did the harvest to their sickle yield,
> Their furrow oft the stubborn glebe has broke;
> How jocund did they drive their team afield!
> How bowed the woods beneath their sturdy stroke! (ll. 25–8)

However, the dead do not quite die, because for Gray we inherit a set of values with which this community was imbued. Such values are political and indicate how the graveyard functions as a synecdoche for British radicalism in which the narrator notes the presence of:

> Some village-Hampden, that with dauntless breast
> The little tyrant of his fields withstood;
> Some mute inglorious Milton here may rest,
> Some Cromwell guiltless of his country's blood. (ll. 57–60)

Gray's pastoral is thus explicitly political rather than literary (Warton) or theological (Young, Blair, Hervey). Gray is self-conscious about this tradition and wishes to mark out an alternative function for the elegy; he notes of the rural dead (not the glorious dead recalled by Hervey) that:

> Their name, their years, spelt by the unlettered muse,
> The place of fame and elegy supply:
> And many a holy text around she strews,
> That teach the rustic moralist to die. (ll. 81–4)

Gray is attempting a different act of memory, one that is communal and which reaches out to the political context in which those lives were lived. However, as Gifford notes, there is a Gothic mood in the poem and the attempt to resurrect the dead for political purposes creates a liminal space that is, in keeping with many of the texts we have looked at, occupied by writing. Instead of speaking for the dead, the poem shifts to engage a voice (one that belonged to the community) that can speak for it and memorialises one of its dead before we are directed to an epitaph that registers his merits. The writing on the tomb is thus not a series of empty signs, as it is for Hervey, but rather it helps to keep the past alive and in doing so creates a bridge between the present and the past and the dead and the living.[21]

Throughout there is a persistent emphasis on how to read and compose messages. There is also an implicit debate staged about what elegies are for. Death and writing are closely linked in these texts, which explore both the meaning of life and the significance of death within what might be termed a metaphysic of writing. These elegies and meditations also employ iconographic images about death and ghosts that contributed to the development of a Gothic symbolism, although significantly they also pursue robustly anti-Gothic ideas as they search for a ground for meaning: theological, epistemological and aesthetic, which is beyond the inertia of the corpse. Pfau argues that these tensions between death and creativity appear at the end of the eighteenth century in the work of Schiller and Kant, but there is an earlier tradition of aesthetics at work, and it is one that is about the Gothic.

Gothic creativity

Edward Young's 'Conjectures on Original Composition' outlines a theory of writing that is exemplified by his earlier *Night Thoughts*. In it he identifies two forms of writing that are defined by imitation – one that imitates nature and one art. For Young, it is important to attempt a representation of nature as, he implies, this brings us closer to God, whereas writing about writing is merely an exercise in aesthetic solipsism. These forms of writing also support different expressions of the imagination, in which writing about nature participates in the growth of the imaginative faculties, which creates originality; or, as Young puts it, 'An original may be said to be of a vegetable nature; it rises spontaneously from the vital root of genius; it grows it is not made'.[22] Young's thesis is that originality can only be produced by copying from nature, as copying from other writers simply generates derivative forms of art. Young also elevates poetry above prose because 'there are mysteries in it not to be explained' (p. 342), but that technically stimulate the imagination above that of the range of 'mere prose-men' (p. 342). Crucially, he separates the natural imagination from the imagination that trades in the type of 'fancy' he critiqued in *Night Thoughts*:

> In the fairyland of fancy, genius may wander wild; there it has a creative power, and may reign arbitrarily over its own empire of chimeras. The wide field of nature also lies open before it, where it may range unconfined, make what discoveries it can, and sport with its infinite objects uncontrolled, as far as visible nature extends, painting them as wantonly as it will: but what painter of the most unbounded and exalted genius can give us the

true portrait of a seraph? He can give us only what by his own or others' eyes, has been seen; thought that indeed infinitely compounded, raised, burlesqued, dishonored, or adorned. (p. 343)

Here the imagination is out of control and is unable to approach the divine; what we have instead are copies of other writers' images. Fancy is thus an illegitimate mode of imitation because its images are second-hand and therefore strangely commonplace.[23] The figurations of fancy are thus, in Young's terms, not properly imaginative because they draw upon pre-existing imagery in order to make sense of them. Implicit is a telling critique of the Gothic night fears that he addressed in his earlier poem. The images of the unreal can only be seen and made cultural sense of if there exists a tacit agreement about what spirits or other fantastical forms look like, so that even a positive spirit such as a seraph requires some common iconographical ground, and such conventions cannot by definition be original for Young.

There is an apparent paradox here because the overactive imagination leads to convention because its solipsistic visions can only be made sense of due to their literary familiarity. For Young, the problem is that the 'genius' of the imagination has been granted 'too great [an] indulgence' (p. 343). Young's essay can be read as both an anticipation of the imaginative freedoms of romanticism and as a critique of those freedoms. This is especially true of the Romantic Gothic and the discourse of death and personification that is found within it (as in *Frankenstein*, for example), and it is an image that Young uses to suggest an internal engagement with one's 'ghost' or animating spirit that also manifests itself through the 'body'. He argues that the subject needs to develop a level of self-reflection in which we can:

> dive deep into thy bosom; learn the depth, extent, bias, and full forte of thy mind; contract full intimacy with the stranger within thee; excite and cherish every spark of intellectual light and heat, however smothered under former negligence, or scattered through the dull, dark mass of common thoughts; and collecting them into a body, let thy genius rise (if a genius thou hast) as the sun from chaos. (p. 345)

The fragments of the internal self thus need to be brought together, and it is tempting to read this as a form of resurrection before the fact that culturally recalls the lines from Blair's 'The Grave' concerning the need to 're-assemble the loose scatter'd parts,/And put them as they were' (ll. 745–6). As we shall see, throughout this study images of fragmentation are repeatedly linked to models of epistemology. During the mid eighteenth century, such links tend to focus on a knowledge of the Protestant self but are given a quasi-scientific turn in the fragmented visions of the spirit world that we find at the end of the nineteenth century.

As Young refutes the potentially Gothic fancies of the night in *Night Thoughts*, so he dismisses the purely imaginative act of fancy as lacking originality, as its conjuring of fantastical visions recycles commonplace literary images. It is a view of originality, writing and fantasy that contrasts with William Duff's enthusiastic engagement with the Gothic in his *An Essay on Original Genius and Its Various Modes of Exertion in Philosophy and the Fine Arts, Particularly in Poetry* (1767). Duff outlines a number of characteristics of 'Original Genius', including the ability to create images of 'Witches, Ghosts, Fairies, and such other unknown visionary beings'.[24] For Duff, there is a conceptual originality to such images that contributes to a developing iconography of fantasy, which also demonstrates the innovation of the form: 'the ideas of those beings, which are common to all, are very general and obscure; there is therefore great scope afforded for the flights of Fancy in this boundless region. Much may be invented, and many new ideas of their nature and offices may be acquired' (p. 140). Duff is explicit that such literary forms could help 'dart a beam upon the dark scenes of futurity' (p. 140) and so enable us to see what happens after death. The inner spirit of the imaginative writer is thus in touch with a wider spiritual dimension that allows for a link to post-mortem experience, so that 'the Poet' can 'give us a glimpse of the other world' (p. 142). For Young, the divine was found in nature and within a self-reflexive engagement with our inner being, whereas for Duff the 'genius' is a figure whose imaginative projections take us beyond nature, and self-knowledge, into a world of ideas and spirits that enable us to engage with death as an aspect of the creative imagination. Death and creativity are thus more closely linked earlier in the eighteenth century than Pfau suggests, even if such aesthetic deliberations are not worked through here as a secular discourse. Revealingly, Duff claims that these visions are not the fancy of Young because they deal with spiritual realities. The relationship between the 'real' and the 'unreal' was later addressed by Nathan Drake.

Drake, a physician, published his essay 'On Gothic Superstition' in 1798 and, after a brief discussion of images of spirits in a range of national, historical and literary contexts, he explores the philosophical significance of spectres. For Drake, literature about spirits depends upon the reality of the spirit world that can now be admitted as a credible aspect of metaphysics via a philosophical 'doctrine of immaterialism', which, although seeming to reference Berkeley's view on subjective experience as an extension of the mind of God, elaborates an alternative secular position based on a model of rationality (although one clearly of a different order from Young's position on 'reason' in *Night Thoughts*), which is linked to an account of poetics.[25] Drake notes of 'gothic' stories concerning spirits that they give:

> considerable latitude to the imagination [and] possess more rationality than almost any other species of fabling; for confined by no adherence to any regular mythological system, but depending merely upon the possible, and to some highly probable, visitation of immaterial agents, it has even in the present metaphysical period still retained such a degree of credit as yet to render it an important and impressive machine beneath the guidance of genuine poesy. (pp. 139-40)

These 'immaterial agents' are founded on 'the appearance of superior, or departed beings' (p. 142). Drake's model of creativity is thus one in which the dead speak to us, if obliquely, and decoding such fables enables us to commune with them.

These various accounts of creativity are clearly concerned about where imaginative inspiration comes from. Spirits could be the product of a disordered imagination, as Young would have it, but they might also suggest that the world is more complex than hitherto thought, as Duff and Drake claim. The writer has access to this otherwise occluded world, which means that the creative and the post-mortem spirit world become aligned. Such a position is attributable to the metaphysical uncertainties of the age in which the moral, and spiritual, status of creative composition is held in considerable ambivalence because new ways of writing about death imply emerging ways of understanding it.

It is important to note how these narratives about creativity are related to the Gothic. Both Duff and Drake regard fancy as underpinning literary forms that enable an engagement with the spirits of the dead. This implies the possibility of living with the dead and implicates a future in which one joins their world, and can communicate from that spirit world via these fantastical narratives. Such a move is different in kind from the more demonstrably religious considerations of Young, Hervey and Blair. For them, the dead may move to another realm, but we do not communicate with them, nor do they speak to us. Indeed, it could be argued that melancholy is generated out of that very communication breakdown. However, the resolution to such feelings of loss rests on the idea of the resurrection in which we are reassembled out of our earthly fragments and brought back to life. Duff and Drake appear to advance a more secular model (notwithstanding Duff's occupation as a Presbyterian minister), which revises such a clear Christian model by suggesting that the relationship between the living and the dead is porous. Whilst these represent different strategies they do share a common view, which is that such engagements (or visitations) are not disturbing and are not intended to be. Melancholy is pushed to the margins, as when it is entertained, as with Warton, it becomes linked to images of the literary rather than tied to the metaphysical. The narratives discussed here clearly come from different cultural and religious positions, but they constitute a body of work that constructs a model of the Gothic that is peculiarly devoid of Gothic emotion. The narratives seem to be either Gothic (as Gifford notes of Grey's 'Elegy') or about the Gothic (here in the guise of 'fancy'), but they do not operate as trauma narratives; indeed, they work towards containing or explaining trauma. This takes us back to Burke and Smith and their view of the role of sensibility as a means of empathetic engagement with those in distress (and, in Smith's case, with the dead).

The issue of containment is key to understanding the genesis of the Gothic. For Burke, as we noted earlier, there is a model of the sublime 'in which a sort of delightful horror, a sort of tranquillity tinged with terror; which ... belongs to self-preservation [and is] one of the strongest of all the passions' (p. 123). Tranquil terror might seem an oxymoron, but it is a position that neatly captures what is happening in Graveyard poetry and these accounts of creativity. Writing becomes the medium that creates distance from authentic feeling, and it is out of this moment that the Gothic emerges as a literary form that is founded on a discourse of containing death. This is why Burke notes that representations of sublimity move the subject in a powerful way because fear does not dominate in this safe engagement with terror. Famously, Burke's lines quoted above were developed by Radcliffe in her 'On the Supernatural in Poetry', where she sees terror as exemplified by images of spectrality in *Hamlet* (1603). Notable in Radcliffe's essay is the repeated suggestion that sources of the Gothic are to be found in Shakespeare and Milton, which grants the Gothic a largely literary provenance. Writing, and writing about the emotions, is closely aligned in these early accounts of feeling and reading that indicate how an emerging language of psychology develops from within models of emotion. Central to Radcliffe's adaptation of Burke's ideas is the notion of 'obscurity', because for Radcliffe 'Obscurity leaves something for the imagination to exaggerate'.[26] This is different in kind (rather than degree) from 'confusion', which 'leaves only a chaos' in 'the mind' (p. 169). Obscurity thus stimulates the imagination, whereas confusion confounds it. How 'obscurity' can be represented underpins many of the diverse voices explored here.

Implicit to our discussion of the elegy is an understanding that the process of personification plays an important function in animating the dead. Death may be construed abstractly (as in Young) but it is also constructed communally (as in Gray), and the latter requires a strategy of personification. Blair and Hervey conclude their explorations of death with images of the recomposed fragmented body that is reassembled at the resurrection. Images of the person are thus central to this process of representation even whilst their presence is used to raise metaphysical questions about the relationship between the living and the dead. It is out of the fragments, or out of Radcliffe's Burkean 'obscurity', that the self is imaginatively, projectively constructed, and this introduces an additional order of interpretation that relates to sight.

Radcliffe discusses Milton in her essay and concludes that his representation of terror 'is seen in glimpses through obscuring shades' (p. 169). Later she profiles the true poet of the sublime as someone who can bring together a disparate range of feelings and aesthetic engagements (including the picturesque) that requires 'an instantaneous perception' (p. 170), which accords an intuitive understanding to the Gothic imagination that enables its reader to see with their eyes. This leads Radcliffe, in her account of *Hamlet*, to suggest that if one walked on the North Terrace at Windsor Castle one would, via Shakespeare's imaginings, populate the terrace with 'a sentinel' whose 'shadow' is 'seen' due to the 'passing ... moonlight' (p. 170) and that an anticipation is created in which one 'expected to see the royal shade' (p. 170) of a ghostly king as the terrace becomes animated by the opening of Shakespeare's play. The Gothic writer enables us to see in a certain way, and part of this process of seeing relates to the personification of death that is often implicit to Graveyard poetry, but explicit to poetry about death at the end of the eighteenth century in which the Burkean debate about terror is developed into an account of psychological fear.

Death and poetry: seeing the Gothic in the 1790s

Stephen Hole's 'Ode to Terror' (1792) is an example of what happens when the usual strategies of Gothic containment break down. The poem is a nightmare vision in which the narrator is haunted by a figure of death that manifests itself via a number of familiar tropes, including murderous robbers and witches. The Gothic terrors come from the type of night that Young had worked so hard to rationalise away in *Night Thoughts*. Hole's narrator is trapped in his body 'as if the hand of death/Lay heavy on me, moisture cold bedews/My shivering limbs' (ll. 9–11).[27] However, such a fear is ascribed to 'fancy' (l. 11), which 'views/Scenes of unknown terrors' (ll. 11–12), even whilst these are seen within the nightmare that awakens the narrator but which extends, rather than dissipates, the anxiety: 'Reluctant, yet compell'd by fear,/I ope my anxious eyes' (ll. 16–17). Indeed, the vision the narrator discovers, which is that of a wood at night, is one that demands to be looked at: 'I gaze – yet all dismay'd,/Would fain, but dare not close their lids again' (ll. 20–1). However, what is also disturbing is that it is, seemingly tautologically, his self-generated fear that is responsible and which leaves him incapable of action: 'And fear, that gave the spectre birth,/Rivets me motionless to earth' (ll. 139–40), as he becomes confronted by a murder that takes place within the wood, which, whilst stimulating the type of sympathy we find in Burke and Smith, nevertheless does not overcome the narrator's paralysis. He notes of the murdered man, 'My pity, hapless man! was thine,/But oh, I could not, durst not give thee aid!' (ll. 68–9). Death takes on human form here and adopts increasingly Gothic hues as the poem develops.

After the murder, the narrator observes the presence of a more supernatural configuration of death:

> now on yon drear heath,
> Hags profane, and hell born sprights,
> Plan schemes of future woe, and scenes of death. (ll. 73–5)

These figures of death are held responsible for the sinking of a ship, which heads 'Down to the unfathom'd deep' (l. 90). The realisation that such visions might be the product of a disordered imagination deepens the anxiety because 'ideal terrors have disjoin'd/My powers of reason, and unhing'd my mind' (ll. 108–9), so that what is required is a repudiation, which concludes the poem, of the visions that he has himself conjured:

> Fell spectre of the haggard eye,
> Wild gesture, and erected hair,
>   Quick from my presence fly!
> Ease, ease awhile my heart opprest,
> Lest, lost and woe-begone, Despair
>   Should seal me for her own,
> And Reason, banish'd from her throne,
> To Madness should resign my tortur'd breast. (ll. 114–21)

Hole's Gothic vision is one without religious, or otherwise sublime, transcendence. Gothic images are projected from within and have their origins within a nightmare, which draws on images of the unconscious that Young explores and moves beyond in *Night Thoughts*. The emphasis on visions is also reflected in the repeated references to sight. Seeing becomes problematic because it requires an inward gaze that could possibly, but here does not, account for the presence of the nightmare. Young had made reference to telescopes turned back on their subjects as a conceit for the exploration of the inner world. Sight provides a defining mode of perception as one tries to discern within the Radcliffean obscurity an imaginative vision that enables us to see the world differently and so populate, for example, the North Terrace with images from *Hamlet*. Problems with seeing are noticeably acute when late-eighteenth-century Gothic narratives explore emerging psychological issues without having the disciplinary language to account for them. In other words, the Gothic of the late eighteenth century captures a move from a discourse of feeling (one that includes sensibility) to a discourse of psychology, which is secular in emphasis, inward looking and morally troubled.[28] However, this is not to assert that this should simply be seen as a precursor to ideas about the uncanny. Rather it indicates that a debate was taking place over the role and status of artistic 'vision', one that seemed to challenge conventional models of Protestant rationality at the time.

Hole's poem represents a Gothic repudiation of the sanitised Gothic iconography of the Graveyard poets. He also suggests that it is within the mind that such fears, and acts of imaginative creativity, are manifested. The status of art and writing and its relationship to fear is captured by Henry Kirke White's 'Ode to H. Fuseli, Esq., R.A., on Seeing Engravings from His Designs' (1807). The poem concerns not only Fuseli but also Dante, whom White regards as the inspiration for Fuseli's artistic vision. Like Hole's poem, White includes reference to drowning mariners but uses this as a conceit for Dante's vision, which represents a 'Genius of Horror and romantic awe,/Whose eye explores the secrets of the deep' (ll. 29–30).[29] Death is never far away in the poem as White makes reference to Norse myths that educate the young Fuseli about death, with reference made to Odin, who shows Fuseli a vision in which he:

> set before his awe-struck sight
> The savage feast and spectred fight;
> And summon'd from his mountain tomb
> The ghastly warrior son of gloom,
> His fabled Runic rhymes to sing,
> While fierce Hresvelger flapp'd his wing. (ll. 63–8)

The feast of death includes Hresvelegr, the corpse-swallower of Norse mythology. This image of the ingestion of the dead captures Fuseli's supposed internalisation of Dante and Norse myths, which are also conditioned by an aesthetic in which 'Taste lately comes and smooths the whole' (l. 89). Indeed, Fuseli's art is celebrated above that of poetry because:

> The Poet dreams: – The shadow flies,
> And fainting fast its image dies.
> But lo! the Painter's magic force
> Arrests the phantom's fleeting course. (ll. 93–6)

White's poem can be read as an account of Gothic art and the ways of looking that it provokes. To that degree it is close to Radcliffe's account of Shakespeare. However, White is also interested in the creative properties of the Gothic imagination and closes on an image that is familiar from Hole:

> The Bard beholds the work achieved,
>   And as he sees the shadow rise,
>   Sublime before his wondering eyes,
> Starts at the image his own mind conceived. (99–102)

Sight and imaginative vision are elided in a process of projection. Fuseli effectively projects the consumed work of others, but in original forms that implicitly challenge Young's idea that only work based upon nature is capable of genuine originality.

This chapter has explored the complex points of contact between ideas about death and creativity in the mid eighteenth century. The elegy represents an early space in which these links are made and can be read as a precursor to the types of debates about death and writing that became typical in the Gothic of the late eighteenth and early nineteenth centuries. How to write about death in new, because self-conscious, ways represents one strand within this emergent Gothic discourse that reflects, rather than fully moves beyond, the metaphysical uncertainties of the period. This emphasis on the writer is clearly linked to a wider discourse of romanticism, although it is also one that is conscious of the role of the reader. As we shall see throughout this study, the emphasis on the creative becomes progressively supplanted by a notion of the reader as a decoder of the seemingly ineffable 'truths' asserted by the creative imagination. This is all a matter of degree, rather than a clearly demarcated paradigm shift as the example of *Frankenstein*, which emphasises Frankenstein's role as a writer and Walton as a reader, suggests. However, what we will witness is a shift in authority in which the space occupied by the reader becomes progressively the place where revelation takes place. The following chapter explores these developments in an account of how memory, in acts of mourning, is imaginatively reconstructed.

Notes

1. For a related discussion of aesthetics, see Eric Parisot's *Graveyard Poetry: Religion, Aesthetics and the Mid-Eighteenth-Century Poetic Condition* (Farnham: Ashgate, 2013).
2. Peter M. Sacks, *The English Elegy: Studies in the Genre from Spenser to Yeats* (Baltimore, MD: Johns Hopkins University Press, 1985), p. 2. All subsequent references are to this edition and are given in the text.
3. Jerrold E. Hogle, 'Elegy and the Gothic: The Common Grounds', in Karen Weisman (ed.), *The Oxford Handbook of the Elegy* (Oxford: Oxford University Press, 2010), pp. 565–84, p. 565. All subsequent references are to this edition and are given in the text.
4. Thomas Pfau, 'Mourning Modernity: Classical Antiquity, Romantic Theory, and Elegiac Form', in Karen Weisman (ed.), *The Oxford Handbook of the Elegy* (Oxford: Oxford University Press, 2010), pp. 546–64. All subsequent references are to this edition and are given in the text. Pfau's wider historical argument is that these new aesthetic theories of the 1790s represent a watershed in 'modernity' that underpins our later theoretical approaches to aesthetics.
5. The reference is, of course, to Schiller's *On Naïve and Sentimental Poetry* (1795).
6. The reference is to Paul De Man's *Blindness and Insight: Essays in the Rhetoric of Contemporary Criticism* (1971).
7. There are other relevant sources, such as John Dennis's *The Grounds of Criticism in Poetry* (1704), John Aikin and Anna Laetitia Aikin's 'On the Pleasure Derived from Object of Terror' (1773) and Nathan Drake's 'On Gothic Superstition' (1798).
8. Adam Smith, *Theory of Moral Sentiments* (Edinburgh: W. Creech, 1813), p. 11. All subsequent references are to this edition and are given in the text.
9. Esther Schor, *Bearing the Dead: The British Culture of Mourning from the Enlightenment to Victoria* (Princeton, NJ: Princeton University Press, 1994), p. 35. All subsequent references are to this edition and are given in the text.
10. Edmund Burke, *A Philosophical Enquiry into the Origins of Our Ideas of the Sublime and the Beautiful*, ed. Adam Phillips (Oxford: Oxford University Press, 1998 [1757]). All subsequent references are to this edition and are given in the text.
11. David Hume, *A Treatise of Human Nature*, ed. L. A. Selby-Bigge and P. H. Nidditch (Oxford: Oxford University Press, 1978), p. 262, cited in Adela Pinch, *Strange Fits of Passion: Epistemologies of Emotion, Hume to Austen* (Stanford, CA: Stanford University Press, 1996), p. 29. All subsequent references are to this edition and are given in the text.

12 Ildiko Csengei, *Sympathy, Sensibility and the Literature of Feeling in the Eighteenth Century* (Palgrave: Basingstoke, 2012), p. 62.
13 Edward Young, *Night Thoughts on Life, Death and Immortality* (London: Baynes and Son, 1824), II. ll. 106-7. All subsequent references are to this edition and are given in the text.
14 Robert Blair, 'The Grave', in *Roach's Beauties of the Poets of Great Britain* (London: J. Roach, 1794), pp. 25-53, ll. 51-3. All subsequent references are to this edition and are given in the text.
15 James Hervey, *Meditations and Contemplations* (Bungay: Brightly and Child, 1816), p. 2. All subsequent references are to this edition and are given in the text.
16 Thomas Warton, *The Pleasures of Melancholy* (London: R. Dodsley, 1747), ll. 1-3. All subsequent references are to this edition and are given in the text.
17 Spenser's 'A Letter of the Authors' from *The Faerie Queene* is also relevant as Spenser indicates that his fantastical figures should be read as participants in a political allegory – that is, they are not pure figures of fancy.
18 Terry Gifford, *Pastoral* (London and New York: Routledge, 1999), p. 46. All subsequent references are to this edition and are given in the text.
19 William Empson, *Some Versions of Pastoral* (London: Chatto & Windus, 1935).
20 Thomas Gray, 'Elegy Written in a Country Church-Yard', in *Gray and Collins: Poetical Works*, ed. Roger Lonsdale (Oxford: Oxford University Press, 1977), pp. 34-9, ll. 1-5. All subsequent references are to this edition and are given in the text.
21 Godwin's account of how to mark the graves of the morally good is also relevant here; see William Godwin, 'Essay on Sepulchres', in *Political and Philosophical Writings of William Godwin*, 7 vols, ed. Mark Philip (London: Pickering & Chatto, 1993), vol. VI, pp. 1-30. For relevant critical readings of Romantic sepulchres, see Paul Westover's *Necromanticism: Travelling to Meet the Dead, 1750-1860* (Basingstoke: Palgrave Macmillan, 2012); Samantha Matthews's *Poetical Remains: Poets' Graves, Bodies, and Books in the Nineteenth Century* (Oxford: Oxford University Press, 2004).
22 Edward Young, 'Conjectures on Original Composition', in *Critical Theory since Plato*, ed. Hazard Adams and Leroy Searle (Andover: Cengage, 2005), pp. 338-47, p. 339. All subsequent references are to this edition and are given in the text.
23 See also Coleridge's discussion of Fancy in relation to the Imagination in the *Biographia Literaria*, ed. and Introd. George Watson (London: Dent, 1975), section 13, p. 167. For Coleridge, Fancy is simply a 'mode of memory' that lacks the dynamism which characterises the secondary imagination.
24 William Duff, *An Essay on Original Genius and Its Various Modes of Exertion in Philosophy and the Fine Arts, Particularly in Poetry* (London: Dilley, 1767), p. 139. All subsequent references are to this edition and are given in the text.

25 Nathan Drake, 'On Gothic Superstition', in *Literary Hours, or Sketches Critical and Narrative*, 2 vols (New York: Garland, 1800), vol. I, pp. 137–49, p. 139. All subsequent references are to this edition and are given in the text.
26 Ann Radcliffe, 'On the Supernatural in Poetry', in *Gothic Documents: A Sourcebook 1700–1820*, ed. E. J. Clery and Robert Miles (Manchester: Manchester University Press, 2000), pp. 163–71, p. 169. All subsequent references are to this edition and are given in the text.
27 Stephen Hole, 'Ode to Terror', in *Gothic Documents: A Sourcebook 1700–1820*, ed. E. J. Clery and Robert Miles (Manchester: Manchester University Press, 2000), p. 139. All subsequent references are to this edition and are given in the text.
28 Gray in an epigram loosely dated between 1742 and 1768 mocked the Master of Trinity College, Cambridge, Dr Robert Smith, for intending to cut down the College's Chestnut Walk, in which he claims, '"Tis not for the prospect, because he's no eyes,/But because he has writ about seeing' (ll. 3–4). Smith was the author of *A Compleat System of Optics* (1738), and Gray's critique is intended to contrast scientific observation with aesthetic considerations. Thomas Gray, 'Lines on Dr Robert Smith', in *Gray and Collins: Poetical Works*, ed. Roger Lonsdale (Oxford: Oxford University Press, 1977), p. 83.
29 Henry Kirke White's 'Ode to H. Fuseli, Esq., R.A., on Seeing Engravings from His Designs', in *Gothic Documents: A Sourcebook 1700–1820*, ed. E. J. Clery and Robert Miles (Manchester: Manchester University Press, 2000), p. 144. All subsequent references are to this edition and are given in the text.

2

Mourning, memory and melancholy: constructing death in the 1790s–1820s

The previous chapter explored the different ways in which death manifested itself in the mid to late eighteenth century. This was a period that was characterised by new ways of writing about death in which the role of memory was implicit. Thomas Gray's 'Elegy Written in a Country Church-Yard' (1751) was instructive in that regard as his narrator imaginatively reconstructs the life of a rural community to which they politically, but not personally, belong. The poem concludes with a move towards this personal element as the narrator passes the narrative to an eyewitness who can recount the life of one of the community's members. Political empathy is therefore surrendered to personal testimony, although one that provides support for the narrator's political vision. However, the poem also identifies memory as playing a key role in establishing the 'reality' of a life that was lived. Memory, and its claim on the subject, has an uneasy, because unstable, presence in the late eighteenth century as its links to authenticity are challenged by constructions of mourning and models of writing.[1]

This chapter begins with an account of memory during the period, before exploring how this links to a popular elegiac discourse of mourning as evidenced by Charlotte Smith's *Elegiac Sonnets*, the first edition of which was published in 1784. The construction of melancholy in *Frankenstein* (1818, revised 1831) develops these issues of mourning and the novel is granted an extended analysis here. However, the new secular psychology sketched by Mary Shelley does not emerge uncontested. James Boaden's *The Man of Two Lives* (1828) constructs a view of reanimation, as self-recollection, that stands as an implicit critique of the apparent ethical bleakness of Shelley's novel.[2] Ann Radcliffe is briefly touched upon here. Her links to discourses of mourning are important, and Terry Castle's reading of the role of the dead in Radcliffe has stimulated significant critical discussion about death and mourning in the Gothic. However, the emphasis will fall on later texts from the period, in part because this is a well-worn critical path on Radcliffe, and in part because Shelley and

Boaden substantially advance the discussion of death and the Gothic during the period by moving death beyond romantic parameters.

Mourning and memory

The tensions between the 'real' and the 'constructed' bear witness to the emergence of the secular uncanny, which Diane Long Hoeveler has explored at length in *Gothic Riffs* (2010). For Hoeveler, 'the gothic needs to be understood, not as a reaction against the rise of secularism, but as part of the ambivalent secularizing process itself'.[3] There has been much critical discussion of the uncanny (by Hoeveler, amongst others), and the argument here attempts to move beyond that focus by exploring how accounts of mourning were closely associated with a model of the artistic imagination at the time. Such a reading enables us to critically reconsider accounts of uncanniness, such as Terry Castle's. Castle's reading of *The Mysteries of Udolpho* (1794) explores how memory shapes an early discourse of the uncanny. She argues that Emily St Aubert is influenced by the dead as her father's moral instruction conditions her view of life after his death. Emily also has anxieties that her paramour, Valancourt, is dead when in fact he is alive. Castle concludes that the novel demonstrates the continuing influence of the dead on the living and also how fears of death impact on life. Radcliffe's characters are thus haunted by the figure of the ghost, which can be read as an example of the persistence of memory. This leads Castle to the conclusion 'that a crucial feature of the new sensibility of the late eighteenth century was, quite literally, a growing sense of the ghostliness of other people'.[4] The dead are not quite dead and the living are haunted by death, and this new manifestation is different in kind from the earlier empathetic engagements of Burke and Smith because this introjection is psychological rather than largely ethical. However, the idea of recollection has an additional complication in the period because of the influence of, as Frances Ferguson has noted, the post-Lockean tradition in which 'memory was identical with reflection, and with a reflection that did not simply reproduce an image of one's past but adapted it in the process'.[5] Romantic memory is thus of a different order than uncanniness because it incorporates a model of the imagination, rather than requiring some form of external verification to confirm whether fears are real or not. Ferguson's position helps us move beyond Castle's reading of Radcliffe because it suggests that memory functions, certainly during the Romantic era, as a dynamic aspect of the imagination, rather than passively confirming the continuing influence of others (such as Emily's father).

According to Ferguson, 'memory stands less for the ability to know that certain events happened or even that one was there to witness them than for the possibility of reflexiveness itself' (514). Also, this is memory free from anxiety because 'one hasn't yet seen things that would make one regret one's past for the consequences that have attended to it' (528). Ferguson also claims, in a reading of Hogg's *The Confessions of a Justified Sinner* (1824), that the Gothic appears to pursue an alternative view of memory that suggests that forgetting can lead to self-destructive acts. However, the picture is more complex than this because in practice it is difficult to isolate a clearly discernible Gothic memory from Romantic conceptions of memory that are also characterised by associations with guilt, mourning and the imagination. Additionally, as we will see in the discussion of Boaden's novel, the links between memory and reincarnation provide an implicit critique of the uncanny as it supplants the uncanny with notions of morality and social value that unite people in death, whilst also evidencing a quasi-scientific context for reincarnation that ambiguously introjects a form of religious sentiment. The debates about memory are also inflected by issues about the imagination and writing, which provide a crucial critical context for any understanding of mourning during the period.

It is important to acknowledge that the Romantic Gothic is also shaped by demonstrably non-Gothic cultural debates about science and by discussions of memory that are more generally considered within romanticism. The roots of the Gothic are to be found within this wider discourse concerning creative self-reflection, which is helpfully illustrated by Samuel Rogers's *The Pleasures of Memory* (1792).

Rogers and the importance of memory

Rogers's poem begins with a reference to an 'old mansion, frowning thro' the trees' rather than a graveyard,[6] but this old building provides an alternative focus on 'Household Deities!' (I. l. 47) rather than the religious feeling inspired by an encounter with a country church. The Gothic fantasies that are exuberantly recalled are childlike and rooted within a recollection of the child's imagination:

> 'Twas here, at eve, we form'd our fairy ring;
> And Fancy flutter'd on her wildest wing.
> Giants and genii chain'd the wondering ear. (I. ll. 37–9)

This past is seemingly innocent, but it takes on greater significance when the narrator asserts that 'The clock still points its moral to the heart' (I. l. 58).

The subject thus needs to resurrect the past in order to appreciate its ethical significance: 'Indulgent MEMORY wakes, and, lo! they live!' (I. l. 83). However, this is not an Augustan order of memory; rather it blends formal recollection with the Romantic idea of imaginative reconstruction:

> Blest MEMORY, hail! Oh, grant the grateful Muse,
> Her pencil dipt in Nature's living hues,
> To pass the clouds that round thy empire roll,
> And trace its airy precincts in the soul. (I. ll. 165–8)

Memory does not quite take you back into the past; rather it constitutes an aspect of Romantic creativity as it encourages the subject to reflect on their past as this will transform their idea of the self, with the poet claiming that memories, 'with magic art' (I. l. 175), can 'Controul the latent fibres of the heart' (I. l. 176). The past informs the present because for Rogers a mesmeric 'magnetic virtue' (I. l. 222) will 'soon unite' (I. l. 222). It requires an engagement with the dead to achieve this and it is also clear that Rogers regards memory as providing a resurrection of the dead because it 'Guards the least link of Being's glorious chain' (I. l. 359), which is held together by a series of associative links.

The first part of *The Pleasures of Memory* is highly impressionistic in its recollection and reconstructions of place and time. In the second part, Rogers elaborates a more complex model of memory that situates it directly within the imagination. In his prefatory comments to Part II, he states that memory 'is often busily employed, when excited by no external cause whatever' (II. p. 37). Memory is what enables the subject to think, whereas sensory perception aligns us with 'other animals' (II. p. 37). However, memory does not just develop the intellectual faculties, it also conditions creativity: 'On her agency depends every effusion of the Fancy, whose boldest effort can only compound or transpose, augment or diminish the materials which she has collected and retained' (II. p. 38). Creativity and death are not implicitly yoked as they were by Young, because memory generates unencumbered imaginative acts. Rogers thus locates the transformative effects of the imagination within the mind rather than claiming that the imagination is stimulated by divine inspiration. Rogers is quick to counter the view that memory so constituted could appear as a disordered solipsism, which Young had regarded as an essential aspect of fancy, when he asserts a proto-Wordsworthian position that 'It is in a calm and well-regulated mind that the Memory is most perfect; and solitude is her best sphere of action' (II. pp. 39–40).[7] Memory thus offers an escape from the physical world, but it is not a spiritual transcendence.

Rogers's prefatory comments to the second part provide an important commentary on memory and subjective experience. The poetry that follows is partially shaped by an Idealism that translates memory into nostalgia, with the second part opening with the lines:

> SWEET Memory, wafted by thy gentle gale,
> Oft up the tide of Time I turn my sail,
> To view the fairy-haunts of long-lost hours,
> Blest with far greener shades, far fresher flowers. (II. ll. 1–4)

This version of memory is decidedly anti-Gothic, and whilst the claims about fancy can be read as an implicit riposte to Young, his view is tinged with an occasional religious colouring that suggests the presence of the ambivalent secularism identified by Hoeveler. He notes of fancy:

> But most we mark the wonders of her reign,
> When Sleep has lock'd the senses in her chain.
> When sober Judgment has his throne resign'd
> She smiles away the chaos of the mind;
> And, as warm Fancy's bright Elysium glows,
> From Her each image springs, each colour flows.
> She is sacred guest! The immortal friend!
> Oft seen o'er sleeping Innocence to bend,
> In that dead hour of night to Silence giv'n,
> Whispering seraphic visions of her heav'n. (II. ll. 78–87)

Memory generates order and continuity, but it is also creative as it enables the construction of worlds that are both 'real' and projected, so that a father who is separated from his children, 'With MEMORY's aid, he sits at home, and sees/His children sport beneath their native trees' (II. ll. 96–7). In Ferguson's terms this identifies the central condition of the liminal Romantic memory that Wordsworth would translate into sensory imagery when making reference in 'Tintern Abbey' (1798) to 'Of eye and ear, – what they half create/And what perceive'.[8] The point for Rogers is that memory enables us to master the past and to generate pleasing visions of it. Despite this seemingly non-Gothic position, Rogers will claim that 'Danger and death a dread delight inspire' (II. l. 153) because we are able to imaginatively overcome such fears by dwelling on occasions when we have quelled our anxieties. Memory, as it were, circumscribes Burke's putatively Gothic terrors.

Memory is constituted by Rogers as a discourse of reason that calms us and induces order where there is threatened chaos. Also, whilst memory might involve solitude it is the thing that unites us all as it identifies a central aspect of our humanity – the ability to self-reflect and to create. Rogers's account of memory does not deny the reality of death, although it posits a vision of the afterlife that closely aligns it with remembrance and friendship rather than with the divine. In Rogers's cosmology the dead can visit us:

> Oft may the spirits of the dead descend,
> To watch the silent slumbers of a friend;
> To hover round his evening-walk unseen,
> And hold sweet converse on the dusky green;
> To hail the spot where first their friendship grew. (II. ll. 395-9)

Here the dead represent the spirit of memory that is abstracted and pure and from which we can learn:

> Correct my views, and elevate my soul;
> Grant me thy peace and purity of mind. [...]

Memory becomes the place where 'Virtue triumphs'. (II. ll. 442)

The Pleasures of Memory can be read as a secular extension of Young's *Night Thoughts*. It might appear to elaborate a non-Gothic model of the subject, but the repeated links between creativity, memory and order should be read as counterpoints to an emerging Gothic tradition in the period – one that questioned the notions of authenticity under which such a model of the subject is organised. As we saw in the previous chapter on the elegy, for Peter M. Sacks Art cancels anxiety by displacing fear onto a manageable aesthetic form. However, the problem is that the aesthetics of Fancy disavows the notion of the 'real' on which Rogers's version of the self depends. In other words, defining reality in this period is subject to considerable debate. For Rogers, 'Fancy' is exonerated, but in part this is because it functions as an antidote to the Gothic vision that he musters elsewhere in his 'Ode to Superstition'.[9]

'Ode to Superstition' incorporates an anti-Jacobean view that demonises forces of revolutionary chaos. The opening lines address 'superstition' as a 'dire Demon' (l. 1) that should be sent 'to the realms of night' (l. 1) rather than allowed to enter 'That little world, the human mind' (l. 3). This chaos is presided over by 'withering demons' (l. 20) that create terrifying political dystopias:

> Thou spak'st, and lo! A new creation glow'd.
>   Each unhewn mass of living stone
>   Was clad in horrors not its own,
> And at its base the trembling nations bow'd.
>   Giant Error, darkly grand,
>   Grasp'd the globe with iron hand. (ll. 53-8)

This world is presided over by a pre-Christian God whose demonic control over vision and revelation is manifested in the figure of Delphi's Sybil, who:

> In vain ... checks the God's control;
> His madding spirit fills her frame,
> And moulds the features of her soul. (ll. 99–101)

The visions of the Sybil represent a Gothic world of darkness, destruction and chaos. It is, however, a Gothic vision that lacks any real power because the forces of light can easily vanquish it:

> Can'st thou, with all thy terrors crown'd,
> Hope to obscure that latent spark,
> Destin'd to shine when suns are dark?
> Thy triumphs cease! thro' every land. (ll. 138–41)

Gothic forces of destruction are in the end defeated by a quasi-divine image of light and reason.

Rogers's politics are a reactionary response to the revolutionary events in France and are typical of their time. However, the images of superstition and false visions are a reworking of Young, but here in political terms that root the discussion firmly in the 1790s. Memory, as construed by Rogers, is a cultural memory in which the recollection of the forces of virtue and light defeat a world of death and chaos. Rogers's themes are therefore grand ones, about politics and models of the subject, but they are also about contrasting images of creativity. The Gothic is opposed to the delights of clarity and the playfulness of Fancy, which indicates the important role that Art plays in these emerging Gothic tensions. How to write about fantasy is key here. Memory functions as a creative drive that overcomes death by uniting us with the dead. Death is not Gothic in this instance, but the picture becomes increasingly complicated when we consider the relationship between memory and mourning, which requires us to take a brief step back to the elegy and its transformation of these themes at the end of the eighteenth century, before discussing their recomposition in *Frankenstein* via an account of Radcliffe.

Charlotte Smith

The fifth edition of Smith's hugely popular *Elegiac Sonnets* (1789) is near-contemporaneous with Rogers's *The Pleasures of Memory*, but represents an explicit attempt to write from within, rather than from without, a model of memory that is associated with mourning.[10] Smith was stung by criticism that earlier editions of her sonnets included unacknowledged sampling of other texts, and the fifth edition provides a list of references to her sources (Rogers also does something similar with his collection). In her dedication to the biographer and poet William Hayley, she claims that 'I can never be more than a distant copyist', although in her prefatory comments she attributes much of this to the limitations of the English language as against the Italian sonnet tradition.

Taken as a whole, the collection illustrates the tensions between a secular and religious view of death. Her self-conscious exercises in the Petrarchan form (sonnets 15 and 16) make reference to a 'heaven' that is conspicuously absent from the rest of the sequence. Indeed, a sonnet such as 'To the Moon' (sonnet 4) seems almost pagan in its conjuring of a lunar space where

> The sufferers of the earth perhaps may go,
> Releas'd by death – to thy benignant sphere. (ll. 9–10)

This suggests that the issue of translation from the Italian to the English is not purely linguistic; it is also a metaphysical relocation.[11] Given the embryonic Romantic context of Smith's work, it is revealing that nature, far from providing a possible discourse of transcendence, functions as a source of alienation. She notes in the concluding lines of 'Written at the Close of Spring' (sonnet 2):

> Another May new buds and flowers shall bring;
> Ah! why had happiness – no second Spring? (ll. 13–14)

Such a claim is rhetorical but also consistent across the collection. Sonnet 8, 'To Spring', notes of spring that:

> Thy sounds of harmony, thy balmy air,
> Have power to cure all sadness – but despair. (ll. 13–14)

If nature fails to provide transcendence then consolation is to be found elsewhere, which marks out a space for memory. Sonnet 10 ('To Mrs. G') begins with a lament that:

> Ah! why will Mem'ry with officious care
> The long lost visions of my days renew. (ll. 1–2)

Memory provides a recollection of a lost happiness that both supports, and sits in tragic counterpoint to, the current state of mourning. However, at the end Smith shifts the focus to the dead and what it is that they remember, which grants the narrator a post-mortem existence through a curious quid pro quo in which the narrator notes of their dead friend:

> Yet of that tender heart, ah! still retain
> A share for me – and I will not complain! (ll. 13–14)

Other poems explore these links between mourning and memory but grant them a literary provenance, with sonnet 24 referencing Goethe's *Sorrows of Young Werther* (1774) and sonnet 32, 'To Melancholy', recalling the Restoration dramatist Thomas Otway. Smith's novels are now widely understood as working within a Radcliffean tradition and, like Radcliffe, Smith includes poems in her early novels, with a selection from *Emmeline* (1788) reproduced in her sonnet sequence. This raises the issue of the literary production of mourning during the period, with Smith's sonnets evidencing a level of literary self-consciousness that complicates the idea of mourning and authenticity.

Stuart Curran has noted that images of distress in Smith's sonnets are 'a literary condition' and would have been understood as such by her readers.[12] Adela Pinch has claimed that 'Smith's sonnets ... highlight the *literariness* of the melancholy they express',[13] and Anne K. Mellor has concluded that in Smith 'emotions are constructed',[14] but that such formulations demonstrate 'the ways in which the emotion of grief is a culturally constructed dimension of gender, and specifically femininity' (p. 450). Pinch concludes, however, that they indicate a wider concern within the discourse of sentimentality where they constitute an 'affective dimension of an epistemological conflict over the origins of feeling' (p. 70). Curran also notes a problem in defining the emotional states within the elegies because 'their emotional affect is defined by what is not present' and which 'would resist therapy because it cannot be articulated' (p. 244). Smith's poems thus demonstrate the presence of a new form of introspection that manifests itself in literary tropes. Memory and mourning provide one way of thinking about this new model of introspection, and, as we shall see, it is *Frankenstein* that emphasises the construction of the self in both bodily and literary terms, which gives a powerful expression to this new shift in how to represent the emotions.

Inscriptions of death and the construction of mourning

Terry Castle accords Radcliffe's *The Mysteries of Udolpho* a special place in the development of a post-Romantic model of the self that underpins Freud's idea of the subject. She claims that '*Udolpho* was more than simply fashionable; it encapsulated new structures of feeling, a new model of human relations, a new phenomenology of self and other' (p. 125). This was because, as touched upon at the start of this chapter, the novel's focus on how the living worry that their loved ones may have died represents a new psychic self-haunting. For Castle, this is linked to a discourse of romantic love in which 'A haunted lover can do nothing, it seems, but haunt the haunts of the other. To love in the novel is to become ghostly oneself' (p. 124). However, because it can be argued that such anxieties represent a possible delusion (because the fears are speculative), they generate a pseudo-mourning that aligns it with melancholy.[15]

In *Udolpho*, Radcliffe's interpolated poem 'To Melancholy' (which is sung by Emily St Aubert) also complicates the idea of an authentic grief as it provides a revealing example of how delusion relates to a wider concern about textual production and ultimately to issues of authorship. The poem begins with an invocation to a Muse of melancholy:

> Spirit of love and sorrow – hail!
> Thy solemn voice from far I hear,
> Mingling with ev'ning's dying gale:
> Hail, with this sadly-pleasing tear![16]

The appeal made is in order:

> To paint the wild romantic dream,
> That meets the poet's musing eye,
> As on the bank of shadowy stream,
> He breathes to her the fervid sigh. (ll. 9–12)

The poem proceeds to request 'O lonely spirit! Let thy song/Lead me through all thy sacred haunt' (ll. 13–14), so that ultimately 'I hear their dirges faintly swell!/Then, sink at once in silence drear' (ll. 17–18), and the muse disappears at the point at which 'Dimly their gliding forms appear!' (l. 20). Whilst the poem concludes in a sentimental evocation of the natural world in which one can 'catch the fleeting moon-light's pow'r/O'er foaming seas and distant sail' (ll. 37–8), nevertheless it is clear that this melancholic mood has been generated through a rhetorical process that requires an initiating muse. The tension between 'feeling' and its origin in 'rhetoric' challenges the type of ontology that Castle observes in the novel. Pinch has argued that in *The Mysteries of Udolpho*, 'melancholy is inseparable from a prose style whose glamour lies in the way it brushes up against the referential status of feelings' (p. 117). Indeed, Pinch goes so far as to claim that understanding melancholy in the novel is 'about recognizing clichés rather than about experiencing the things to which these images refer' (p. 117). Pinch also provides an unspoken modification of Castle's claim that the dead become introjected in *Udolpho* when she pursues an approach from Abraham and Torok, who had argued that the subject inherits the repressed lives of those who have been psychologically close to them, but without inheriting the problems that had led to such repression, which now appears as an emptiness in the subject that cannot be adequately explained.[17] For Pinch, evidence for such a claim is to be found in the very form of the Gothic, which supports, in the case of Radcliffe, 'a theory of transgenerational and social practices; of mental processes fixed on words' (p. 133); it is an idea that will be pursued in Chapter 4 in a reading of *The Mystery of Edwin Drood* (1870). The repetition of clichés of mourning, within the stylised and repetitive form of the Radcliffean Gothic, represents an attempt, for Pinch, at desperately trying to assert meaning and presence even whilst such frantic acts of repetition serve to draw attention to the emptiness of the tropes employed. However, this sense of an empty rhetoric of death also represents a moment of dissonance that has its roots within a more generalisable sense of Romantic melancholy.

Thomas Pfau, in *Romantic Moods: Paranoia, Trauma, and Melancholy, 1790–1840* (2005), argues that Romantic melancholy is self-consciously textually produced, concluding that 'Inasmuch as both its cause and symptoms pivot on a deep awareness of its strictly textual constitution, melancholy cannot be classified as a "feeling" in any ordinary sense'.[18] Instead, melancholy is constituted as an allegoric mode that is *about* emotional loss, rather than articulates or captures authentic feelings of loss. It functions as a pseudo-mourning, although one that harbours within it a wider epistemological malaise, because 'The excessively emblematic quality of allegoric expression corresponds to a thoroughly overdetermined world in which all objects, identities, and possible forms of action appear owned and exhausted a priori' (p. 326). Romantic melancholy thus represents loss, but in the form of alienation, because melancholy provides an 'implicit repudiation of the realist model that posits the empirical world as an authentic epistemological source' (p. 348); a repudiation that is enacted with a particular power within the Gothic's challenge to the 'realist model' – a process that can be helpfully illuminated by a reading of *Frankenstein*.[19]

Frankenstein is both an exercise in melancholy and a self-conscious textual production. For Pfau, this Romantic self-consciousness can be traced back to Robert Burton's *Anatomy of Melancholy* (1621), which emphasises the rhetorical conjuring of melancholic moods. Significantly, Burton also sketches a nascent Gothic imagination that in its delusions forms a version of melancholia in which the subject 'suspects every thing he heares or sees to be a Divell, or enchanted, and imagineth a thousand Chimeras and visions, which to his thinking he certainly sees, like bugbeares, talkes with black men, Ghosts, goblins &c'.[20] This alienated imagination underpins *Frankenstein*, but this emphasis on delusion also informs Robert Walton's optimistic and non-Gothic pursuit of a lost tropical paradise at the North Pole that 'ever presents itself to my imagination as the region of beauty and delight'.[21] Shortly after this claim, Walton recounts how in his youth 'I also became a poet and for one year lived in a Paradise of my own creation' (p. 64). The idea of paradise is thus framed as a largely rhetorical one, as it has its provenance within a poetic ambition that is later reworked in how Milton's *Paradise Lost* (1667) shapes the imaginative expectations of Frankenstein's creature. The novel also evidences an early distrust of writing, with Walton noting in his second letter to his sister, Margaret Saville, 'I shall commit my thoughts to paper ... but that is a poor medium for the communication of feeling' (p. 67). This prepares the scene for the arrival of Frankenstein, whom Walton describes as 'generally melancholy and despairing ... sometimes he gnashes his teeth' (p. 75), as the novel proceeds to be dominated by Frankenstein's melancholy confession of the events that have led up to his arrival at the North Pole.

How to communicate this melancholy in 'a poor medium for the communication of feeling' is the textual subtext that associates melancholy with the type of absence that Pfau sees as central to Romantic melancholy. In *Frankenstein*, writing itself becomes an empty medium that cannot compensate for the novel's repudiation of a Romantic conception of nature. The creature is both real and unreal, authentic in his sense of feeling, but physically constructed and intellectually formed by textual encounters with Milton, Volney, Goethe, Plutarch and Gibbon. Nature thus becomes linked to the artificial as Shelley challenges the notion of sublime transcendence that Frankenstein repeatedly pursues as an antidote to his melancholy suffering. Walton, who is acutely conscious of how the narrative will be read by his sister, also suggests that reading leads to an estrangement from nature as it introduces principles of taste that might unsettle his description of the seemingly wasted but still 'noble creature' (p. 76) that Frankenstein has become. He notes that her problem is that 'You have been tutored and refined by books and retirement from the world, and you are therefore somewhat fastidious' (p. 78). However, the creature is a self-conscious creation that takes on the mantle of Gothic text, one that is imbued with a discourse of melancholic estrangement as Frankenstein's feelings of loss are played out as a textual alienation from his own production. To this degree the creature can be read as text and Frankenstein as its author, and this enables a reconsideration of Shelley's description of her inspiration for the novel in the Introduction to the 1831 edition, where she claims that for the scientist who could raise the dead, 'His success would terrify the artist; he would rush away from his odious handiwork, horror-stricken' (p. 59). This image of the 'artist' is contextualised by earlier comments in the Introduction that refer to writing. Mary Shelley notes that 'It is not singular that, as the daughter of two persons of distinguished literary celebrity, I should very early in life have thought of writing' (p. 55). She also notes of Percy Shelley that 'He was forever inciting me to obtain literary reputation, which even on my own part I cared for then, though since I have become entirely indifferent to it' (p. 56). This precedes her discussion of the genesis of the novel in a ghost story competition, which also supports the fundamentally self-conscious textual production of the novel. As Mary Shelley notes after the competition, 'I busied myself *to think of a story*' (p. 57, italics in original), which eventually overcame 'that blank incapability of invention which is the greatest misery of authorship, when dull nothing replies to our anxious invocations' (p. 58). Mary Shelley is thus also reflected, or doubled, in the image of Walton, who can also be seen as a type of struggling author who is concerned about his narrative reconstruction of Frankenstein's tale.

How the novel addresses the implicit doubling between the creature and Frankenstein can also be read as reworking a Romantic context in which the self becomes increasingly alienated from nature through the intervention of the cultural forms that underpin the creature's education. Hegel in the *Phenomenology* of 1807 argues that:

> It is ... through culture that the individual acquires standing and actuality. His true *original nature* and substance is the alienation of himself as Spirit from his *natural* being. This externalization is, therefore, both the purpose and existence of the individual ... This individuality *moulds* itself by culture into what it intrinsically is, and only by so doing is it an intrinsic being that has an actual existence; the measure of its culture is the measure of its actuality and power. Although here the self knows itself as *this* self, yet its actuality consists solely in the setting-aside of its natural self.[22]

Pfau notes of this that, 'For Hegel, culture does not simply negate the theoretical fantasy of immediacy and autonomy; it also reorients the experience of that negation toward productive ends by identifying expressive genres and techniques that allow the individual to articulate such self-alienation in objective and social form, namely, as aesthetic work' (pp. 311-12). The self becomes recomposed as text, but because that takes place within a stylised rhetoric the self is lost, or at best only partially projected, and this explains the self-conscious authorial anxiety expressed by both Mary Shelley and Walton concerning the struggle to find an idiom in which to represent Frankenstein's plight. However, Frankenstein is repeatedly confronted by representational versions of melancholy, as in his reading of Henry Clerval's Orientalist writers with their 'soothing' version of 'melancholy' in which 'life appears to consist in a warm sun and a garden of roses' (p. 116). Later Frankenstein refers to a portrait of his mother, which represented her 'in an agony of despair, kneeling by the coffin of her dead father' (p. 125). Such representations are precursors to the creature's self-consciously aware tale of melancholy, one in which the creature invites Frankenstein to function as a discerning reader: '"Listen to my tale; when you have heard that, abandon and commiserate me, as you shall judge that I deserve"' (p. 146). However, this is quickly followed by a disagreement between them over the notion of authorship, which is closely linked to the idea of melancholy. First, Frankenstein blames the creature for referring to the unhappy circumstances of William's death, '"circumstances of which I shudder to reflect, that I have been the miserable origin and author?"' (p. 147). The creature repeats that Frankenstein should wait until he has '"heard my story and can decide"' (p. 147); however, this decision will determine whether the creature leads '"a harmless life"' (p. 147) or becomes '"the author of your own speedy ruin"' (p. 147). Earlier the creature implicitly acknowledges Frankenstein as the author of the creature's tale when he requests, '"listen to me, and then, if you can, and if you will, destroy the work of your hands"' (p. 146). The links between melancholy, text and analogies to authorship are reiterated in this encounter that ultimately settles on a notion of the reader and *their* feelings of affect as the ultimate adjudicator of the authenticity of melancholy.

How the creature's tale is read is also dependent upon a model of fact because it needs to be both affecting and real. It is in this spirit that the creature tells Frankenstein that he managed to acquire access to letters sent by Safie to Felix and made '"copies"' of them, and '"Before I depart I will give them to you; they will prove the truth of my tale"' (p. 169). However, given that they are 'copies', their reality is questionable. Nevertheless, the creature repeatedly regards textual affect as *the* source of genuine feeling. He recounts his discovery of Milton, Plutarch and Goethe's *Sorrows of Young Werther* and notes that '"They produced in me an infinity of new images and feelings, that sometimes raised me to ecstasy, but more frequently sunk me into the lowest dejection'" (p. 173). Such affect is beyond that of a purely intellectual apprehension because, after reading of Werther's suicide, '"I wept, without precisely understanding it'" (p. 174). The guarantor of emotional authenticity is displaced from author to reader as their affect reveals the truth of a text's claim on the subject. The creature, for example, observes the blind Mr De Lacey play on his guitar '"several mournful but sweet airs, more sweet and mournful than I had ever heard him play before. At first his countenance was illuminated with pleasure, but as he continued, thoughtfulness and sadness succeeded'" (p. 178). Melancholy may be generated through art, but the emotion is no less real for all that. However, the novel's interrogation of the status of this emotional 'truth' is subject to further analysis in a largely critically neglected passage in which Frankenstein recounts his tale to a magistrate in an attempt to enlist legal support for the pursuit of the creature.

Frankenstein's confession is subject to a different order of testing as it is scrutinised by the fact-based system of the law, whereas Walton is prepared to grant the tale an authenticity that depends on both its emotional affect and his reading of Frankenstein's character. Frankenstein tells the magistrate: '"It is indeed a tale so strange that I should fear you would not credit it were there not something in truth which, however wonderful, forces conviction. The story is too connected to be mistaken for a dream, and I have no motive for falsehood'" (p. 242). The initial incredulity of the magistrate is overcome by the force of the narrative, which provokes a Coleridgean suspension of disbelief. Frankenstein notes of the magistrate that 'I saw him sometimes shudder with horror; at others a lively surprise, unmingled with disbelief, was painted on his countenance' (p. 243). This archetype of the Gothic reader is, however, dispelled when his legal identity is reasserted, so that 'when he was called upon to act officially ... the whole tide of his incredulity returned' (p. 243), and ultimately 'He endeavoured to soothe me as a nurse does a child and reverted to my tale as the effects of delirium' (p. 244). The tale is denied its authenticity in this instance, although the poetic Walton will attempt to uphold its emotional affect as an indicator of its emotional truth. Walton's sister is a reader of this tale and Walton asks her, 'You have read this strange and terrific story, Margaret; and do you not feel your blood congeal with horror, like that which even now curdles mine?' (p. 252). Whilst Frankenstein, ever self-conscious about the accuracy of his narrative, corrects Walton's manuscript because '"I would not that a mutilated one should go down to posterity'" (p. 253).

Walton notes of Frankenstein that 'His eloquence is forcible and touching' (p. 253) and this glosses Frankenstein's claim about the creature that '"He is eloquent and persuasive, and once his words had even power over my heart; but trust him not"' (p. 252). Story-telling thus lies at the heart of the novel as it attempts an examination of how writing constitutes a moment of loss. Melancholy, which is repeatedly referred to, is the emotion that is produced or conjured by rhetorical forms whose fictive quality is consistently asserted.

Melancholy appears as a bogus form of mourning because it represents loss in an allegorical mode. *Frankenstein*'s obsession with story-telling serves to make visible the narrative construction of melancholy that repudiates a Romantic conception of nature. To that degree, the novel departs from Romantic aesthetics by asserting a domestic narrative, associated with Margaret Saville, which becomes a characteristic of later Victorian fiction. Emily Brontë's *Wuthering Heights* (1847), for example (discussed in the following chapter), which blends the Romantic with the Gothic and the domestic, can be read as looking back to the Romantic and as anticipating the domestic novel, and builds upon the ideas that emerge in *Frankenstein*.[23] The roots of that development can be discerned in *Frankenstein*'s movement beyond the Romantic as the novel associates such change with the doubled melancholy of Frankenstein and his creature, who head towards the nothingness of the blank white page of the polar ice cap. However, Brontë's novel attempts to recuperate a Romantic language of nature that *Frankenstein* problematises because, as Anne K. Mellor notes, in *Wuthering Heights* 'books are a barrier between the mind and passionate experience', even though it is the bookish Nelly Dean who narrates the tale.[24] *Frankenstein*, in other words, initiates a cultural debate about the emotions and narrative forms that Brontë inherits and reworks. How melancholy functions as a pseudo-mourning also requires scrutiny as it forms an alternative version of mourning that is elaborated in the novel around feelings of grief for Henry Clerval.

After the death of Clerval, Frankenstein contemplates: 'And where does he now exist? Is this gentle and lovely being lost forever? Has this mind, so replete with ideas, imaginations fanciful and magnificent, which formed a world, whose existence depended on the life of its creator – has this mind perished? Does it now only exist in my memory?' (p. 201). Immediately preceding this passage, Frankenstein describes Clerval as 'a being formed in the "very poetry of nature"', which is then followed by some lines from 'Tintern Abbey'. These movements suggest that Frankenstein's feelings of grief are produced within a version of the poetic imagination. Melancholy yet again, as in Radcliffe, becomes a matter of textual production despite the attempt to evoke a feeling of subjective and emotionally authentic loss.

Mary Shelley discussed this model of grief in an article titled 'On Ghosts', published in the *London Magazine* of March 1824, in which she explored the question of the authenticity of ghosts. She admits that 'I never saw a ghost except once in a dream', before exploring feelings of loss in which she becomes haunted by a sense of another's passing presence.[25] She recounts visiting a house where she had once visited a now deceased friend and records that 'I walked through the rooms filled with sensations of the most poignant grief. He had been there; his living frame had been caged by those walls, his breath had mingled with that atmosphere, his step had been on those stones, I thought: – the earth is a tomb, the gaudy sky a vault, we but walking corpses' (p. 282). Memory is not indulged in the way that Rogers had conceived it. However, it does have links to ideas of writing and creativity. Timothy Morton, for example, has noted that this melancholic moment is established through a variety of rhetorical techniques (including metonymy, parataxis and apophasis), all of which contribute to how 'Shelley's sense of present absence becomes embodied in her own reaction: she is modeling how a reader should thrill to her prose', and 'On Ghosts' therefore reproduces the rhetorical origins of melancholy that are worked out to a considerable extent in *Frankenstein*.[26] For Morton, '"On Ghosts" is a masterpiece of sensational writing; through a series of sophisticated rhetorical devices, Shelley renders the concrete but slippery experience of the void' (p. 271). Pfau's model of Romantic melancholy is to some degree instructive here. He concludes that such narratives 'expressly identifies as a self-conscious, fatigued, indeed symptomatic form that disables the (romantic) paradigm of spontaneity and expressivity before our very eyes. The melancholic idiom unravels the project of an authentically expressive poetics as an illusion of subjective mastery premised on an inaccessible pre-text' (p. 326). This 'pre-text' relates to a conception of an organising aesthetic principle that is made invisible within formulations of melancholy that either attempt to disguise such rhetorical processes or incorporate them as an associated aspect of emotional affect. Natural feeling and natural modes of expression cannot, however, logically be elided, and so for Pfau such texts fragment because the 'pre-text' cannot coherently assemble the narrative pieces that constitute the performance of melancholy, so that 'the romantic image ... disintegrates as its symbolic aesthetic is rendered in shards or fragments without any credible claim to a pre-existing totality' (p. 326). This is developed in *Frankenstein* when Frankenstein recounts his construction of the creature:

His limbs were in proportion, and I had selected his features as beautiful. Beautiful! Great God! His yellow skin scarcely covered the work of muscles and arteries beneath; his hair was of a lustrous black, and flowing; his teeth of pearly whiteness; but these luxuriances only formed a more horrid contrast with his watery eyes, that seemed almost of the same colour as the dun-white sockets in which they were set, his shrivelled complexion and straight black lips. (p. 105)

The conception cannot contain the reality. A Gothic text is produced rather than a more 'beautiful' one that would retain its beauty by concealing its aesthetic construction. In Morton's terms, the 'void' is made visible as the labour ('the work of muscles and arteries') that inhabits a notion of the aesthetic is indiscreetly manifested. The creature also falls into fragments as the aesthetic conception fails to keep the pieces together. Ultimately this becomes ascribed to a discourse of melancholy that is embodied in the creature who is repeatedly linked with melancholy and who, by virtue of overcoming, or transcending, death, is placed beyond an association with a temporary mourning.

Castle's reading of *Udolpho* accords it an element of emotional authenticity when she claims that 'To be haunted, according to the novel's romantic myth, is to display one's powers of sympathetic imagination; the cruel and the dull have no such hallucinations' (p. 123). Even if terms such as 'myth' and 'hallucinations' are used here, they are not intended as challenges to a notion of a rhetorically contrived emotional experience. Castle's focus is on mourning, but given that the account is of imaginary fears about the death of the living – 'those who mourn, as it were, for the living' (p. 123) – this is closer to melancholy. The issue is how what Castle sees as 'this new obsession with the internalized image of other people' (p. 125) is aesthetically produced. *Frankenstein* arguably makes explicit what is implicit in *Udolpho* (although it is overtly addressed in the interpolated 'To Melancholy'), which is that melancholy becomes inauthentic when it is generated via visible narrative devices, and its affect is recorded in the reader's response even though the reader may ultimately (as in the example of the magistrate) question the reliability of the narrative. Castle's version of the self becomes complicated when this aesthetic factor is introduced into the argument.

The creature functions as Frankenstein's affective melancholic text that is read as both 'monster' and as abandoned innocent, as both a projection of Frankenstein's melancholy and as an introjection of the creature's dystopian reading. Feelings become fictionalised and fiction becomes the site of emotional affect. However, it is also important to address the central role that death plays in the novel, not only as it illustrates how an emerging secularism was established through a nascent psychological discourse, but also because it is closely linked to ideas of remembrance.

Constructing the self

At one level *Frankenstein* is focused on the idea of the constructed self, as the creature is assembled from dead body parts and intellectually assembled through aural engagement with literary texts such as *Paradise Lost*, Plutarch's *Lives* and Goethe's *The Sorrows of Young Werther*. The creature is both 'real', in the sense that he possesses recognisable human emotions, and completely manufactured. His sense of self is rooted in the pursuit of Frankenstein, who can explain his origins and who might pity him. The creature's account of his childhood centres on the senses and corresponds to a Lockean notion of the mind as a tabula rasa that is constructed through associations. This form of abstract recollection contrasts with the account of Frankenstein's childhood that centres on the type of family relations from which the creature is excluded. The novel also addresses how the differently gendered educational engagements of Frankenstein and Elizabeth conditioned whether they saw nature as an object for scientific investigation or aesthetic contemplation.

Frankenstein thus establishes childhood memory as *the* site of recollection and this begins with Walton's account of his early years when he read about 'the various voyages which have been made in the prospect of arriving at the North Pole' (p. 64). As with Frankenstein's early reading and the creature's language lessons, it is text that defines the ambitions of selfhood. Walton notes, 'My education was neglected, yet I was passionately fond of reading' (p. 64). This bookishness ghosts the context in which a new psychology emerges, a psychology that requires a new form of interpretation in order to read its cryptic messages. How to read, and how to read the self, are the two demands posed in the novel and both are connected to images of childhood that compromise the ambitions set by childhood reading. As Walton sees his abstract, because bookish, ideals for adventure undermined by his experiences at the North Pole, so Frankenstein notes the discrepancy between his aesthetic ideal and the reality of his creation, as we have noted earlier: 'His limbs were in proportion, and I had selected his features as beautiful. Beautiful! Great God! His yellow skin scarcely covered the work of muscles and arteries beneath'; indeed, with his 'dun-white sockets' and 'shrivelled complexion and straight black lips' (p. 105) he resembles a corpse. Here the death that

Frankenstein is seeking to overcome remains a persistent presence, and yet it is a form of death that also manifests the life that it has lost as the 'muscles and arteries' suggest a latent energy that Frankenstein's ministrations will reinvigorate. The dead are not quite dead and the living are not quite alive, and this new psychology poses novel demands on interpretation. These tensions are ultimately settled by a withdrawal into the mind as the place where this new Romantic subjectivity becomes constituted on the denial of the corporality of the corpse. *Frankenstein* clearly illustrates this when Frankenstein's account of the reanimated patchwork corpse is supplanted by a troubled dream that takes us within Frankenstein's psyche, where we bear witness to how it connects these issues of life and death and suggests an explanation, if not a resolution, for their origins in Frankenstein's life.

Frankenstein recollects that:

> I slept, indeed, but I was disturbed by the wildest dreams. I thought I saw Elizabeth, in the bloom of health, walking in the streets of Ingolstadt. Delighted and surprised, I embraced her, but as I imprinted the first kiss on her lips, they became livid with the hue of death; her features appeared to change, and I thought I held the corpse of my dead mother in my arms; a shroud enveloped her form, and I saw the grave-worms crawling in the folds of the flannel. (p. 106)

Life becomes desire, which becomes death, which becomes incestuous, and Frankenstein awakens from this nightmare to be confronted by his creation who is represented as both a reanimated corpse and as an infant: 'He held up the curtain of the bed; and his eyes, if eyes they may be called, were fixed on me. His jaws opened, and he muttered some inarticulate sounds, while a grin wrinkled his cheek' (p. 106), an image from which Frankenstein flees.

Death and life are intrinsically linked in the novel, but this new life represents the death of the old. The creature does not recollect its previous lives, but rather represents an image of creativity that mimics the Romantic rupture with the past in its pursuit of the transcendent. The dead may live again, but this represents a renewal or a rebirthing – an image captured in the figure of the creature as both corpse and baby. However, he is also an aspect of Frankenstein's inner life, and the painful truth that he comes to acknowledge is that the creature represents in projected form his implicit hostility towards domesticity (his dead fiancée and mother) and that the creature's desire for family mocks his aversion to such ties. Mellor has noted the gendered narrative here that critiques a discourse of masculine ambition (represented as science) that is predicated on what

Schoene-Harwood has termed 'domophobia'.[27] The creature can thus be read as the product of a particular type of politics as well as a troubled aspect of Frankenstein's inner world. The psychological elements of the drama transform the narrative into a secular one, and even though it may be possible to argue that Frankenstein has usurped God's role in creating life, it is not apparent that there is a God in the text who is profaned. Rather the psychological links between Frankenstein and the creature challenge any coherently applied notion of 'evil' and constitute a mode of writing that works beyond the pursuit of moral certainty that is typically found in Radcliffe. The final battle at the polar ice cap illustrates this as Frankenstein struggles against a self-projected personification of death in a dead place – a battle in which death both wins and loses.

Reanimating the dead is figured as a mode of projection in *Frankenstein* and this echoes Shelley's resurrection of the dead in 'On Ghosts'. The dead are manifested from within – which implies the presence of an inner 'spirit' that would be explored in depth at the end of the century by F. W. H. Myers through his ideas of sublimation and astral travel, which are discussed in Chapter 6. The dead are with us, argues Shelley's novel, and we can never escape them. However, this secular account of death does not go uncontested during the period. An alternative model of death, one that seeks to put back the type of moralising eschewed by Shelley, is developed in James Boaden's *The Man of Two Lives*.

Reanimating the dead: the ethics of memory in *The Man of Two Lives*

James Boaden had some success as a dramatist in the late eighteenth century. His *Fountainville Forest* (1794) was based on Radcliffe's *The Romance of the Forest* (1791), whilst *The Italian Monk* (1797) was based on her *The Italian* (1797). In 1799 he produced *Aurelio and Miranda*, which reworked some of the central scenes from M. G. Lewis's *The Monk* (1796). He published theatrical biographies including accounts of Kemble and Mrs Siddons in the 1820s. He later wrote Gothic novels that achieved some popularity at the time, including *The Man of Two Lives* in 1828 and *Doom of Giallo, or the Vision of Judgment* in 1835. Diane Long Hoeveler has noted that in his plays Boaden used ghosts to explore both religious and secular provenances for ideas about spirits, and these tensions appear in his 1828 novel (p. 131).

The Man of Two Lives can be read as a critique of the apparently bleak amorality of *Frankenstein* as it provides an alternative story about resurrection that establishes an ethical dimension by asserting the demands of past-life memory. The narrative, which begins in 1778, is told retrospectively from the point of view of an Englishman, Edward Sydenham, who is sent to Germany to complete his university education. Sydenham has intimations of a previous life in which he had been one Frederic Werner. As Werner he had led a dissolute life and Sydenham feels that he has a responsibility to return to those now aged figures from Werner's past in order to recompense them for the wrongs that he did. It transpires that many of those he had seemingly corrupted had in the main led virtuous lives, as they had been able to reflect and come to terms with their own misdemeanours. Memories that could be painful become a means through which to reflect on the possibilities of virtue. The living, as in Sydenham, recall the dead, but in an ethical context that helps to establish notions of value that unite an otherwise fragmented group of individuals. Noteworthy is the role that Franz Mesmer plays in the novel, as a character who prompts Sydenham towards various conclusions about the relationship between the living and the dead and who appears as a mysterious character until his identity is revealed at the end. A loosely configured notion of animal magnetism enables characters from Werner's past to discern some qualities that he possessed in Sydenham and also to suggest ways in which the inanimate (the dead) establish links to the living.

Werner is not a ghost in Boaden's novel as he is reanimated through reincarnation in Sydenham, and it is a link established through a continuity of consciousness that establishes the presence of a coherent identity: 'If consciousness alone establishes our identity, (for our body is in a constant state of change,) that principle in me might render other proof necessary ... I am the man now writing his present history, and am equally sure that I was that other being whose life I also record, because I know it to have been mine.'[28] Werner is granted a return because he wishes to make amends for the lives that he has damaged but is unsure if the voice that grants him this was 'really some immortal spirit' or 'fancy' (vol. I, p. 5). He then realises that he has been 'united to a helpless infant' and reborn (vol. I, p. 6), as the early pages of the novel provide a gloss on *Frankenstein*'s creature's account of their infancy in which they understand the world through the senses before 'began the work of imitation' when they acquire language (Boaden, vol. I, p. 8). The novel blends images that are familiar from Frankenstein's education with that of the creature and these appear as knowing references to Shelley's novel. However, whereas *Frankenstein* can be read as a critique of the Romantic idea of 'nature' (by asking questions about what 'natural' means), Boaden works to build continuities with the past so that the effect is to move beyond the potential autobiographical solipsism (Frankenstein's narrative) of *Frankenstein* by asserting an ideal of positive biographical reflection. Sydenham's mother is unconcerned by his early claims about a previous life as, although she dismisses them as fantasy, '"To imagine a previous life is but as the biography of another man; and a fancied being, like a real one, may supply incidents for meditation and improvement"' (vol. I, p. 26). Indeed, Sydenham is in the unusual position of writing both an autobiography and a biography, which raises issues of agency that are familiar from our earlier discussion of authorship in *Frankenstein*. Boaden also explores issues about representation when Sydenham indicates that he had purchased a book of engravings of the university at Frankfurt from a period when, as Werner, he had studied there; also the youthful Sydenham 'filled my sketch-books with views which I derived from memory, though they were uniformly attributed to the fertility of my fancy, and a happy turn to composition' (vol. I, pp. 29–30), which are admired by the artists Benjamin West and Henry Fuseli (in keeping with Boaden's incorporation of real figures, such as Mesmer, in the novel), with Fuseli taking over the artistic education of the young Sydenham. The links to Fuseli are used to develop a discussion about art in which Fuseli is praised for the narrative qualities of his paintings because his characters are captured at moments of passionate intensity, so that in Fuseli 'every single figure [represents] the impersonation of its ruling passion' (vol. I, p. 34). Sydenham goes so far as to assert that art provides the template by which life is understood because 'nature herself submits to the limitations of art', and as art aspires to perfection so the anti-*Frankenstein* position is reached that 'The exterior bears the moral character of the being. We are formed to be guided by this sympathy between the mind and the body' (vol. I, pp. 38–9). The psychological complexities and the problems posed in the discussion of constructions of nature in *Frankenstein* are redirected for more positive, if simplified, ends.

Sydenham's interest in art also engages with ideas of the Gothic. The references to Fuseli illustrates this, as does the enthusiasm for a certain type of music that was 'solemn and mysterious, sweet and unearthly' (vol. I, p. 45). His moral education is derived from reading the sermons of Dr Isaac Barrow (the seventeenth-century theologian and scientist), which demonstrates the presence of a Christian will at work through the dictates of 'reason' rather than faith (vol. I, p. 51). Sydenham's arrival in Frankfurt brings confirmation that his visions of an earlier life are reflected in the places he sees and the people that he seeks out. Whilst in an inn he discusses the evidence for the presence of ghosts with his friend Herman (who in the novel functions as a type of Clerval and who, like Clerval, is a linguist): 'we ventured to enquire into the possibility of such beings, and to estimate that testimony on which they had been received in all ages ... As a kindred theme we touched upon the occult sciences, and the possessors, real or fanciful, of extraordinary powers' (vol. I, p. 76). They are joined by a mysterious individual who provides a sceptical overview of the history of spirits and directs their consideration to a more quasi-scientific basis as a support for genuine metaphysical speculation. At the end of the novel it will be revealed that this individual is Franz Mesmer. The, at this stage, unidentified Mesmer is questioned on his view about reincarnation and responds: '"If," said he, "you are once satisfied that the thinking part of us is utterly different in its nature from body, and that ideas have no dimensions ... it is little likely that such a being should be capable of decomposition with the body: why should it not ... become the spiritual ... parts of other beings?"' (vol. I, pp. 89–90). Mesmer then claims that he knows that such is the case for one Frederic Werner. Sydenham is confused by this encounter, and shortly afterwards embarks on a tour of Europe. The encounter emphasises that the spirit survives death and so develops an alternative renunciation of the corpse than that outlined in *Frankenstein*. In Boaden's novel the dead are psychically introjected rather than projectively personified, and this has different moral consequences for agency.

After these opening, if lengthy, discussions about death, art and the transmigration of spirits, Sydenham embarks on a European tour in which he encounters a number of people who knew Werner and whose lives have been subject to some ethical readjustment, which leads Sydenham to the conclusion that Werner's acts ultimately provoked people to positively re-evaluate their lives. Nevertheless, the novel repeatedly comes back to abstract discussions about spirits. In one such conversation with his Cambridge tutor, one Dr Hervey (a supposed descendant of the seventeenth-century William Hervey), he is informed of the Mesmeresque view that '"The spiritual substance, be it creation or effusion, can hardly be kept inactive; it is an energy, and must operate on something else"' (vol. I, p. 132), before exploring how the work of Herder argues for the presence of a spiritual dimension, a view that Dr Hervey claims '"is directly opposed to some of our anatomical physiologists"' (vol. I, p. 135), who, like Frankenstein, emphasise the presence of a material world.[29]

Initially Sydenham is appalled by what he learns of Werner's alleged sexual and financial improprieties and by a document written by him titled 'Self-examination', which he sees as 'a striking sketch of moral disorganization' (vol. I, p. 254), even whilst these papers help give 'life, and voice' to Werner (vol. II, p. 3), with much of the second volume devoted to the good that Werner, often unintentionally, did. Indeed, Werner's background is a mixture of the religious and the scientific, which in part explains his fickle nature that functions as a secular counterpoint to his father's resolution of science with religion, with Sydenham informed that '"The father of Werner was a man of science. His studies of nature were of the greatest value; he was a clergyman, his experiments increased his piety"' (vol. II, p. 42). On the other hand, '"Frederic was by nature *critical;* did that beget distrust of excellence?"' (vol. II, p. 42), which led him to flout conventional morality in starting an affair with an opera singer, Leonora, whilst engaged to Francina, although Francina refers to Mesmer's idea of animal magnetism to account for this when she asserts that 'The really correct woman, like the magnet, can either attract or repel as she presents herself' (vol. II, p. 71). This discourse of science sits alongside a religious discourse that addresses the idea of the Fall, which shapes the perception of the world maintained by the creature in *Frankenstein*. Sydenham meets with the Abbé Ponto, an acquaintance of Leonora's, who, far from leading a monastic life, 'lives as much in the world as any man' (vol. II, p. 82). Sydenham is struck by his sage view that '"The liberal mind will not ... refuse to applaud what is good amongst the fallen; and the philosopher may properly view the whole species as a compound of contradictions"' (vol. II, pp. 98–9), which functions as a preface to Sydenham's visit to Leonora. He discovers that Leonora, via animal magnetism, has learnt morality from the suffering she inflicted on Francina, who came to see Leonora perform as Medea and who admired her performance despite the pain she had caused her, leading Leonora to acknowledge that '"It was this woman's greatness of soul that ultimately awakened my OWN"' (vol. II, p. 148). Consequently she broke from her previous associates and followed a programme of corrective reading and self-reflection, so that '"My character, by imperceptible degrees, became firm and principled"' (vol. II, p. 149). She notes the similarities between Sydenham and Werner, but also the moral transformation that has taken place – '"You inherit, in some inconceivable way, his taste, his feelings, his attachments; but they are purified and exalted by their new medium"' (vol. II, pp. 162–3) – as the novel works towards establishing a morality that is incorporated within a model of subjectivity, one that functions as a counterpoint to the troubled psychology asserted in *Frankenstein* in which self-knowledge is irredeemably painful.

The Man of Two Lives explores the relationship between science (Mesmer) and ethics. It does so by redirecting a model of reanimation that Shelley develops in more challenging terms in *Frankenstein*. Where

Shelley works to outline a new version of the subject as troubled by their inner impulses, Boaden invalidates the idea of impulse by replacing it with a discourse of morality. In Boaden the emphasis is on overcoming the individual to become part of the collective, whereas in *Frankenstein* the norms of the collective (and in particular its way of looking at 'nature') are exploded. Death is in some fashion the end in *Frankenstein*, whereas in *The Man of Two Lives* it constitutes a moral rebirth. Also, whilst writing is implicated in this new psychology in *Frankenstein*, Boaden aligns art with a more conventional model of beauty. *The Man of Two Lives* thus sanitises the predominantly secular considerations of death in *Frankenstein* by exalting the nobility of the spirit beyond the coarse materiality of the corpse. In doing so, Boaden evacuates uncanniness of emotional affect because the novel does not demonstrate an anxiety about the presence of the dead. The novel tacitly argues for an alternative formulation of life and death, which, whilst secular in emphasis, does not collapse into the bleak psychology of *Frankenstein* because it emphasises the importance of agency, as the Abbé Ponto says of the now redeemed Leonora: '"she can be whatever she chooses to become"' (vol. II, p. 168).

The Man of Two Lives also celebrates the emotional transportation of art, which functions as a vehicle for displaying moral credibility. Leonora's performance of Medea is praised by Sydenham for its evocation of the 'divine' within the 'profane' (vol. II, p. 179), and so Leonora transmits a moral message within her performance, which, for the Abbé, turns her into a '"MUSE"' (vol. II, p. 180). The moral message is also tempered by a medical one as it is revealed that Mesmer had treated the dying Werner and, through his friendship with Fuseli, had noted Sydenham's drawings of German scenes that demonstrated a link to Werner. This disclosure is made in a letter to Sydenham that concludes with Mesmer's ambitious sense of the project which lay before him, and it is a passage that bears rhetorical similarity to the discourses of ambition that are familiar from Walton and Frankenstein in Shelley's novel. Mesmer writes:

> In now taking my leave of my young friend, a little may be said, without vanity, as to myself. Objects of infinite importance to mankind claim ME wholly. In addition to simplifying the healing art, I design to work a mighty revolution in philosophy. I am destined to unfold unknown principles to the world, leading all to profound and benevolent results. (vol. II, pp. 300-1)[30]

The concluding comments articulate a degothicised uncanny that is rooted within an idea of benevolence, which stands as a synopsis of the novel's moral message concerning the transformative properties of ethical self-reflection. Sydenham claims that 'most men are permitted TWO LIVES ... *one* of ACTION, with its usual attendant ERROR; the *other* of REFLECTION, and, as it ought to prove, of ATONEMENT' (vol. II, pp. 302–3), which is elaborated through 'the power of conscience' (vol. II, p. 303). Self-knowledge and self-reflection plus the capacity to be magnetically purified by the good acts of others establish a view of death as simply an aspect of life. The spirit inhabits a narrative of improvement that implies the presence of a secular evolution of morality, one that conquers death and so moves the subject beyond the claims of mourning and melancholy via a form of emotional transcendence.

Death during the 1790s–1820 undergoes a radical transformation. The horrors of a finite life are ghosted by a parallel discourse of artifice that links death with emerging models of aesthetics. Mourning and melancholy become heavily stylised and appear as elements within a culture of writing and representation. How to write about death involves constructing death – and even two highly divergent novels such as *Frankenstein* and *The Man of Two Lives* repeatedly refer to books, poems and plays, which illustrates the fundamentally rhetorical status of death in the period. At one level, the significance of death becomes organised by point of view. William Hazlitt, for example, in his essay on Byron in *The Spirit of the Age* (1825) provides a coda on Byron's death, which was announced whilst he was composing the conclusion to his essay. For Hazlitt, 'Death cancels every thing but truth; and strips a man of every thing but genius and virtue. It is a sort of natural canonization. It makes the meanest of us sacred – it installs the poet in his immortality, and lifts him to the skies. Death is the great assayer of the sterling ore of talent.'[31] Death thus bestows immortality. That this is all a matter of point of view is borne out by Hazlitt's contrary position expressed in his essay 'On the Fear of Death' from *Table-Talk* (1822), where he argues for a rather more bleak position in which:

> People walk along the streets the day after our deaths just as they did before, and the crowd is not diminished. While we were living, the world seemed in a manner to exist only for us, for our delight and amusement, because it contributed to them. But our hearts cease to beat, and it goes on as usual, and thinks no more about us than it did in our life-time.[32]

Whilst this might be an 'ordinary' death, it is not one that 'makes the meanest of us sacred'. Such a view might seem far removed from that of Smith and Burke's idea of empathy with the dead, but in a further *Table-Talk* essay, 'On Will-Making', Hazlitt discusses the obligation that the living have to honour the terms of a will because 'we sympathise with the dead as well as with the living, and are bound to them by the most sacred of all ties, our own involuntary fellow-feeling with others!'[33] Hazlitt might seem to be an unusually fickle commentator on death, but his shifting perspective is a consequence of moving between the demands of eulogy and the innovations expected from the polemical essay. From where you write about death shapes the expressions granted to it – and this singular change indicates the presence of a newly emerging vision of death during the period.

A key question concerns the role of the Gothic. Whilst one would categorise many of the texts discussed in this chapter as classic Gothic narratives, they are ones that draw upon images of memory, as in Rogers, which are part of the wider non-Gothic culture. The Gothic becomes the place in which ideas about death are subject to some considerable critical scrutiny, and this represents the desire to find new languages in which one can make sense of death within a largely secular context. And yet it is difficult to thereby assert that death is itself 'Gothic'. Indeed, as illustrated by Boaden, there is an implicit debate about death that is staged within the Gothic, and his version of the uncanny is far removed from that of either Radcliffe or Shelley. The Gothic provided a forum for these discussions about how to gain an understanding of death that did not necessarily turn death into an object of Burkean Terror. How to know death and how one acquires a way of knowing about others through models of death is given a quasi-scientific turn in the work of Poe and George Eliot, a turn that builds upon the scientific contexts of the time but also upon the Gothic engagements with science we have witnessed in Shelley and Boaden, and this will be addressed alongside a discussion of death in *Wuthering Heights* in the following chapter.

Notes

1 See Mark Sandy's *Romanticism, Memory, and Mourning* (Aldershot: Ashgate, 2013), for an in-depth analysis of mourning within a Romantic context.
2 It should also be noted that Shelley also produced various tales about reanimation: 'Valerius the Reanimated Roman', 'Roger Dodsworth: The Reanimated Englishman' and 'The Mortal immortal', which address themes about history, love and nation.
3 Diane Long Hoeveler, *Gothic Riffs: Secularizing the Uncanny in the European Imaginary, 1780–1820* (Columbus: Ohio State University Press, 2010), p. 6. All subsequent references are to this edition and are given in the text.
4 Terry Castle, 'The Spectralization of the Other in *The Mysteries of Udolpho*', in *The Female Thermometer: Eighteenth-Century Culture and the Invention of the Unconscious* (Oxford: Oxford University Press, 1995), pp. 120–39, p. 125. All subsequent references are to this edition and are given in the text.

5 Frances Ferguson, 'Romantic Memory', *Studies in Romanticism*, 35:4 (Winter 1996), 509–33, 510. All subsequent references are to this edition and are given in the text.
6 Samuel Rogers, *The Pleasures of Memory* (Boston: Manning and Loring, 1795), I. l. 13. All subsequent references are to this edition and are given in the text.
7 The reference being to Wordworth's claim in the Preface to the *Lyrical Ballads* about the importance of 'emotion recollected in tranquillity'.
8 William Wordsworth, 'Lines Written a Few Miles above Tintern Abbey', in *William Wordsworth: Selected Poetry*, ed. and Introd. Stephen Gill and Duncan Wu (Oxford: Oxford University Press, 2008), pp. 57–61, ll. 106–7.
9 Samuel Rogers, 'Ode to Superstition', in *The Pleasures of Memory* (Boston: Manning and Loring, 1795), pp. 93–104. All subsequent references are to this edition and are given in the text.
10 Charlotte Smith, *Elegiac Sonnets* (London: T. Cadell, 1789). All subsequent references are to this edition and are given in the text.
11 Given the period it would also be tempting to assert a potential difficulty of translating from the Catholic to the Protestant.
12 Stuart Curran, 'Romantic Elegiac Hybridity', in Karen Weisman (ed.), *The Oxford Handbook of the Elegy* (Oxford: Oxford University Press, 2010), pp. 238–50, p. 243. All subsequent references are to this edition and are given in the text.
13 Adela Pinch, *Strange Fits of Passion: Epistemologies of Emotion, Hume to Austen* (Stanford, CA: Stanford University Press, 1996), p. 66. All subsequent references are to this edition and are given in the text.
14 Anne K. Mellor, '"Anguish No Cessation Knows": Elegy and the British Woman Poet', in Karen Weisman (ed.), *The Oxford Handbook of the Elegy* (Oxford: Oxford University Press, 2010), pp. 442–62, p. 451. All subsequent references are to this edition and are given in the text.
15 Freud, in 'Mourning and Melancholia' (1917), distinguishes between mourning and melancholy by ascribing the first to a necessary, and naturally arising, period of grief during which the subject is confronted by the overwhelming loss of a loved one, but also of 'one's country, liberty, [or] an ideal'; from *On Metapsychology: The Theory of Psychoanalysis*, The Penguin Freud Library, vol. XI, trans. James Strachey, ed. Angela Richards (Penguin: Harmondsworth, 1991), pp. 251–72, p. 252. For Freud, melancholy closely resembles mourning, but whereas the latter represents a temporary condition, the former is a persistent emotion that is also characterised by a lack of 'self-regard' which is 'absent in mourning' (p. 252). This leads Freud into analysis of the fragile and narcissistic ego development that informs states of melancholy. Freud is mentioned here as his model of the subject underpins Castle's analysis.
16 Ann Radcliffe, *The Mysteries of Udolpho*, Introd. Terry Castle, ed. Bonamy Dobrée (Oxford: Oxford University Press, 1998 [1794]), pp. 665–6, ll. 1–4. All subsequent references are to this edition and are given in the text.

17 Nicholas Abraham and Maria Torok, *The Wolf Man's Magic Word: A Cryptonymy* (Minneapolis: University of Minneapolis Press, 1986 [1976]).
18 Thomas Pfau, *Romantic Moods: Paranoia, Trauma, and Melancholy, 1790–1840* (Baltimore, MD: Johns Hopkins University Press, 2005), p. 324. All subsequent references are to this edition and are given in the text.
19 The 1831 edition is referred to here as the complete version of the text produced by Shelley. It is not an edition that responds to Boaden, so there is no supplementary dialogue between them that has been overlooked.
20 Robert Burton, *The Anatomy of Melancholy* (1621), in *The Nature of Melancholy: From Aristotle to Kristeva*, ed. Jennifer Radden (Oxford: Oxford University Press, 2000), pp. 129, 142–56.
21 Mary Shelley, *Frankenstein; or, the Modern Prometheus*, ed. and Introd. Maurice Hindle (Penguin: Harmondsworth, 1985 [1831]), p. 63. All subsequent references are to this edition and are given in the text.
22 George Hegel, *Phenomenology* (1807), cited in Pfau, *Romantic Moods*, p. 311 (italics in original).
23 For a relevant discussion of the relationship between *Frankenstein* and *Wuthering Heights*, see Sandra M. Gilbert and Susan Gubar's *The Madwoman in the Attic* (New Haven, CT and London: Yale University Press, 2000).
24 Anne K. Mellor, *Romanticism and Gender* (London: Routledge, 1993), p. 200.
25 Mary Shelley, 'On Ghosts', in *Gothic Documents: A Sourcebook 1700–1820*, ed. E. J. Clery and Robert Miles (Manchester: Manchester University Press, 2000), pp. 280–5, p. 282. All subsequent references are to this edition and are given in the text.
26 Timothy Morton, 'Mary Shelley as Cultural Critic', in Esther Schor (ed.), *The Cambridge Companion to Mary Shelley* (Cambridge: Cambridge University Press, 2003), pp. 259–73, p. 271. All subsequent references are to this edition and are given in the text.
27 See Anne K. Mellor, *Mary Shelley: Her Life, Her Fiction, Her Monsters* (London: Routledge, 1990); Berthold Schoene-Harwood, *Writing Men: Literary Masculinities from 'Frankenstein' to the New Man* (Edinburgh: Edinburgh University Press, 1999).
28 James Boaden, *The Man of Two Lives: A Narrative Written by Himself*, 2 vols (London: Henry Colburn, 1828), vol. I, p. 3. All subsequent references are to this edition and are given in the text.
29 The reference is to Johann Gottfried Herder's *Another Philosophy of History* (1774).
30 See Walton's first letter to Margaret Saville, pp. 63–6; see Frankenstein's speech on pp. 101–2 concerning how 'A new species would bless me as its creator'. For a recent study of the popular reception of mesmerism and hypnotism, see William Hughes's *The Devil's Trick: Hypnotism and the Victorian Popular Imagination* (Manchester: Manchester University Press, 2015).

31 William Hazlitt, 'Byron', in *The Spirit of the Age* (London: Henry Colburn, 1825), pp. 160–85, pp. 180–1.
32 William Hazlitt, 'On the Fear of Death', in *Table-Talk* (London: Dent, 1942), pp. 321–30, p. 327.
33 William Hazlitt, 'On Will-making', in *Table-Talk* (London: Dent, 1942), pp. 113–21, p. 121.

3

From writing to reading: Poe, Brontë and Eliot

Why cannot a man talk after he is dead? *Why* – *Why* – that is the question.
Edgar Allan Poe.[1]

The previous chapter explored the complex relationships that emerged in the Gothic at the end of the eighteenth century and early nineteenth century as representations of death, and its ethical and artistic significance, became subject to critical scrutiny. One persistent theme that emerged concerns the role of creativity and its links to images of death and dying. In one sense there is an implied metaphysical narrative at work here that claims that death tells us something about life. This is constructed in predominantly aesthetic terms as death becomes a subject for artistic and intellectual contemplation. How to write about death becomes a way of animating the dead, and this plays a crucial role as the narrative of death progresses into the nineteenth century as the exploration and confirmation of death-like experiences becomes increasingly foregrounded in the Gothic. This is a repeated issue, as we shall see, in the work of Edgar Allan Poe. The nineteenth-century Gothic builds upon an earlier tradition of Gothic death even as it progressively attempts to externalise (through science and through rituals of mourning) the newly internalised models of death and the psychological states on which they depend. At one level, how to narrate death runs through Poe's tales, Brontë's *Wuthering Heights* (1847) and Eliot's 'The Lifted Veil' (1859), but, in parallel, there emerges an interest in recording how death becomes constructed as a potential object of knowledge, one in which the shift from writing to reading plays a significant role. Science, as in mesmerism and accounts of animal magnetism, provides a context for some of these approaches, but also functions as a narrative framework in which subjectivity is constructed. Poe's tales provide us with a clear example of how these new changes in representations of death, from writing to reading, are developed in the Gothic.

Voicing death: Poe

J. Gerald Kennedy has argued that 'Poe's responsiveness to the problem of death led to self-conscious reflection upon writing and the power of words'.[2] Kennedy further notes that writing for Poe functioned 'as a mode of discovery and analysis' (p. 28). The problem with Poe, however, is isolating a particular strand of writing about death because death takes on myriad forms and is linked to different contexts such as mesmerism, accounts of psychopathology and models of beauty. The role of aesthetics will be returned to later in a discussion of George Eliot, but it is worth noting that Poe's view of beauty is linked to how narratives about death suggest an aesthetic return, most frequently in which beautiful women embody an idea of art that appears in reanimated Gothic forms. However, it is also important to explore the more seemingly abstract (quasi-scientific) tales such as 'Mesmeric Revelation' (1844) and 'The Facts in the Case of M. Valdemar' (1845), as they provide an interesting bridge to the earlier Gothic tradition.

We noted in the previous chapter that James Boaden's *The Man of Two Lives* (1828) makes explicit engagement, via Franz Mesmer, with ideas about mesmerism and animal magnetism. Indeed, Boaden's influence on Poe's 'William Wilson' (1839) has been suggested by one critic.[3] The concluding paragraph of Boaden's novel asserts the importance of developing a conscience, and Poe's tale addresses what happens when that conscience is killed off in a narrative that is also framed by issues of magnetic influence that link the narrator to his unnamed, but twin-like, double. These issues are given more extensive treatment in Poe's tales about mesmerism.

'Mesmeric Revelation' reads like an abstract and theoretical account of subjectivity and its relationship to a spiritual world, but the dying narrator, Vankirk, is clear that his tale is intended as a refutation of 'the mere abstractions which have been so long the fashion of the moralists of England, of France, and of Germany'.[4] Doris V. Falk has noted that Poe had read early accounts of mesmerism that were heavily indebted to ideas about animal magnetism which emphasised the cosmic and physical aspects of the 'force', rather than later accounts that asserted a psychological influence.[5] Nevertheless, the tale attempts to work beyond abstractions by asserting the eye-witness testimony of Vankirk's encounter with a world that exists beyond death as he recounts what he feels in his dying state. The philosophical argot of the tale is supported by feelings that are close to religious ecstasy in their embracing of the effects of the mesmeric trance, which grants a 'mesmeric exaltation' (p. 89) that enables Vankirk to escape his 'normal condition' (p. 89). Unusual to the story is the blending of a quasi-scientific diction relating to matter and rationality and its substantiation of the divine. The magnetic pull of the cosmos reveals to Vankirk that 'The ultimate or unparticled matter not only permeates all things, but impels all things; and thus *is* all things within itself. This matter is God' (pp. 90–1). Mind and body are brought together because 'To create individual, thinking beings, it was necessary to incarnate portions of the divine mind', so that humans are aspects of the divine, but are different from God by virtue of their physical formation. Death returns the subject to their ultimate destination, which is to rejoin the divine world that had created them so that 'Our present incarnation is progressive, preparatory, temporary. Our future is perfected, ultimate, immortal' (p. 93). In the end is our beginning because we never really die, and the mesmeric trance grants us a foretaste of that as it enables the suspension of our corporality and gives us a hint of what the 'unparticled' life anticipates.

The tale may seem like a confirmation of a divine presence that implicates the existence of a 'full design' (p. 93). However, the tone of the tale is at odds with its subject matter because the pursuit of the divine is expressed in secular, quasi-scientific terms. The discovery of God is the consequence of an application of rationality that makes the tale read like an exercise in experimental discovery. Also, it is notable that the intimation of the divine does not imply the existence of a theologically conventional discourse of ethics, which we witnessed in the eighteenth century in the work of Young and Hervey, amongst others. Falk claims that Poe's version of what mesmerism uncovers is merely 'an amoral force' (536), which underpins the peculiar paradox that God seems like an aspect of physics in which science functions as a way of demonstrating the existence of the divine. The tale is both religious *and* secular and death is celebrated as the state to which we are naturally evolving. Death may therefore seem to be represented in a positive light in 'Mesmeric Revelation'; the same, however, could not be said of 'The Facts in the Case of M. Valdemar', published the following year.

'Mesmeric Revelation' can be read as an exercise in clairvoyance. Vankirk's sense of the cosmos is intimated through his medium-like mesmeric trance. The seemingly privileged subject who exploits scientific procedure in order to reveal a truth that is concealed from others meets its counterpart in the figure of his detective, C. August Dupin. However, before looking at Poe's detective it is helpful to explore how 'The Facts in the Case of M. Valdemar' rework the premise of 'Mesmeric Revelation' in Gothic terms.

The doctor–patient paradigm is revised in 'The Facts in the Case of M. Valdemar', with the focus shifting to the narrator rather than staying on the mesmeric subject. The shift is significant because death becomes registered in terms of its physical effects. The dying Valdemar (who, like Vankirk, has terminal pulmonary tuberculosis) is placed in a mesmeric trance that arrests the symptoms of physical dissolution. Initially the narrator acknowledges a difficulty in placing Valdemar into a mesmeric trance: 'His will was at no period positively, or thoroughly under my control, and in regard to *clairvoyance*, I could accomplish with him nothing to be relied upon.'[6] Indeed, the tale focuses on responses to Valdemar, who is in no state to reproduce the conceptually complex discourse of Vankirk. If science is co-opted for a divine cause in 'Mesmeric Revelation', here science is baffled by what it observes.

Valdemar's retreat into his dying self, which is enabled by the mesmeric trance, generates an intellectual consideration of what he discovers. The narrator notes that the mesmerised Valdemar's 'glassy roll of the eye' leads only to an 'uneasy *inward* examination' (p. 354, italics in original). Sleeping becomes synonymous with dying when Valdemar claims that he is '"still asleep – dying"' (p. 355), and so does not generate the possibility for the application of reason found by Vankirk.

The tale functions as an explicit rebuttal of the type of consolation literature from the period that centred on the deathbed scene. Philippe Ariès has noted how in nineteenth-century America the once private and intimate recollections of the dead (as referenced in family elegies and epitaphs) took on a more public turn, as witnessed by the production of 'true stories and novels in which the authors ... try to convince their readers that death has not really taken away those dear to them', despite the crucial role of the deathbed scene and the significance that was attached to last words.[7] Valdemar, in contrast, is not surrounded by the family and his death cannot be construed in such superficially positive terms. After having been maintained at the point of death for seven months by virtue of a mesmeric trance, an effort is made to relieve Valdemar of what has clearly become a traumatising state of simultaneous life and death. The narrator recounts the horror of Vankirk's claim that '"*I say to you that I am dead!*"' (p. 359, italics in original) as he pleads for release. His final cries of '"dead! dead!"' and rapid physical degeneration into 'a nearly liquid mass of loathsome – of detestable putridity' (p. 359) function as an explicit critique of that 'happy death' usually recorded in contemporary consolation literature. Poe is not, however, simply mocking the sentimentality of consolation literature; he is, across both tales, exploring a theory of life and death and how that relates to a version of the cosmos that he would examine in his long essay, *Eureka*.

Life, death and the cosmos

Eureka was published in 1848 and is based on a two-hour lecture titled 'The Cosmogony of the Universe' delivered by Poe at the Society Library, New York in February of that year. It is indebted to Newton and engages with some of the new understandings of the universe mapped by Alexander von Humboldt in *Kosmos* (1845), to whom Poe's treatise is dedicated. G. R. Thompson has noted that *Eureka* appears to contain the key to understanding why images of 'Nature and Death, as well as madness, perversity, and terror' can be seen as part of a coherent 'grand design' across Poe's texts that is rooted in his quasi-scientific evaluation of the universe.[8] The treatise contains a series of narrative tones, employing comedy, parody and scientific discourse. It can also be read in a tradition of reflection on the cosmos that echoes the deliberations of Young's *Night Thoughts*. Indeed, in the Preface Poe claims that he wants the treatise to be granted the status of a 'Poem' and, in keeping with the themes of morbidity and the discourse of creativity that ghosts it, he states that 'it is as a poem only that I wish this work to be judged after I am dead'.[9]

Poe's thesis is that the end of the universe is implied in its beginning and that the 'annihilation' of the universe is inevitable (p. 211). As it arose from nothing, so it heads back towards nothing. The life and death of the universe are in turn recapitulated in the life and death of the subject, who is thereby united with all other subjects because 'A man ... becomes Mankind; Mankind a member of the cosmical family of intelligences' (p. 213). For Poe, the universe has been created by God, who has become sublimated within the particles of the universe, and for this reason the universe appears to operate through divinely created laws. However, we are denied proper access to this divine presence because it eludes our attempts at detection. This is because although ideas about 'God' may well exist in 'nearly all languages', such labelling 'stands for the possible attempt at an impossible conception' (p. 222). It represents an effort at understanding rather than true knowledge. This type of position was mapped in 'Mesmeric Revelation', where it is claimed that 'There is no immateriality; it is a mere word' (p. 90). Instead, we find God in the seeming paradox of 'unparticled matter' that 'permeates all things' and in effect 'is God' (pp. 90–1). For Poe, the universe is created out of nothingness by the creative mind of God who is the '*First Cause*' (p. 251, italics in original), and from this original unity there is the dispersion of God within the discrete parts of matter. Tellingly, he claims that God is everywhere and nowhere, and Poe asserts that the universe is both divinely created and oddly secular because this God has seemingly absented themself. For Poe, 'The Thought of God is to be understood as originating the Diffusion – as proceeding with it – as regulating it – and, finally, as being withdrawn from it on completion' (p. 251). Also, this now absent God has only presided over one aspect of the universe because, for Poe, matter is not infinite and therefore neither is God, and he regards any alternative view as 'impossible and preposterous' (p. 256). The universe is thus finite and inhabited by this diffused God whose rules condition the laws pertaining to the universe even whilst they no longer inhabit it in any viable way. God is both absent and present. God is also simultaneously conceived as both alive and dead, and the implication is that we all inhabit a liminal world like that of Vankirk and Valdemar – we just do not, yet, know it. For Poe, we need to understand that we live within a divinely constructed narrative, which our own attempts at art mimic. To write, therefore, is to take us close to God, even though 'The plots of God are perfect' whereas ours are fallible 'because it is a finite intelligence that constructs' (p. 292). But our plots, Poe claims, can provide us with a dim echo of what is to come, because the universe, like any tale, has a sense of an ending. Poe appears to privilege writers as having a finely tuned 'Conscious Intelligence' (p. 305) that is the consequence of the subtle ministrations that the ether plays upon the refinement of the soul. Crucially, the end of the universe will be defined by the end of matter, which will release God, who 'will be but the re-constitution of the *purely Spiritual* and Individual God' (p. 308, italics in original) that existed before the universe was created. In the end is the beginning and our capacity to plot (to create) takes us towards the divine, so that 'The pleasure which we derive from any display of human ingenuity is in the ratio of *the approach* to this species of reciprocity. In the construction of *plot*, for example, in fictitious literature, we should aim at so arranging the incidents that we shall not be able to determine, of any one of them, whether it depends from any other or upholds it' (p. 292, italics in original). The search is therefore for unity, but to write plots that are close to the divine they need to have a sense of an ending because it is there, at the end, at the moment of death, that meaning is generated.

The central claim is that the universe, whilst structured, contains no obvious ethical presence. God has been transformed into unparticled matter, and awaits their recomposition at the end of days. Thompson claims that in *Eureka*, 'the essence of the Universe is neither creative nor destructive ... – but simply Void' (p. 298). However, Thompson ignores the fact that Poe is trying to find meaning in the 'Void', and that is why he gives voice to Vankirk and Valdemar. Death in *Eureka* is only a prelude to another type of living that is, in the end, found in narrative. In the end is the beginning, and this idea of repetition makes sense of why in Poe the dead seem to come back. The idea is given treatment in his other tale about hypnotism and animal magnetism, 'A Tale of the Ragged Mountains' (1844), which completes Poe's closely produced series of narratives about death and trance-like states.

Death and the repeated life

Whilst 'Mesmeric Revelation' and 'The Facts in the Case of M. Valdemar' address the immediacy of death, 'A Tale of the Ragged Mountains' functions as a resurrection narrative that has more in common with Boaden's *The Man of Two Lives*. The narrator of the tale notes of Augustus Bedloe, its principal protagonist:

> Whence he came, I never ascertained. Even about his age – although I call him a young gentleman – there was something which perplexed me in no little degree. He certainly *seemed* young – and he made a point of speaking about his youth – yet there were moments when I should have had little trouble in imaging him a hundred years of age.[10]

He is young and old and of obscure origins that need to be explored in order to account for why Bedloe is as he is. Also, the suggestion that he '*seemed* young' is somewhat belied by his corpse-like appearance: 'His limbs were exceedingly long and emaciated ... His complexion was absolutely bloodless' and his eyes usually resembled 'the eyes of a long-interred corpse' (p. 679). The mystery of Bedloe's appearance is solved by animal magnetism in the rapport that develops between Bedloe and one Dr Templeton, who believes in the efficacy of 'magnetic remedies' (p. 680). The excitement induced in Bedloe by his contact with Templeton, plus Bedloe's use of morphine, generates a strange vision when, on a walk around a familiar country terrain, Bedloe is apparently transported to a late-eighteenth-century British colonial scene populated by Malays and British soldiers. The scene is that of a rebellion in which Bedloe attempts to make good his escape but is speared in the head by a Malay, whose spear resembles a snake. He then recounts leaving his body, which is accompanied by 'a violent and sudden shock through my soul, as if of electricity' (p. 685). Templeton, on hearing this tale, produces a portrait of a friend, one Mr Oldeb, who had been killed during an uprising in the Indian city of Benares in 1780. When treating Bedloe for a fever he had acquired during his walk, Templeton accidently bleeds his head with a 'venomous' leech, which results in his death from an alternative type of head wound.

The striking features of this synopsis are the role of repetition and the brief mention that is made of electricity as a form of energy that jolts the spirit out of the dead Bedloe. Animal magnetism is also, as Falk (540) has noted, an electromagnetic force, and its use shifts the emphasis away from Bedloe and on to Templeton, who makes possible the reincarnation of his dead friend (with 'Oldeb' functioning as a near anagram of Bedloe). Falk has also observed how the tale makes 'time and space unreal and relative', which demonstrates the type of thinking that Poe would elaborate in *Eureka*. It also bears striking structural similarities to the cosmology elaborated by Poe in his essay, as it too suggests that at the end of a life a new form of life is released. For Falk, Poe ultimately asserts an optimistic sense of an ending in which 'either identity would be preserved after death, or annihilation would itself be purposeful in absorbing man into God' (546). Bedloe's corpse-like appearance at the start thus contains within it a reassurance that the dead do not properly die, they are either reborn or recycled into the unparticled matter that is God. In effect the tale reasserts the conclusion of 'Mesmeric Revelation' in which the self becomes absorbed into the unity of the cosmos. The end of life cannot be separated from its origin, just as God, in *Eureka*, is a force that is explicitly manifested at the beginning and at the end.

Crucially, the tale focuses on the hypnotist as the generator of knowledge, and although 'A Tale of the Ragged Mountains' is different in structure and tone from the two other tales of mesmerism, they too focus on the analyst as the figure who tries to make sense of what they see and hear. All three tales, and *Eureka*, focus on how we can gain knowledge of this ethereal world that is both spiritual and subject to natural laws. Poe introduces science into this debate in order to place the idea of the divine on a more sure footing than that found in the consolation literature of the time. Art becomes the medium through which the divinely inspired plots can be intimated, and this suggests a different order of knowledge than that found in mesmerism, which is abstract and detached in its explorations even whilst Poe's mesmerists become pulled into the plots of others (as in Templeton's apparent resurrection of his friend Oldeb through Bedloe). Art, as in *Eureka*, takes you closer to the divine, and it is through models of beauty that a rebirth, or a resurrection, becomes possible. Repetition becomes key in understanding how Poe explores this process, and tales such as 'Morella' (1835) and 'Ligeia' (1838) demonstrate how Poe initially formulated his metaphysical deliberations on life and death as aesthetic ones. Poe brings together these concerns in 'The Philosophy of Composition' (1846), which also anticipates many of the issues subsequently addressed in *Eureka*.

Writing death

Kennedy has argued that in tales such as 'Berenice' (1835), 'Morella', 'Ligeia' and 'The Fall of the House of Usher' (1839), death is portrayed 'not as annihilation or separation but as an ambiguous, temporary parting. In a revolting parody of the death of the Other, Poe depicts the return of the beloved not in spiritual terms but as a ghastly reanimation tinged with vampirism' (p. 78). There are clear gender implications involved in discussing the different representations of the death of women in these earlier tales and the images of dead and dying men in the later mesmeric ones. Poe's now famous dictum from 'The Philosophy of Composition', that 'When it most closely allies itself to *Beauty*: the death of a beautiful woman is unquestionably the most poetic topic in the world', has been the subject of much critical scrutiny.[11] Elisabeth Bronfen in *Over Her Dead Body* (1992) has produced a critically canonical assessment of the cultural history of representations of dead women, including Poe's contribution to that history. Her view is that Poe's assertion about the return of Beauty represents an aesthetic ideal that was missing in life. The real woman disappears, is killed off, only to be replaced by a beautiful facsimile of herself. Mourning and melancholy thus becomes highly ambiguous states that for Bronfen refer to 'the indeterminacy, hesitation or contradiction in respect to meaning inscribed in any representation'.[12] For Poe, 'Beauty of whatever kind, in its supreme development, invariably excites the sensitive soul to tears. Melancholy is thus the most legitimate of all the poetical tones' (p. 484). However, it is clear that this is male melancholy and its engagement with death may seem to be of a completely different order than that found in the tales of mesmerism, but it is through the idea of narrative structure and forms of repetition that these diverse images formulate a model of death that reflects Poe's view on the cosmos.

If Bedloe seemed like a recognisable corpse in life, Ligeia resembles a corpse of a different kind, which is repeatedly associated with her whiteness, as represented by 'her marble hand', her skin, which is described as 'rivalling the purest ivory', and the 'brilliancy almost startling' of her white teeth.[13] If Bedloe had the dull eyes of a corpse, Ligeia inspires metaphysical contemplation – 'What was it ... which lay far within the pupils of my beloved?' (p. 656) – that is linked to memory. The narrator discerns in the eyes something that has been forgotten, but which he appears to be on the point of remembering. It represents a different order of memory than that implied by how Oldeb is recalled by Bedloe (and is clearly different from the type of Romantic memory advanced by Samuel Rogers, which was discussed in Chapter 1). The fascination with Ligeia's eyes also implies that the narrator has been in some way hypnotised by them and that he is subject to animal magnetism. His feelings when looking at her eyes are likened to the type of transportation that one might find in art, as he acknowledges a similar feeling generated 'by certain sounds from stringed instruments, and not unfrequently by passages from books' (p. 656). As Poe would map it in *Eureka*, this takes you towards the divine, but it is a divinity that can only be released in death. The narrator acknowledges that Ligeia has placed him on a path that leads 'to the goal of a wisdom too divinely precious' (p. 657). He recalls that 'Her presence ... rendered vividly luminous the many mysteries of the transcendentalism in which we were immersed' (p. 657). Bronfen has noted of Ligeia that 'Alive she has a truth that is beyond worldly knowledge, but she will not yield it. She not only marks the limit of mortal knowledge but also represents that truth which is beyond' (p. 332). Ligeia represents the struggle with death as the narrator bears witness to how 'she wrestled with the Shadow' (p. 658). Her anxieties are revealingly given aesthetic form in the guise of her poem about 'the conqueror Worm' (p. 659, l. 39), which records her fear of death in specifically theatrical terms. The opening stanza notes how angels watch over the human tragedy of existence:

> Lo! 'tis gala night
>   Within the lonesome latter years!
> An angel throng, bewinged, bedlight
>   In veils, and drowned in tears,
> Sit in a theatre, to see
>   A play of hopes and fears,
> While the orchestra breathes fitfully
>   The music of the spheres. (p. 658, ll. 1–8)

Subsequent references are made to 'Mimes' (l. 9) and 'puppets' (l. 11) that represent mortals who are part of the 'motley drama' (l. 16), who are trapped in a narrative arc of life and birth that positions them as within:

> a circle that ever returneth in
>   To the self-same spot;
> And much of Madness, and more of Sin
>   And Horror, the soul of the plot! (ll. 20–3)

It is out of this scene of horror that a vampiric 'blood-red thing' emerges (l. 26), and this leads to the conclusion 'That the play is the tragedy, "Man,"/ And its hero, the conqueror Worm' (ll. 38–9). Kennedy (p. 82) reads the poem as an explicit challenge to consolation literature, but surely what is more striking is the engagement with plot and story, one that is presided over by spiritual and then increasingly physical forces. Death becomes the logical outcome of the divine plot that Poe would elaborate in *Eureka*.

Ligeia dies, but is kept subliminally alive through images the narrator records on the tapestries that decorate the walls of a German abbey that he purchases after her death and which he inhabits with his new wife, Lady Rowena. Anxieties about death and the trauma of mourning are echoed in the representational horrors with which he surrounds himself that seem to move from the unreal to the real. He notes of these images that, to the visitor,

> they bore the appearance of simple monstrosities; but upon a farther advance, this appearance gradually departed; and step by step ... the visitor ... saw himself surrounded by an endless succession of the ghastly forms ... The phantasmagoric effect was vastly heightened by the artificial introduction of a strong continual current of wind behind the draperies – giving a hideous and uneasy animation to the whole. (p. 661)

The progressively cosmic horror registered in Ligeia's poem is here given a dramatic force. The representation becomes seemingly animated by the wind and the effect is to bring such images to life even as Poe asserts, in *Eureka*, that death leads to a new creativity. This creativity aligns the narrator with this Gothic impulse to destroy in order to conjure a lost aesthetic that is associated with Ligeia and not with Rowena, whom 'I loathed ... with a hatred belonging more to demon than to man' (p. 661). Rowena's sudden illness is attributed by the narrator to either 'the distemper of her fancy' or 'the phantasmagoric influences of the chamber' (p. 662). The implication is that Rowena is killed by representation and in death is transformed by the 'visions of Ligeia' that the narrator is repeatedly haunted by as Rowena lies dying. As Rowena suffers death by representation, so Ligeia is reborn out of his vision of her, as if his very grief has conjured her back into existence. Life is thus generated out of death as the beauty of Ligeia is restored. For Bronfen, the narrator's mourning of a vision of Ligeia means that 'this image requires its materialisation first as another body then as a text' (p. 333). In the end the tale represents the triumph of a type of narrative vision, and significantly this is developed through images of repetition.

It is tempting at this stage to advance a reading of Poe that argues that such images of repetition anticipate Freud's idea of the uncanny; after all, Freud asserts that 'Many people experience the feeling in the highest degree in relation to death and dead bodies, to the return of the dead, and to spirits and ghosts'.[14] Freud also elaborates links between the uncanny and its representation in literary forms when he claims that 'Apparent death and re-animation of the dead have been represented as most uncanny themes. But things of this sort too are very common in fairy stories' (p. 369). Indeed, Freud will even extend this argument about representation further when he argues that the uncanny, as it is represented in literature, 'is a much more fertile province than the uncanny in real life, for it contains the whole of the latter and something more besides, something that cannot be found in real life' (p. 372). This will lead to the conclusion that perhaps it is in literature that a genuine provenance for the uncanny can be found: Freud claims that '*in the first place a great deal that is not uncanny in fiction would be so if it happened in real life; and in the second place there are many more means of creating uncanny effects in fiction than there are in real life*' (p. 373, italics in the original). Poe's fascination with how representation, creativity and death conceptually pivot could be read as a logical precursor to this position.[15] The central place of repetition would also seem to suggest this, as we see Ligeia return from the dead, for example, or as in Poe's use of doubles (as typified by 'William Wilson'). However, there is an additional complexity. We saw earlier in this book that images of death might look Gothic but actually function as a form of anti-Gothic because they elicit sympathy rather than fear (as in Adam Smith and Edmund Burke), so in Poe we have a version of the uncanny that, because it is the product of a highly self-conscious artistic vision, seems to evacuate the uncanny of any meaningful uncanny affect.

In 'The Philosophy of Composition', Poe states that the author should have an idea of how the narrative will end and begin to head towards that ending (in structural terms recapitulating what is metaphysically asserted in *Eureka*). As Poe puts it, 'Nothing is more clear than that every plot, worth the name, must be elaborated to its *denouement* before anything be attempted with the pen' (p. 480, italics in original). In his account of the composition of 'The Raven' (1845), he claims that 'the work proceeded step by step, to its completion, with the precision and rigid consequence of a mathematical problem' (p. 482). The element of mood is also discussed within the context of matters of scale, so that 'the extent of a poem may be made to bear mathematical relation to its merit' (p. 483), with a short poem being better as it can be read at one sitting, thus enabling the reader to focus on the mood of the piece without the mental distractions that a longer work would induce, and so supports the desired 'ratio ... of intensity' (p. 483). This is followed by a discussion of why melancholy was a suitable tone that should be rooted in feelings of male grief for a dead lover. He even acknowledges that in 'The Raven' he used a type of rhyme scheme that was meant to emphasise a sense of repetition that was appropriate to the theme of a subject who is trapped by feelings of grief. Poe thus engages with a number of issues about death, mourning, creativity and repetition that will constitute familiar elements of the uncanny, but they are issues that are self-consciously developed as structural forms within a narrative. Poe's model of composition outlines, in literary terms, a way of thinking about representation that would be translated into quasi-scientific principles in *Eureka*. Bronfen neatly summarises what this self-conscious engagement with representations of a dying woman leads to:

> Because her dying figures as an analogy to the creation of an art work, and the depicted death serves as a double of its formal condition, the 'death of a beautiful woman' marks the *mise an abyme* of a text, the moment of self-reflexivity, where the text seems to comment on itself and its own process of composition, and so decomposes itself. (p. 71, italics in original)

This is also closely allied to Poe's sense that a narrative's end is worked towards from the beginning, so that 'Death is ... from the start integral to his notion of poetics' (p. 61). Poe's uncanny is thus, at the level of composition, devoid of uncanny affect.

The theme of repetition is given an unusual inflection in 'Morella', which can be read as a counterpoint to images of return in 'Ligeia' and as working in a different idiom of death than that expressed in 'The Philosophy of Composition'. The tale bears many similarities to 'Ligeia', with the narrator noting that he and Morella share a passion for metaphysical speculation, and that she is the guide in such matters. However, for the narrator, Morella's engagement with 'the ashes of a dead philosophy' lead to horror rather than enlightenment.[16] Crucially, this appears to be due to a matter of tone rather than content. The problem is Morella's voice. The narrator notes:

> hour after hour would I linger by her side, and dwell upon the music of her voice – until, at length, its melody was tainted with terror, – and there fell a shadow upon my soul – and I grew pale and shuddered inwardly at those too unearthly tones. And thus, joy suddenly faded into horror, and the most beautiful became the most hideous. (p. 667)

Morella is associated with an anti-aesthetic (which is opposed to 'beauty'), and Poe attempts to challenge this Gothic aesthetic even whilst he works within it. Beauty is linked to melancholy grief, which bestows a paradoxical pleasure in which the subject is, as Poe states in 'The Philosophy of Composition', 'impelled ... by the human thirst for self-torture' (p. 491). However, the narrator does not love Morella, and she refers to this when she becomes ill whilst pregnant and cryptically informs him that '"in life thou didst abhor, in death thou shalt adore"' (p. 669). The narrator acknowledges that he has a particular interest in death, specifically in where the person goes after death, an interest that he shares with Morella.

Morella dies in childbirth and the daughter appears as the physical embodiment of Morella. Initially, the narrator states that 'I loved her with a love more fervent than I had believed it possible to feel for any denizen of earth' (p. 669). However, these feelings are quickly turned to 'horror' as the child expresses views held by Morella, so that 'the lessons of experience fell from the lips of infancy' (p. 669). The child is effectively inhabited by the spirit of Morella and what is truly horrifying for the narrator is her apparent return. The child dies at the point at which the narrator gives her 'Morella' as her baptismal name, and when he goes to place her in the family tomb he discovers that it is empty, so that in effect Morella dies twice. At one level the tale centres on the loss of innocence represented as the loss of childhood. But much of the horror is related to the tone of Morella's voice, which reappears in the daughter as 'the sad musical tones of her speech' (p. 670). The voice is accorded a different significance than how the voice is constructed in the tales of mesmerism, where it is granted insight and authority, whereas here it is associated with a more traumatic, because more personal, form of revelation. The narrator did not love Morella, but he did love his daughter until that was taken away from him by Morella's apparent return. For Kennedy (p. 82), the tale explores the unavoidability of death, as the narrator's distance from Morella had suggested his refusal to engage with her death only to be confronted with it through the death of the daughter. And whilst that subsequent death may seem to be the end of the matter, the narrator cannot escape the memory of it: 'Years – years may pass away, but the memory of that epoch – never!' (p. 671). It is not a death that is a new beginning, as it is in the other tales; instead it represents death as trauma, not as release, and so Poe produces a counterpoint to images of death that he elaborates elsewhere. Important to note in this context is that Morella at no point functions aesthetically. By virtue of the horror she produces, she does not generate the type of transcendence that Art, because of Poe's suggestions of its divine provenance, can provide. Instead, 'Morella' indicates that the narrator is trapped within an alternative Gothic aesthetic that is without transcendence.

As we have seen, *Eureka* is a key text in Poe's aesthetic theory, and there are links between it and 'The Philosophy of Composition' that provide a context for the images of beauty in his tales. There are a number of other Poe texts that could have been discussed here, such as 'The Fall of the House of Usher', 'Berenice', 'The Oval Portrait', and poems such as 'The Raven' and 'Annabel Lee'. The grouping selected here demonstrates how models of death, writing and art can be linked to a consideration of animal magnetism and to Poe's theory of cosmology. These issues may seem to have an American provenance, but it is telling how many of Poe's intellectual frameworks combine a mixture of Emersonian transcendentalism with some implicit aspects of European romanticism (notably Kant on cognition), notwithstanding his apparent refutation of European philosophy in 'Mesmeric Revelation'.[17] Poe's model of death and the images of creativity with which it is associated are complicated by a shift from writing to reading, which can be illustrated by an exploration of death in *Wuthering Heights*.

Wuthering Heights: knowing death?

Ariès has noted of *Wuthering Heights* that 'Everything that in an earlier novel would have been erotic, macabre, and diabolical becomes here passionate, moral and funereal. The book is a symphony on the intertwined themes of love and death' (p. 443). However, such images are not divorced from aesthetic considerations, and Carol Margaret Davison has argued that the fascination with death that we find across the work of the Brontë sisters is rooted in their juvenilia, 'especially their use of voice, atmospherics, and poetic/narrative elements', which shape the representations of death in their adult writing.[18] She argues that such juvenilia 'constitute a type of Graveyard Poetry in that they render poetic visions of the beyond/next world while exploring the interrelated Christian themes of faith, doubt, and divine judgement' (p. 5). Emily Brontë's poems, such as 'No Coward Soul is Mine' (1846), can be read as part of a Christian tradition in which divine solace supports a strength of moral purpose that enables the subject to overcome the fear of death. However, it is a tradition that *Wuthering Heights* complicates by emphasising that it is Nelly Dean's piety that makes her an unreliable narrator. Nelly is unable to interpret events, so much as censure them by demonising the apparent wilfulness of Heathcliff and Cathy. To that degree the Gothic appears as a type of negative labelling in which Heathcliff is repeatedly demonised and dehumanised, leading Nelly to question '"Is he a ghoul or a vampire?"'[19]

However, before Nelly begins her narration we see Lockwood struggling to come to terms with life at the Heights, and during his overnight stay he first discovers on a window ledge the repeatedly scratched name of Catherine, followed by those of Earnshaw, Heathcliff and Linton. The ledge doubles as a table that 'was covered with writing scratched on the paint', which takes on an increasingly ghostly nature as Lockwood falls asleep and records that 'a glare of white letters started from the dark, as vivid as spectres – the air swarmed with Catherines' (p. 20). The ghost of Cathy is thus invoked through language and this in turn is related to the pile of 'mildewed books' on the table that includes a copy of Cathy's Testament. This and other books have, according to Lockwood, been scribbled over, and they include a diary. Lockwood's attempt to read the diary is initially challenged by a problem of decoding when he recalls that 'I began, forthwith, to decipher her faded hieroglyphics' (p. 20). The story he reads relates to similar acts centred on reading. He recounts Cathy's tale of her, Heathcliff and Hindley's attendance at one of Joseph's religious services that requires them 'to take our Prayer-books' (p. 20), which are subsequently referred to as '"good books"' by Joseph when, after the service, he berates Cathy and Heathcliff for playing and tells them to read their prayer-books instead. However, Cathy had noted before the service that 'H. and I are going to rebel' (p. 20), and they enact this Romantic rebellion by throwing their books into the dog kennel, with Cathy 'vowing I hated a good book' (p. 21). Lockwood then becomes drowsy over *Seventy Times Seven, and the First of the Seventy First: A Pious Discourse Delivered by the Reverend Jabez Branderham in the Chapel of Gimmerden Sough*, which has been defaced by Cathy. In the dream that follows, Lockwood renounces a sermon by Branderham and attempts to get the congregation to attack Branderham by calling out '"Fellow martyrs, have at him! Drag him down, and crush him to atoms, that the place which knows him may know him no more!"' (p. 24). Cates Baldridge has noted that Lockwood's rebellion echoes that of Cathy and Heathcliff, but it is one that is couched in 'the repressive rhetoric which has tormented him' so that Lockwood's rebellion becomes effectively negated.[20] For Baldridge, Lockwood is a voyeur, although one who tries to decode the strange scenes that he observes at the Heights. Lockwood, however, has a tendency to translate these dramas into other, symbolic forms, so that he copies rebellion whilst also becoming aware of a dead Cathy who is available for similar symbolic projection.

As Lockwood's rebellion becomes trapped by Branderham's rhetoric, so he sees the dead Cathy as lost in her scratched names, which appear like a mass of writing that then leads him to her books. Her names become 'spectres' that are resurrected out of the rotting books, an image developed in the peat bog that surrounds the chapel where Branderham preaches, 'whose peaty moisture is said to answer all the purposes of embalming on the few corpses deposited there' (p. 23). This dream is followed by the tapping on the window by a spectral Cathy who claims that she has come from '"the moor!"', which is populated by such bogs (p. 25). Death, for Lockwood, cannot be separated from writing, reading, books and acts of symbolic haunting. This is why he will see that the key to understanding is narration, which means that when Nelly takes over the story she needs to demonstrate her credentials as a narrator, telling Lockwood '"I have read more than you would fancy, Mr Lockwood. You could not open a book in this library that I have not looked into"' (p. 63). How to read death and its significance pervades the novel, and it requires a process of interpretation that rests on the reassembly of parts, of manuscripts, memories and signs.

Ingrid Geerken has noted the presence of fragmentation in the novel, a presence that Lockwood only voyeuristically observes but which the grief-stricken Heathcliff powerfully feels as an act of persistent recollection.[21] He tells Nelly:

> 'what is not connected with her to me? and what does not recall her? I cannot look down to this floor, but her features are shaped on the flags! In every cloud, in every tree – filling the air at night, and caught by glimpses in every object by day I am surrounded with her image ... The entire world is a dreadful collection of memoranda that she did exist, and that I have lost her!' (pp. 323-4)

Geerken advances a theory of 'Mortal Regret' that is different in kind from melancholy and which functions in the novel as an attempt to bring fragments together into their whole, in a strategy that has Heathcliff's fragmented Cathy (who is found in floors, clouds and trees) as the dismembered being who lies behind it all. For Geerken, in such acts 'a perfect assemblage of parts will resurrect the dead' (376). Geerken acknowledges links to *Frankenstein* in an argument about Frankenstein overcoming his mourning for his mother by symbolically resurrecting her through the figure of the creature. Significantly, she links this to the narrative structure of Shelley's novel in which 'the act of bodily reparation is paralleled on a formal level by the many layers of narration that envelop the central act of revivification. The work of mourning literally becomes one of restoration' (376). This enveloping may seem maternal but it also implicates textuality in the production of mourning. An act of restoration, considered in these textual terms, requires a process of interpretation that brings the signs together to form a coherent narrative. We saw in Chapter 1 that a concern with assembling fragmentary messages into a complete narrative was addressed in Young's *Night Thoughts*, and it is an issue that will also be explored in an account of knowledge of the occult in Chapter 6. In *Wuthering Heights* Heathcliff's hostility towards books keeps alive his grief, and implies that the terms under which a plausible resurrection can be affected have to be on grounds other than the purely textual. The ghost of Cathy, for Lockwood, comes out of his reading of her texts, but the status of the ghost is unclear as it is a child's spirit that is manifested (out of her child writings), rather than the adult Cathy that died. Texts thus keep alive frozen versions of the self rather than provide possibilities for spiritual release or regeneration – which is also suggested in the young Cathy and Heathcliff's renunciation of the prayer-book. Any resurrection is thus on terms other than those suggested in the textual resurrections that Geerken links to *Frankenstein* (and by association with *Wuthering Heights*).

In part this suspicion about texts is suggested in Nelly's highly partial narration. However, it is also evident in the dying Cathy's anger and bewilderment at her projected vision of Edgar watching her die. She tells Nelly that she has a vision of '"Edgar standing solemnly by to see it over; then offering prayers of thanks to God for restoring peace to his house, and going back to his *books*! What in the name of all that feels, has he to do with *books*, when I am dying?"' (p. 122, italics in original). Later, Heathcliff will confiscate the second-generation Catherine's books, with her lamenting to Lockwood, '"Mr Heathcliff never reads; so he took it into his head to destroy my books"' (p. 301). Some of her other books have been stolen by Hareton, whose clumsy recitations from them provoke Catherine's anger, as she notes, '"Those books, both prose and verse, were consecrated to me by other associations, and I hate to have them debased and profaned in his mouth!"' (p. 302). The link to 'associations' glosses Heathcliff's reading of the signs of Cathy's presence, which he also sees as reflected in the face of Hareton, with Heathcliff acknowledging the difficulty in emotionally describing '"the thousand forms of past associations, and ideas he awakens; or embodies"' (p. 323). An idea of memory links the bookish to the signs of Cathy, but they are, in the novel, assigned to different models of experience. Books do not resurrect the dead in the same way that 'ideas' are awakened, and Heathcliff's use of 'awakens' implicates a different order of knowledge, one that is related to the dead.

We have noted how Lockwood's dreams are rooted within a problematic, because partial, attempt to make sense of Cathy's childlike narratives.

There the problem is one of interpretation but also of epistemology. When he sees 'a child's face looking through the window', he conjectures that he has conjured Cathy's spirit, although it is a palpable one that he physically assaults, cutting its wrist on the broken windowpane. Lockwood has a rational explanation for this 'dream'. After repeatedly reading her scratched name, it 'produced an impression which personified itself when I had no longer my imagination under control' (p. 28). However, it also suggests that dreams produce a certain type of knowledge because they symbolically incorporate versions of the 'truth' (in which the dream of Cathy reflects her feelings of exclusion, or when the dream about Branderham reveals Lockwood's ambivalent feelings on rebellion). Later Cathy will tell Nelly, "'I've dreamt in my life dreams that have stayed with me ever after, and changed my ideas; they've gone through me, like wine through water, and altered the colour of my mind'" (p. 80). Dreams effect emotional and intellectual changes and they provide a space where covert understandings are formed. They are also represented as occulted places that challenge Nelly's pursuit of moral clarity and desire for well-formed social and ethical structures. She refuses to listen to Cathy's dream because "'We're dismal enough without conjuring up ghosts, and visions to perplex us'" (p. 80), and she also concedes 'I was superstitious about dreams then, and am still' and feared that the thought of Cathy's dream 'made me dread something from which I might shape a prophecy, and foresee a fearful catastrophe' (p. 80). Later the dying Cathy relates what Nelly interprets as a dream when Cathy claims to see a face in the wall, leading Cathy to believe that "'the room is haunted!'" (p. 123) by a personification of death.

Cathy's anxieties about death are not matched by Nelly, who is able to recuperate this crisis by transforming it into a manageable deathbed scene, although only after the event when she notes in general terms that 'I see a repose that neither earth nor hell can break; and I feel an assurance of the endless and shadowless hereafter' (p. 169). For her, faith is restored at such moments, but the novel entertains a more secular version of death in Cathy's fears, which has led Geerken to argue, in a view which challenges that of Davison, that *Wuthering Heights* 'repudiates two main cultural forms of consolation: the genre of elegy, and the concept of the Christian afterlife' (p. 374).

Dreams offer a secular liminal space in the novel. They are figured as ghostly – populated by strange, possibly Gothic visions that provide a symbolically and critically complex analysis of the subject's world. Heathcliff claims that the sight of Hareton 'awakens' an image of Cathy that has been introjected as a memory, and it is one that leads to Heathcliff's decline and death. Heathcliff now withdraws into himself and observes his body as an almost independent entity, so that '"I have to remind myself to breathe – almost to remind my heart to beat!"' (p. 324); a type of spiritual memory associated with Cathy supplants an embodied, and more automatic, sense of memory.

These concerns may seem to be far removed from Poe, but they indicate a way of complicating his view that forms of narration can be linked to the divine. It should be noted, however, that Poe also claims a link between sleeping and dying when he has Valdemar claim that he is '"still asleep – dying"' (p. 355). The dream becomes the place where the dead are alive in their last moments, and this introjection of death would later be developed into a quasi-scientific area for investigation in the work of F. W. H. Myers, which is explored in Chapter 6.

In terms of narrative, however, *Wuthering Heights* pursues an alternative line of enquiry to that found in Poe, because the novel argues that whilst writing evokes the dead, it is not the place where they are to be found. The dead inhabit an alternative symbolic realm that is linked to memory and dreams, and the fact that it is secular is demonstrated by the location of the graves of Cathy and Heathcliff (and indeed Edgar) outside the churchyard, which permits metaphysical freedom 'for the sleepers in that quiet earth' (p. 337). Death is, however, as it is in Poe, a form of liberation, albeit not one that generates a wider knowledge about the cosmos (which distances it from Young's account of the universe in *Night Thoughts*). *Wuthering Heights* in part affects this complication of what we have witnessed in Poe by shifting the emphasis from writers to readers. This highlights the importance of decoding death; it is an issue that Poe addresses in his detective tales, but it is also found in Eliot's 'The Lifted Veil', which also examines links between art, creativity and models of death.

Lifting the veil

Thomas Albrecht has noted that the type of animal magnetism addressed by George Eliot in 'The Lifted Veil' has its roots in her 1856 essay, 'The Natural History of German Life'. There she formulates a theory of art which argues that it fosters a sympathetic engagement with life that brings readers into a shared culture of empathetic understanding. For her, 'Art is the nearest thing to life; it is a mode of amplifying experience and extending our contact with our fellow-men beyond the bounds of our personal lot'.[22] For Albrecht, this identifies a desire to find a communal experience that is 'an extension beyond the limitations of the self' that implies (although Albrecht does not assert this) the models of empathy that we found in the works of Smith and Burke, discussed in Chapter 1.[23] Albrecht's reading of the tale moves it beyond the discourse of animal magnetism that has typically been advanced as a critical context for it. For Albrecht, Latimer's insight into the minds of others does not elicit 'pity and compassion', but rather 'boredom and contempt' (439). However, Eliot does not leave it there because, argues Albrecht, Latimer projects these feelings on to Bertha, whereas when confronted by the earlier emotional crisis caused by the death of his father, Latimer is able to feel a type of empathy that suggests the presence of an ethical understanding which is otherwise lost in mind reading.

This view of Latimer, and why he needs to be corrected, rests on an assumption that he is a potentially failed reader of art – which in the instance of his father's death is manifested as a vision of love that binds Latimer not only to his father, but to all those who love the dead. The issues of writing, which was explored in relation to Poe, and reading, which was addressed in *Wuthering Heights*, are brought together in 'The Lifted Veil', and their intersection and links with models of death and dying indicate epistemic shifts in the literary narrative of death during the period.[24]

It is important to note that Latimer not only sees visions and can read some minds at some points (although he is unable to read Bertha's murderous intent), but also has ambitions to become a poet, even whilst the tale works through a defamiliarised sensation narrative concerning secrets, threats of murder and images of death that are reconstituted so that, in Poe-like fashion, the beginning is also, explicitly, about the end. The tale should fail as a sensation narrative because Latimer notes at the start, 'I foresee when I shall die, and everything that will happen in my last moments'.[25] This also emphasises the idea of 'knowing' that runs through the texts discussed in this chapter.

The tale is explicit in these engagements as Latimer struggles to reconcile his occasional visions with his aspiration to become a poet. He claims an early poetic sensibility that is not matched by his ability to write poetry. There is a space between feeling and aspiration that Latimer associates with his inability to communicate his feelings. He notes that 'A poet pours forth his song and *believes* in the listening ear and answering soul, to which his song will be floated sooner or later' (p. 7, italics in original). Art without a readership is not art, in Eliot's terms (as she would address it in 'The Natural History of German Life'); it is solipsism (which indicates that Latimer wants different things from his listeners than Eliot wants from her readers).[26] He subsequently relates an incident when he sees a vision of Prague, a place Latimer is unfamiliar with, which is generated by his father's reference to it. Latimer doubts the status of the vision: 'Was this a dream ... of a strange city, quite unfamiliar to my imagination?' (p. 9). It is a question that leads him to consider, 'was it the poet's nature in me, hitherto only a troubled yearning sensibility, now manifesting itself suddenly as spontaneous creation?' (p. 10). However, a subsequent troubled vision of Bertha (before he has met her) as a 'fatal-eyed woman' (p. 12) makes him wonder '*was* it a power? Might it not rather be a disease – a sort of intermittent delirium' (p. 12, italics in original). Latimer is thus unsure whether such visions are a gift or a curse, but these are issues that are repeatedly expressed in literary terms. He notes, for example, of the seemingly demonic Bertha's interest in him that 'The most prosaic woman likes to believe herself the object of a violent, a poetic passion', which enables her to think of Latimer as 'dying with love and jealousy' (p. 16) as she becomes romantically involved with his brother, Alfred. So far Bertha seems like a femme fatale who is familiar from sensation fiction, and links to the mode of sensation fiction help to widen the discussion about sympathy.

Susan David Bernstein has noted that the issue of *Blackwood's Edinburgh Magazine* (July 1859) in which the tale was published included an item (which immediately followed the tale) concerning H. L. Mansel's 'Bampton Lectures', on 'The Limits of Religious Thought', on theology and rationalism, delivered at Oxford University in 1858. Mansel's lectures on the relationship between the inner self and the external world share an implicit context with Eliot's tale, but more importantly Bernstein notes that Mansel wrote an anonymously published review, titled 'Sensation Novels', in the *Quarterly Review* of April 1863, of twenty-four sensation novels. In it Mansel suggested that reading such fiction aims at 'electrifying the nerves of the reader' through strategies that are akin to employing 'heat, electricity, galvanism'.[27] As Bernstein notes, this implies that the form has an effect on the reader similar to that of the animal magnetism that is attributed to Bertha in the story. Readers are therefore potentially united by some form of emotional response, even whilst Eliot attempts to subvert the form by addressing the role of secrets in a culturally complex way.

The problem confronted by Latimer is that he knows too much (the time when he will die) and too little (that Bertha wishes to have him poisoned). His visions of creativity do not, ultimately, produce a discourse of Romantic transcendence that could unite him with other readers and writers. Instead he is trapped by the knowledge of his impending death. This has led Helen Small to claim that 'The fundamental opposition in this story is not between art and science, or even between the ideal and the real, but between the fearful prospect of absolute knowing and the saving possibility of doubt and speculation'.[28] For Small, this is because Eliot was conscious of the anti-vitalist agenda that G. H. Lewes was developing in *The Physiology of Common Life* (1860), which argued that the principles of life were unknowable, even whilst science appeared to provide new revelations that suggested that the dead, perhaps, do not quite die. For Lewes, this is because we cannot be confident about pinpointing the exact moment at which death occurs: 'Hours after a man is dead, his muscles live, and will contract; his glands live, and will secrete; his heart lives, and will beat; his stomach lives and will digest.'[29] This leads Lewes to the conclusion that, considered in molecular terms, 'There can be no such thing as matter essentially dead: there can be no such thing as matter essentially living' (vol. II, p. 416). These secular considerations are reworked in 'The Lifted Veil' because, as Small notes, death is all too knowable for Latimer, who is denied the consolation of faith because '[h]is entire narrative is, of course, silently predicated on the disappearance of God' (p. xxvi).

In Poe, God has left the cosmos that they created, but will return at the end as they are recomposed out of their diffused atoms. In *Wuthering Heights*, the God that Emily Brontë frequently refers to in her poetry is strangely absent as death becomes a metaphor for freedom, and in Eliot's tale the absent God is the cause of Latimer's despair. Eliot suggests that understanding is located within the body, which takes us beyond Poe's claims about what is recalled within 'unparticled matter'. It is significant therefore that the tale's chief revelation is voiced by the already dead when the revived Mrs Archer incriminates Bertha in the intended poisoning of Latimer. The blood transfusion made by Latimer's friend Meunier only revives Mrs Archer long enough to make the accusation, but it creates another point of contact with Lewes, who had examined the possibility of blood transfusions in *The Physiology of Common Life* where he discussed whether blood has a life of its own that makes it similar to any other bodily tissue (vol. I, p. 255). In Eliot's hands it becomes transformed into a metaphor for the revelation of secrets, and Jill Galvan has noted in the tale how 'the flow of blood is roughly tantamount to the flow of information'.[30] Mrs Archer thus transmits information as transfused blood enables her to do so. The tale also demonstrates a formal engagement with medical issues, with Kate Flint observing that Latimer's scientific education enables him to discuss the death of his brother and Mrs Archer in medical terms as well as identifying his own demise from angina pectoris.[31] Flint claims that Latimer tacitly indicates that 'not only are bodies important in their own right but ... our comprehension of their workings may be analogous to our interpretation of texts' (460). Latimer is indeed a reader of some minds and bodies, and their ailments, so that 'truth' ultimately becomes established not through the power of his 'visions', but by an interpretation of those visions. For this reason, blood takes on both a medical and a symbolic function in the tale: it is about life and death and about the knowledge of life and death (as illustrated in Mrs Archer's revelation about Bertha's plot). Such a slip from fact to symbol invites a literary interpretation. As in Brontë, the shift is from writing to reading, and in Eliot physical bodies and textual bodies become conflated so that the signs of illness function as clues about what will, textually, happen next – as in, for example, the revelation that the tale will end with heart failure. Bodies are made to surrender their textual secrets, which indicates that death is not simply a bodily process but also a moment that generates symbolic forms that are organised into a narrative structure. The tale reads like a detective story even whilst its beginning declares its conclusion, and, as in a detective tale, everything becomes known via a process of investigation and interpretation, which in this instance also has links to Lewes.

Lewes's account of blood indicates that its function cannot be separated from any other organic function and that bodies must be seen within the context of how each organ relates to another. Bodily life is sustained through these interactions and provides us with clues about the role each plays in sustaining the body. Reading the body thus depends upon decoding organic function. Knowledge is gained by the assimilation of different forms of understanding so that we gain a complete picture of how the body operates. Knowledge of an organ is thus a clue about how the wider body works, which is why blood in Eliot's tale functions as a transmitter of knowledge. However, Eliot's tale plays out this level of knowledge as a tragedy for Latimer, as his visions, and understanding of disease, mean that he knows too much, and ultimately these insights become reconstituted as a troubling clairvoyance (even if Latimer is a poor interpreter of what he supposedly knows).[32] The focus at the end is on Latimer as a reader and develops these ideas in which 'these figures I have just written, as if they were a long familiar inscription' are a prelude to his imminent 'dying struggle' (p. 43). However, on a purely textual level this revelation takes us back to the beginning of the tale where his impending demise is first noted. It is possible to identify a quasi-Poesque inflection here in which the tale's end is established at the start and the death of the subject is underpinned by the stories of deaths and dying that accompany it – so that death and narrative are intimately related. Death in this reading constitutes a new beginning as it is the moment that both ends the narrative and starts it (as the close takes us back to the claims made at the beginning). Lewes's concluding chapter of *The Physiology of Common Life* is titled 'Life and Death' and there he argues that 'Death is a new birth: with it certain forms of existence are completed, and certain others are commenced ... the unwound watch is silent, but it is not destroyed' (vol. II, p. 445). In Eliot's tale, death is both physical and tragic, but metaphorical in its relation to a model of epistemology. The idea that death is not the end because it inaugurates a new mode of understanding was a central concept of Poe's *Eureka*; it also plays an important function in his detective stories, which, like 'The Lifted Veil', assert links between apparent clairvoyance, knowledge and death.

A science of death

Lewes's scientific influence on 'The Lifted Veil' has been outlined, and Anthony Evans has noted that Poe's tales of mesmerism were consciously written as scientific investigations, which resulted in their publication in scientific journals including *The American Phrenological Journal* and the *London Popular Record of Modern Science*. Evans notes that we should not dismiss this as Poe's attempt at a hoax because 'it is important to acknowledge that these works were published and received as legitimate contributions to the field of science, and thus they offer an insight into the assumptions and expectations of the scientific community'.[33] Eliot in 'The Natural History of German Life' also uses the scientific idea of natural history as a model for the development of an enlightened social policy that needs to acknowledge the different legal, class, economic and cultural factors that constitute any society, just as natural science acknowledges the different contributions made by various scientific disciplines such as physics, biology, chemistry and mathematics.[34] *Wuthering Heights* is clearly beyond such scientific considerations, but its secular vision is based on the notion that death constitutes a problem for knowledge that cannot be purely resolved by reference to religion.

In Poe's detective fiction we can observe a model of the scientific imagination at work. This is in a form that fits well with his account of composition in which the end is in sight from the very start, indeed in which one writes back from the end to the start (a view that Poe famously related to Dickens and which is recalled in the opening of 'The Philosophy of Composition'). At one level this, yet again, reworks Poe's idea of death as something that, as in the tales on mesmerism, we work back from in order to make sense of. Poe's detective, Dupin, also works in this way, and his approach, whilst appearing to suggest clairvoyance, rests upon principles of observation. Dupin's theory of observation is given sustained treatment at the beginning of 'The Murders in the Rue Morgue' (1841), where he demonstrates to the narrator how he had deduced that he was thinking of the actor, Chantilly, by a series of associations on their city walk. The narrator notes of Dupin, 'His results, brought about by the very soul and essence of method, have, in truth, the whole air of intuition'.[35] It is a process that rests upon a model of the subject that transforms into psychological terms what Eliot would develop into a theory of sympathy. The narrator notes how the true analyst can win at draughts by mastering their opponent rather than simply focusing on the game at hand. The narrator claims that, 'Deprived of ordinary resources, the analyst throws himself into the spirit of his opponent, identifies himself therewith, and not infrequently sees thus, at a glance, the sole methods (sometimes indeed absurdly simple ones) by which he may seduce into error or hurry into miscalculation' (p. 142). In this process the analyst enters a trance-like state, as the narrator notes of Dupin when he is working on a problem: 'His manner at these moments was frigid and abstract; his eyes were vacant in expression' (p. 144). Dupin's way of solving the mystery of the apparent murders of Madame L'Espanaye and her daughter rests, however, on rather more empirical grounds, such as the identification of the handprint on the throat of the daughter as belonging to an Ourang-Outang, which reveals the killer.

Dupin might, at an abstract level, represent the extension of a type of animal magnetism that enables him to read minds, but he is also an empiricist who is able to read the clues produced by 'hard' evidence. Dupin is also independent and intellectually superior – someone who is able to solve the problem of their deaths without emotionally empathising with them. His sympathy is, so the tale suggests, reserved for those who deserve it. The tale hints that what is at stake here is what it means to be a person. The Ourang-Outang is clearly off the human spectrum, but Dupin's dispassionate assessment of the killings renders him similarly inhuman. The tale is about the investigation of a death in which the ferocity of the killings contrasts with the coldness of Dupin's rationality, and this sense of death, and how to discuss it, represent it and draw conclusions from it, is a feature found in Poe, Brontë and Eliot.

Death is seemingly not the end; it provides a pretext for investigation. A tale such as 'The Murders in the Rue Morgue' shifts the emphasis away from the dead bodies of the victims and on to the detective, but this is in part because in Poe death has a largely rhetorical status. Death has a narrative force, but it is also an aspect of the divine and is related to creativity. Creativity appears in how the mind of the detective reassembles the clues to complete the tale, once told as mystery and then retold with its solution. Indeed, in Poe's review of Hawthorne's *Twice-Told Tales* (1842) he emphasises the importance of 'establishing this preconceived effect. If his very initial sentence tend not to the outbringing of this effect, then he has failed in his first step'.[36] In essence this would be repeated in his later theory of composition and can clearly be witnessed in the tales. At one level, Poe attempts to recode death as a principle of art in which the divine is released at the moment of artistic completion, because narrative, for Poe, as we have seen with *Eureka*, takes you close to the divine. His artistic and scientific conceptions thus work towards a confirmation of a divine force that exists beyond the end of the narrative so that stories reach out for a presence that ensures meaning, and this view provides its perfect gloss in the model of the detective story. However, there is a paradox here, because Dupin is devoid of human empathy. Logic on its own cannot be the answer, which is why in 'The Purloined Letter' (1844) Dupin is reconfigured as a combination of poet and mathematician in an attempt to emotionally redeem him. Such a combination also elides creativity with deduction, and whilst Poe's writings discussed here should be seen within the context of a shift from writing to reading, it should also be noted that many of his texts also observe this new, emerging tendency in which death constitutes a mystery that may become 'solved' as long as one possesses the requisite analytical skills, which in symbolic terms suggests the ability to read metaphysically.

'The Lifted Veil' does not make death horrifying, but the foresight that anticipates death. Latimer has to live with the constant knowledge that his life is finite and that for him death is the end, even whilst in rhetorical terms the end implies the beginning. The key feature of these texts is that death becomes divided into a painful emotional truth *and* into a rhetorical device. *Wuthering Heights*, however, represents a sceptical engagement with this rhetorical death that is evidenced through its ambivalence about textual authority.

The problem is that death no longer feels quite real (because of its links to narrative), but also feels totally overwhelming (because the unreality of the text cannot function as an emotional salve). The problem with death in the mid nineteenth century, as it is developed in these Gothic images, is one of interpretation. Poe, Brontë and Eliot in different ways illustrate how the eighteenth-century links between death and creativity became reworked in a secular context that made death more, rather than less, troubling. The reason why is because death is becoming familiar, it is now part of life, part of mourning and memory; however, shorn of any explicit theological context this familiarity is introjected, as illustrated by Latimer's horrified emotional solipsism. A sense of aloneness links Poe, Brontë and Eliot, even if Poe seems the most optimistic of the three with his sense that at the end a new type of life may emerge.

Death in the mid nineteenth century represents a moment when the putative links between death and creativity appear to unravel. Poe provides a coherent system in which he forms an alignment between art, death and notions of the creative, but the shift from writers to readers that we see in Brontë and Eliot demonstrates an alternative direction that death will take as it becomes reconstituted as a problem for interpretation. Death starts to migrate inwards around alternative figurations of the 'soul', and it is one in which dreams will provide the place where the subject's inner world, or 'ghost', resides. These reconceptualisations become clear at the end of the nineteenth century, partly through spiritualism and the quasi-scientific ideas that it advanced. These changes are mapped here in relation to the Gothic tradition and there is, of course, a strong case to be made that Tennyson's *In Memoriam* (1850) should also be seen as part of this wider culture of doubt, faith and reflection.[37] However, death in the Gothic produces another way of looking at these concerns as it works through issues about creativity and interpretation that it has inherited from an earlier Gothic tradition. It is also characterised by the ambivalent secularism that Hoeveler has identified in the period. Even Poe's apprehension of the divine is one predicated on an absent God who may come back to us at the end (rather than that we are taken to God after *our* death). The shift from writing to reading represents a turning point in the representation of death in the Gothic.

The death of the subject is given a new twist in the work of Dickens; it is one in which the literary dimensions of death are paralleled by feelings of alienation and estrangement, but there is also a precarious discourse of doubling that emerges in Dickens that sketches a version of the subject that will be elaborated around feelings of death and dying at the end of the nineteenth century. Dickens's principal contribution to the literary history of death in the period will be in the development of a model of the conscience, which will be explored in the next chapter.

Notes

1 Edgar Allan Poe, 'Editorial Miscellany', *Broadway Journal*, 2:23 (13 December 1845), 359, italics in original.

2 J. Gerald Kennedy, *Poe, Death and the Life of Writing* (New Haven, CT and London: Yale University Press, 1987), p. viii. All subsequent references are to this edition and are given in the text.
3 The suggestion is by Woodberry in the Stedman and Woodberry ten-volume set of Poe's work published in 1894–95, vol. IV, pp. 358, 359.
4 Edgar Allan Poe, 'Mesmeric Revelation', in *The Complete Tales and Poems of Edgar Allan Poe* (Harmondsworth: Penguin, 1982), pp. 88–95. All subsequent references are to this edition and are given in the text.
5 Doris V. Falk, 'Poe and the Power of Animal Magnetism', *PMLA*, 84:3 (May 1969), 536–46, 536–7. All subsequent references are to this edition and are given in the text.
6 Edgar Allan Poe, 'The Facts in the Case of M. Valdemar', in *Edgar Allan Poe: Selected Writings*, ed. and Introd. David Galloway (Harmondsworth: Penguin, 1982), pp. 350–9, p. 351, italics in original. All subsequent references are to this edition and are given in the text.
7 Philippe Ariès, *The Hour of Our Death*, trans. Helen Weaver (New York: Random House, 2008), p. 453. All subsequent references are to this edition and are given in the text.
8 G. R. Thompson, 'Unity, Death, and Nothingness: Poe's "Romantic Skepticism"', *PMLA*, 85:2 (March 1970), 297–300, 297.
9 Edgar Allan Poe, *Eureka: An Essay on the Material and Spiritual Universe*, in *The Science Fiction of Edgar Allan Poe*, ed. and Introd. Howard Beaver (Harmondsworth: Penguin, 1979), pp. 205–309, p. 209. All subsequent references are to this edition and are given in the text. It is tempting, given the context, to read Poe's 'I am dead' as a gloss on Valdemar's final cries.
10 Edgar Allan Poe, 'A Tale of the Ragged Mountains', in *The Complete Tales and Poems of Edgar Allan Poe* (Harmondsworth: Penguin, 1982), pp. 679–87, p. 679, italics in original. All subsequent references are to this edition and are given in the text.
11 Edgar Allan Poe, 'The Philosophy of Composition', in *Edgar Allan Poe: Selected Writings*, ed. and Introd. David Galloway (Harmondsworth: Penguin, 1982), pp. 480–92, p. 486, italics in original. All subsequent references are to this edition and are given in the text.
12 Elisabeth Bronfen, *Over Her Dead Body: Death, Femininity and the Aesthetic* (Manchester: Manchester University Press, 1992), p. 61. All subsequent references are to this edition and are given in the text.
13 Edgar Allan Poe, 'Ligeia', in *The Complete Tales and Poems of Edgar Allan Poe* (Harmondsworth: Penguin, 1982), pp. 654–66, pp. 654, 655. All subsequent references are to this edition and are given in the text.
14 Sigmund Freud, 'The Uncanny', in *Art and Literature: Jensen's 'Gradiva', Leonardo Da Vinci and Other Works*, The Penguin Freud Library, vol. XIV, ed. Albert Dickson (Harmondsworth: Penguin, 1990), pp. 335–76, p. 364. All subsequent references are to this edition and are given in the text.

15 For an account of how Poe can be read as anticipating Freud, see Clive Bloom's *Reading Poe, Reading Freud: The Romantic Imagination in Crisis* (Basingstoke: Macmillan, 1988).
16 Edgar Allan Poe, 'Morella', in *The Complete Tales and Poems of Edgar Allan Poe* (Harmondsworth: Penguin, 1982), pp. 667–71, p. 667. All subsequent references are to this edition and are given in the text.
17 I have sketched these theoretical points of contact with Kant in my *Gothic Radicalism: Literature, Philosophy and Psychoanalysis in the Nineteenth Century* (Basingstoke: Macmillan, 2000), see ch. 5, 'The Urban Sublime: Kant and Poe', pp. 103–28, which includes some discussion of 'Mesmeric Revelation'.
18 Carol Margaret Davison, 'The Brontës and the Death Question', unpublished article, p. 5. All subsequent references are to this edition and are given in the text.
19 Emily Brontë, *Wuthering Heights*, ed. and Introd. Pauline Nestor (Harmondsworth: Penguin, 2003), p. 330. All subsequent references are to this edition and are given in the text.
20 Cates Baldridge, 'Voyeuristic Rebellion: Lockwood's Dream and the Reader of "Wuthering Heights"', *Studies in the Novel*, 20:3 (Fall 1988), 274–87, 281.
21 Ingrid Geerken, '"The Dead Are Not Annihilated": Mortal Regret in "Wuthering Heights"', *Journal of Narrative Theory*, 34:3 (Fall 2004), 373–406. All subsequent references are to this edition and are given in the text.
22 George Eliot, 'The Natural History of German Life', in *Essays of George Eliot*, ed. Thomas Pinney (New York: Columbia University Press, 1963), pp. 266–99, p. 271.
23 Thomas Albrecht, 'Sympathy and Telepathy: The Problem of Ethics in George Eliot's *The Lifted Veil*', *ELH*, 73:2 (Summer 2006), 437–63, 438. All subsequent references are to this edition and are given in the text.
24 I discuss 'The Lifted Veil' in a wider context about death in relation to Poe, Haggard and Stoker in 'Victorian Gothic Death', in Andrew Smith and William Hughes (eds), *The Victorian Gothic: An Edinburgh Companion* (Edinburgh: Edinburgh University Press, 2010), pp. 156–69.
25 George Eliot, 'The Lifted Veil', in *The Lifted Veil; Brother Jacob*, ed. and Introd. Helen Small (Oxford: Oxford University Press, 1999), pp. 3–43, p. 3. All subsequent references are to this edition and are given in the text.
26 I am indebted to my colleague Helena Ifill for this observation.
27 H. L. Mansel, 'Sensation Novels', *Quarterly Review* (April 1863), 481–514, 488–9, 487. Cited in Susan David Bernstein, 'Transatlantic Magnetism: Eliot's "The Lifted Veil" and Alcott's Sensation Stories', in Jennifer Phegley, John Cyril Barton and Kristin N. Huston (eds), *Transatlantic Sensations* (Aldershot: Ashgate, 2012), pp. 183–206, p. 190.
28 Helen Small, 'Introduction', in *The Lifted Veil; Brother Jacob*, ed. and Introd. Helen Small (Oxford: Oxford University Press, 1999), pp. ix–xxxviii, p. xxvi.

29 George Henry Lewes, *The Physiology of Common Life*, 2 vols (Edinburgh and London: Blackwood, 1860), vol. II, p. 446. All subsequent references are to this edition and are given in the text.
30 Jill Galvan, 'The Narrator as Medium in George Eliot's "The Lifted Veil"', *Victorian Studies*, 48:2 (Winter 2006), 240-8, 242.
31 Kate Flint, 'Blood, Bodies, and *The Lifted Veil*', *Nineteenth-Century Literature*, 51:4 (March 1977), 455-73, 459. All subsequent references are to this edition and are given in the text.
32 I am indebted to my colleague Helena Ifill for this observation.
33 Anthony Evans, 'Mesmerism and the Electric Age: From Poe to Edison', in Martin Willis and Catherine Wynne (eds), *Victorian Literary Mesmerism* (Amsterdam and New York: Rodopi, 2006), pp. 61-82, p. 65.
34 Such a view is also in accord with Lewes's view of the organic integrity of the body in which we need to observe how the organic parts relate to the bodily whole.
35 Edgar Allan Poe, 'The Murders in the Rue Morgue', in *The Complete Tales and Poems of Edgar Allan Poe* (Harmondsworth: Penguin, 1982), pp. 141-68, p. 141. All subsequent references are to this edition and are given in the text.
36 Edgar Allan Poe, '*Twice-Told Tales*, A Review', *Graham's Magazine*, 20 (May 1842), 298.
37 See Julian Wolfreys, *Victorian Hauntings: Spectrality, Gothic, the Uncanny and Literature* (Basingstoke: Palgrave, 2001), for an account of *In Memoriam*. The book also includes a chapter on 'The Lifted Veil'.

4

Gothic death and Dickens: executions, graves and dreams

So far this study of death has argued that death fails to signify in any explicitly Gothic way. Death is either not the end or is turned into a subject for scientific enquiry. The work of Charles Dickens, however, demonstrates the presence of an emerging Gothic vernacular, one centred on a metaphysics of death, which progresses the history mapped so far in this study. Dickens explores death in a variety of contexts, and initially this chapter examines how Dickens's attitude towards capital punishment is informed by a metaphysical concern that images of death may awaken a latent desire to both kill and die. This view of the self-destructive self is further elaborated in representations of damaged family relations that are also associated with death. Finally, we shall see that dreams about death become the site where a model of the uncanny is elaborated and such concerns constitute an inward turn in Dickens that has implications for the model of creativity we have explored so far.

Robert Mighall has claimed Dickens as a lost Gothic voice in the Gothic hiatus between 1820 and the popular *fin de siècle* Gothic of Stevenson, Stoker, Wilde, Machen and Wells. For Mighall, Dickens was the first to resituate the Gothic in the present day and to reposition it within the urban landscape, whilst still utilising familiar Gothic tropes concerning the continuing influence of ancestral secrets.[1] For Mighall, Dickens finds 'the Gothic useful both as a rhetorical structure and metaphorical repertoire to serve his progressive and reformist agenda' (p. 86). However, the precise political flavour of that agenda is not as clear as this suggests, and although Mighall acknowledges that Dickens developed a version of Gothic London that implicated a number of institutions (most notably the law) in the creation of destitution, the issue of capital punishment complicates this.[2] Mighall concludes his essay by asserting that 'From Landscapes to mindscapes, the Gothic found and came to rest in a new domain. The transformation can be traced through the Dickensian canon' (p. 95). This chapter explores this internalisation by examining how the conscience came to function as an introjected form of self-policing. The presence of a conscience implies the possibility of redemption, but by the time we get to the later narratives, most notably *The Mystery of Edwin Drood* (1870), images of the conscience have been supplanted by troublesome dreams.

Dickens was indebted to a Gothic tradition, and whilst some of those points of contact are clear, as in the Christmas ghost stories or in the constructions of his villains, for example, there are other, more oblique psychological and emotional impulses at work. These issues of the self are worked through Dickens's ostensibly reformist social agenda, and it is difficult to isolate images of subjectivity from his complex, because shifting, political views. These issues can, however, be located within a discourse of empathy with implicit links to Smith, Burke and Eliot, and how Dickens works within, and beyond, that discourse provides a helpful starting point for a discussion of the Gothic self in Dickens.

The issue of empathy in Dickens registers a cultural shift towards the reader that we explored in the previous chapter. Mary-Catherine Harrison has noted that Dickens repeatedly represents failed readers as amoral and emotionally estranged. Scrooge in *A Christmas Carol* (1843) had, in his early years, been an enthusiastic reader of *Robinson Crusoe* (1719) and the *Arabian Nights* (1704–17), which, Harrison argues, introduced him to 'the moral value of imagination' that the ghosts compel the adult Scrooge to re-engage with.[3] A less redemptive figure is that of Harold Skimpole in *Bleak House* (1853). Despite his seemingly warm nature, Skimpole is dismissive of Jo the crossing-sweeper, regarding him as a potential source of disease. Skimpole's seemingly sympathetic rendering of the ballad 'The Peasant Boy' is intended to be in ironic contrast to his dismissal of Jo. Crucially, Skimpole cannot link his engagement with the literary to the real world and so lacks any genuine empathetic feeling, meaning that 'Skimpole is [Dickens's] model of how *not* to read' (Harrison, 265). How to interpret texts is thus central to Dickens's model of empathy and reflects how his novels are meant to be read – as encouragements for political reform.

We briefly saw in the previous chapter how George Eliot sketched a model of empathetic bonding with the reader in her essay 'The Natural History of German Life' (1856). For her, it was important to represent class-bound experience in psychological terms. By getting into the mind of characters, she claims, the reader can empathetically engage with their experiences. However, she regards Dickens as deficient in that regard because he captured only the outer form of character and not 'their conceptions of life, and their emotions'.[4] Whilst it would be difficult to claim

Dickens as part of a tradition of realism, as Eliot conceived it, nevertheless there is a level at which he attempts to engage with his readers and to elicit their sympathies. For Dickens, it is in the fabulation of texts such as the *Arabian Nights* that a model of the imagination emerges that can be used to convey the type of political message that Eliot was looking for in realism. Dickens makes specific demands on his readers by directing them to read within the melodrama for the political realities he wants them to consider. As the example of Skimpole illustrates, readers need to connect texts to wider political dramas. Nowhere is this issue of empathy so pressing, and for Dickens so lacking, as in the example of capital punishment.

State killing

Before discussing representations of executions (and pending executions) in *Oliver Twist* (1837) and *A Tale of Two Cities* (1859), it is helpful to explore Dickens's views on public execution, which were set out in a series of letters published in 1846 and 1849. Dickens wrote five letters to the *Daily News* between 23 February and 16 March 1846 that were prompted by his attendance at the public execution of François Courvoisier, a footman who murdered his employer, Lord William Russell, in May 1840. The execution took place on 6 July 1840 before a crowd of 40,000 outside Newgate prison. It was an event that William Makepeace Thackeray recalled in his essay 'On Going to See a Man Hanged' (1840), which shares with Dickens some of the horror of the occasion.[5] In his letter of 28 February, Dickens argues that the media has glamorised murder and that this debases the moral sensibilities of those who follow the progress of murder trials in the press. The interest in such cases, according to Dickens, is due to the death penalty that the murderer faces. He argues that other crimes that also once attracted the death penalty, such as burglary, for example, were devoid of glamour, whereas 'a criminal under sentence of death, or in great peril of death upon the scaffold, becomes immediately, the talk of the town'.[6] Edmund Burke had suggested that scenes of distress naturally awaken in us an empathetic desire to help. He notes of scenes of misery that 'the pain we feel, prompts us to relieve ourselves in relieving those who suffer'.[7] Burke claims that written accounts of despair elicit our empathy, but that true suffering will always play a more significant role than representations of it. The example he gives is of how a public execution would empty a theatre full of people who had gone to see a tragedy, so that 'let it be reported that a state criminal of high rank is on the point of being executed in the adjoining square; in a moment the emptiness of the theatre would demonstrate the comparative weakness of the imitative arts, and proclaim the triumph of real sympathy' (p. 43). Dickens, however, perceives a waning of affect. The press reports of murder trials generate 'a horrible fascination, which, in the minds – not of evil-disposed persons, but of good and virtuous and well-conducted people, supersedes the horror legitimately attracting to crime itself, and causes every word and action of a criminal under sentence of death to be the subject of a morbid interest and curiosity'.[8] Dickens does not leave it there as he cites a report from 1841, presented to the State Assembly of New York, that advocated the abolition of the death penalty. The passage quoted by Dickens asserts that:

> Whether there sleep within the breast of man, certain dark mysterious sympathies with the thought of that death, and that futurity which await his nature, tending to invest any act expressly forbidden by that penalty, with an unconscious and inexplicable fascination, that attracts his thoughts to it, in spite of their very shuddering dread; and bids his imagination brood over its idea, 'till out of those dark depths in his own nature, comes gradually forth a monstrous birth of Temptation.[9]

This subject is quite different from the one mapped by Burke. Here 'sympathies' are psychological, not social. This new subject is a Gothic one, defined by unaccountable 'unconscious and inexplicable' impulses, enthralled by the death drive and is inward rather than outward looking. Dickens affirms that this passage 'shadowed out a metaphysical truth, which, however wild and appalling in its aspect, was a truth still'.[10] That accounts of murder might inspire murder in the emotionally susceptible is in part attributed by Dickens to the effect that public executions have on the crowds that witnessed them. His account of Courvoisier's execution is very far removed from the rush to sympathy that Burke had claimed would empty a theatre. Rather the theatre of the scaffold demonstrates a morally bleak view of the self. Dickens recalls:

> From the moment of my arrival, when there were but a few score boys in the street, and those all young thieves, and all clustered together behind the barrier nearest to the drop – down to the time when I saw the body with its dangling head, being carried on a wooden bier into the gaol – I did not see one token in all the immense crowd; at the windows, in the streets, on the house-tops, anywhere; of any one emotion suitable to the occasion. No sorrow, no salutary terror, no abhorrence, no seriousness; nothing but ribaldry, debauchery, levity, drunkenness, and flaunting vice in fifty other shapes.[11]

Dickens's crowd lacks the emotional refinement of Burke's theatre-goers and there is a class narrative here about middle-class sensibility versus working-class leisure (as Dickens emphasises the holiday mood of the audience – the execution is also that of a servant rather than a 'criminal of high rank'). There is also a worry that the social contract disintegrates because the precautionary warning that the execution is intended to enact is reconstituted as entertainment. This may seem a separate issue to the concern about how accounts of murders can corrupt the morals of the 'good and virtuous and well-conducted people', but in fact it implicates a wider failure of the social contract. The death penalty sensationalises death because it grants it a glamour that undermines the ostensible function of the public execution to act as a deterrent. In the letter of 13 March he also claims that the spectacle of the execution, far from deterring would-be murderers, awakens within them a desire to take the centre-stage role of the executed criminal because 'a morbid tendency to brood over the sight until temptation is engendered by it, are the inevitable consequences of the spectacle, according to the difference of habit and disposition in those who behold it'.[12]

Dickens's subject struggles with the demands of the social contract as their strength of feeling is out of tune with it. The inward look reveals the presence of something barbaric that is also manifested in the cruelty of the execution. William Calcraft, the hangman who carried out the execution of Courvoisier, was known for his use of the short-drop method in which the condemned would be dropped only three feet, meaning that they would often be slowly asphyxiated. As part of the 'entertainment', Calcraft, who was known for his vulgar jokes, would sometimes pull on the condemned's legs or sit on their shoulders to hasten their end and to amuse the crowd. Public execution, for Dickens, fails on all levels: it does not work as a deterrent, it awakens a latent death wish and it is cruel. This position can be helpfully clarified by Jacques Derrida whose account of the death penalty is relevant to a discussion of how this new, emerging, troubled self is articulated within the abolitionist rhetoric of the mid nineteenth century.

Derrida addresses Nietzsche's critique of Kant's claim that execution constitutes a categorical imperative. For Kant, capital punishment is the ultimate sanction for those who breach the social contract. It grants the condemned dignity because it makes their death meaningful. It also restores a moral equilibrium policed by the social contract. Nietzsche, however, in *On the Genealogy of Morals* (1887), argues that Kant's position is flawed. He asserts that the application of punishment as rectifying a grievance cannot be turned into a simple process of like-for-like retribution, because in reality it is impossible to gauge the level at which exact restitution should be made. This is true of all crime: why, for example, does burglary have a specific prison tariff attached to it? How can that be precisely calculated? For Nietzsche, such matters are economic judgements, so that a life is worth a life, rather than a more complex, but nevertheless also unsatisfactory, attempt to calculate what exactly a life sentence should constitute. Derrida notes that for Nietzsche, 'The origin of the legal subject, and notably of penal law, is commercial law; it is the law of commerce, debt, the market, the exchange between things, bodies, and monetary signs, with their general equivalent and their surplus value, their interest'.[13] Not only is punishment therefore predicated on a rhetoric of economics, it also replicates the terms of a credit-based economy that is built upon a model of credit and loss which is also potentially abstract and intangible, so that forms of punishment also become intangible. For Derrida, Nietzsche highlights a shift from a religious notion of divine justice to a more secular version of faith, so that 'what makes us believe in an equivalence between crime and punishment, at bottom, is belief itself; it is the fiduciary phenomenon of credit or faith' (p. 152). Nietzsche, however, argues that the assertion that execution functions as a categorical imperative, because it honourably applies the needs of the social contract, fails because we do not believe it. The act of execution demonstrates state cruelty, not the ethical ties that bind a community together. Burke's pursuit of the grounds under which sublime experience can be made socially meaningful is instructive in this regard. Throughout his *A Philosophical Enquiry* (1757), there is an assertion that collective behaviour is the consequence of a shared moral and sympathetic vision. However, for Dickens execution brings out the worst in people, not the best. It represents the failure of the social contract by demonstrating the presence of what one is meant to surrender as a condition of entry into society – the obscure, anti-social demands of the 'unconscious' and the unique 'disposition' of the subject. Derrida writes about this process in terms that gloss Dickens's view of the wholly negative effects of public execution. For Derrida, following Nietzsche, the problem is that the failure of belief identifies a rift in the subject: 'this internal division, this properly analytic dissociation, this cleavage, this split of believing haunted by non-belief is almost quasi-hypnotic, one might say spectral, quasi-hallucinatory, or unconscious' (p. 154). In the instance of the public execution, we do not believe that we are witnessing the restoration of order; instead, as Dickens notes of the volatile crowds attracted to executions, we see the disintegration of social order.

This new, Gothic version of the self ultimately struggles to elude the dictates of an economic rhetoric as the subject becomes formed through a shadowy version of the economy, which is reflected in Dickens's account of the pickpockets and petty thieves that populate the execution-day crowd. The alternative economic strategies represented by criminal activity were, of course, given full treatment by Dickens in *Oliver Twist*, which will be discussed below. What is noticeable, however, is how the state apparatus creates the possibility under which criminality occurs. Dickens is clearly not on the side of Gothic disorder, but bears witness to what he regards as a troubling outlet for all that is socially, emotionally and psychologically reprehensible. However, he is on the side of Nietzsche *avant la lettre* when he claims that the nihilistic bleakness of the condemned is reflected in the assertion that "'I took his life. I give up mine to pay for it'".[14] The economic metaphor fails for Dickens because it is not a fair trade.[15] He sees murder as the result of a 'coward character' that cannot be properly corrected through execution. To that degree his is a conservative critique of these economic metaphors. The problem is that the condemned is likely, for Dickens, to inspire hero-worship, which in turn invites emulation. Dickens's abolitionist stance is therefore motivated by support for, as he states in his final letter to the *Daily News* on 16 March, 'the advantage of society' rather than for 'any individual malefactor' whom he regards with contempt.[16]

Our narrative about death is thus developed in terms that relate to what the value of a life is and these repeatedly appear in debates about abolition. Dickens is regarded as having revised his view when, after witnessing the dual execution of Frederick and Marie Manning on 13 November 1849, he returned to the issue in two letters published in *The Times*. In the first, written in the immediate aftermath of the execution (which was witnessed by a crowd of up to 50,000), he notes, as he did in 1846, the demeanour of the crowd. He recalls that after the crowd's night of largely drunken revelry, 'the sun rose brightly … it gilded thousands upon thousands of upturned faces, so inexpressibly odious in their brutal mirth or callousness, that a man had cause to feel ashamed of the shape he wore, and to shrink from himself, as fashioned in the image of the Devil'.[17] The religious language employed by Dickens is striking. In the 1846 letters, however, he had been suspicious of those who used the Bible to assert the necessity of execution, regarding this as an abuse of scripture. Likewise he had been sceptical about accounts of last-minute religious conversions made by the condemned. This later religious rhetoric also conditions his account of how the crowd responded to the Mannings' execution:

> When the two miserable creatures who attracted all this ghastly sight about them were turned quivering into the air, there was no more emotion, no

more pity, no more thought that two immortal souls had gone to judgement, no more restraint in any of the previous obscenities, than if the name of Christ had never been heard in this world, and there were no belief among men but that they perished like the beasts.[18]

This is not empty rhetoric. Whilst his development of a particular form of psychology advances our understanding of the history of a Gothic subjectivity, it is important to note that Dickens would not have seen it like that. Juliet John has argued that Dickens was opposed to an emerging emphasis on character psychology in literature, and that in his texts psychology is repeatedly related to deviance because it takes the subject out of the social sphere and so beyond the ties that are central to the social contract.[19] However, what is often overlooked is that for Dickens the way out to a Burkean world of empathy requires a reworking of a Christian ethos that in the end, as we shall see in the instance of *Edwin Drood*, cannot be sustained. Ultimately, Dickens's vision collapses into a dream world that reconstitutes a discourse of creativity which emphasised the importance of the subconscious as the place where the Gothic imagination resides. Before we get to that point, Dickens will underline the significance of the conscience in both modifying behaviour and articulating a genuine sense of remorse.

Oliver Twist and the Christian uncanny

In the Preface to the second edition of *Oliver Twist* Dickens countered accusations that the novel was improbable given that its apparent condemnation of corrupting social forces was belied by the virtuous dispositions of Oliver and Nancy. Dickens states that he wanted to suggest the presence of redemption within what otherwise appear as 'adverse circumstance'.[20] For Dickens, moral choice is always an option; thus the novel explores the point where one would refuse to be willingly involved in certain crimes, on a hierarchy from pickpocketing to murder. The conscience of the individual steps in to stop progression or compels a character, such as Nancy, to work for the good of Oliver. Dickens therefore does not see such virtue as anomalous to the social context in which his criminals operate; rather any such anomaly is harboured within a divided model of the self, although one that is defined theologically rather than psychologically. Such goodness found within adversity 'is emphatically God's truth … It involves the best and worst shades of our nature; much of its ugliest hues, and something of its most beautiful; it is a contradiction, an anomaly, an apparent impossibility; but it is a truth' (p. 37). The conscience is the thing that, in *Oliver Twist*, persecutes the law-breaker and nowhere is this more clear than in the context of death and fears of death. Sikes's haunting after the murder of Nancy is revealing for how it runs together both a fear of death and an anxiety that the conscience taunts you with your bad acts.[21]

Sikes is destined for a form of public execution that is self-inflicted when he slips in attempting to secure a noose intended to go around his waist to help him descend from the roof of a building surrounded by those intent on arresting him. The novel notes: 'The noose was on his neck. It ran up with his weight, tight as a bowstring, and swift as the arrow it speeds. He fell for five-and-thirty feet. There was a sudden jerk, a terrific convulsion of the limbs; and there he hung' (p. 453). The cause of his misadventure is not the crowd gathering to try to capture him but the eyes of Nancy that have persecuted him since his killing of her. His departure from London soon after the murder is one in which he is accompanied by Nancy's corpse:

> He could trace its shadow in the gloom, supply the smallest item of the outline, and note how stiff and solemn it seemed to stalk along. He could hear its garments rustling in the leaves ... If he stopped it did the same. If he ran, it followed – not running too: that would have been a relief: but like a corpse endowed with the machinery of life, and borne on one slow melancholy wind that never rose or fell. (p. 428)

Sikes is beyond redemption and this is made clear in his rejection by his former criminal associates and in his self-execution. Published eight years before Dickens's letters on capital punishment in the *Daily News*, it anticipates the position that those who kill may be influenced by motives other than purely murder. The suggestion of a death drive is mapped here as a type of non-transcendent solipsism that is articulated through projection. The spectral but also very physical image of Nancy (it walks, its movements captured by the sound of rustling leaves) becomes supplanted by what appears to be another figure who is seemingly manifested out of this dead Nancy. It anticipates Sikes's death and is construed as his corpse. Sikes notes of this figure: 'He had kept it before him that morning, but it was behind him now – always. He leaned his back against a bank, and felt that it stood above him, visibly out against the cold night-sky. He threw himself upon the road – on his back upon the road. At his head it stood, silent, erect, and still – a living grave-stone, with its epitaph in blood' (p. 428). This grave is both his and Nancy's. The dead Nancy conjures the dead Sikes so that self-destruction is inevitable as he reads on the tombstone a record of his own death. On his journey he is accompanied by the dead eyes of Nancy, 'so lustreless and so glassy' (p. 428), which haunt him until the very end. The novel also records at this point, 'Let no man talk of murderers escaping justice, and hint that Providence must sleep' (p. 428), which emphasises the Christian vision that underpins Sikes's punishment and which also helpfully explains Sikes's subsequent involvement in bravely attempting to extinguish a farmhouse fire. Initially, Sikes senses danger and is then confronted by a seemingly apocalyptic vision in which 'The broad sky seemed on fire. Rising into the air with showers of sparks, and rolling one above the other, were sheets of flame, lighting the atmosphere for miles round, and driving clouds of smoke in the direction where he stood' (p. 429). Valentine Cunningham has noted that Dickens's interest in religion was in part reflected through images of the apocalypse that can be found in the conflagrations that engulf the rioters in *Barnaby Rudge* (1841), Krook in *Bleak House* (1853) and Miss Havisham in *Great Expectations* (1861) and which are associated with the revolutionaries in *A Tale of Two Cities* (1859). Some of these images are more political than others and the judgements suggest different agendas, with Cunningham noting: 'The socially transgressive might expect to meet their end in some such revolutionary conflagration of the kind Dickens ... fear[s] might be coming Britain's way. But eternal punishment for sinners in the fires of Hell is not on Dickens's agenda.'[22] The reason for this rebuttal of a model of hell (at least on a theological if not on a political level) was because Dickens supported the version of forgiveness found in the New Testament, whereas Old Testament advocates (such as Mrs Clennam in *Little Dorrit* (1857)) are shown as eaten up by feelings of vengeance (Cunningham, p. 268). The narrator notes of Sikes that 'in every part of that great fire was he; but he bore a charmed life, and had neither scratch nor bruise, nor weariness nor thought, till morning dawned again, and only smoke and blackened ruins remained' (p. 430). Sikes's attempt to help seems to suggest his desire for self-destruction, and his escape from harm indicates that an alternative form of condemnation is required. Sikes may be beyond redemption, but he is also beyond an externally imposed Old Testament judgement.

The example of Sikes indicates that a horror of death is internalised as a form of self-awareness through which one becomes conscious of a conscience. Death is not neutral, or, as Derrida puts it, 'Death is not natural' (p. 117), in this context because we are looking at violent, and so premature, death. Sikes, as it were, internalises the principles of the death penalty, which anticipates the type of self-destruction that Dickens would map in his later letters on capital punishment.

The novel's penultimate chapter centres on Fagin in the condemned cell. Fagin has been driven to the point of insanity as he awaits his fate, seemingly reliving some of the crimes that had led him to this point; it is noted that 'He grew so terrible ... in all the tortures of his evil conscience' (p. 470). Fagin is not redeemed here, despite his informing Oliver and Mr Brownlow about the whereabouts of Oliver's father's will. Fagin is driven mad by fear (and by an 'evil conscience') and in the end is rendered incomprehensible. Symbolically, however, an alternative image of death and resurrection is available.

Derrida recalls in one of his early lectures on the death penalty his childhood familiarity with the case of Eugen Weidmann, who was the last person to be publicly executed in France on 17 June 1939.[23] Derrida recalls an iconic photograph of Weidmann in which his head had been bandaged and notes that Weidmann is the first word of Jean Genet's *Our Lady of the Flowers* (1943). Genet's novel addresses the issue of capital punishment within a theological context that construes the condemned as Christ-like, as punished for their sins but subject to redemption and resurrection. In this context, Derrida reads the real-life image of the bandaged Weidmann as symbolically echoing the wrapping of Christ's body in linen before his resurrection. Christ was also subject to capital punishment, and for Derrida this establishes a symbolic link between punishment, martyrdom and resurrection that Genet explores in his novel.

It is noted of Fagin as he awaits his fate in the condemned cell that 'He had been wounded with some missiles from the crowd on the day of his capture, and his head was bandaged with a linen cloth' (p. 470). Derrida, in his account of Genet, recalls the moment in the Bible where it is noted (in John 19: 38–40) that after crucifixion the followers of Jesus 'took the body of Christ and wound it in linen clothes' (Derrida, p. 32). The symbolic point that Derrida wants to make, following Genet, is that capital punishment does not quite kill the condemned, because they survive their literal death by being kept alive in the public imagination. This is relevant to Dickens because he too, in his letters to the newspapers, claims (in a conservative way) that a type of inappropriate posterity is granted to the condemned through the circulation of popular street narratives about them, which were typically peddled at the execution, and by media interest in the life and imprisonment of the condemned. The dead are therefore resurrected after death in the instance of capital punishment, and Fagin's symbolic association with the linen that the post-crucifixion Christ was wrapped in suggests this connection. Dickens uses these links to argue that capital punishment fails in a fundamental way: it grants a posthumous life that challenges the social order that the execution is meant to protect. It is an issue that Dickens sought to rectify in his second letter to *The Times*, published on 19 November 1849.

Dickens begins his letter by emphasising the type of crowd that an execution appeals to, claiming that 'they chiefly attract as spectators the lowest, the most depraved, the most abandoned of mankind; in whom they inspire no wholesome emotions whatever'.[24] The sight of the death of the condemned on such a crowd has 'a debasing and hardening influence'.[25] For Dickens, the solution is for executions to be held in private. Whilst this would eliminate the deleterious effects of the sight of capital punishment, Dickens also proposes an addition that would ensure that the condemned cannot be culturally resurrected. Dickens argues that: 'From the moment of the murderer's being sentenced, I would dismiss him to ... dread obscurity ... I would allow no curious visitors to hold any communication with him; I would place every obstacle in the way of his sayings and doings being served up in print on Sunday mornings for the perusal of families.'[26] Death is now final because it can be done in secret. Dickens's letters to *The Times* were regarded as a renunciation of the pro-abolitionist stance of the 1846 letters. However, the picture is more complex than that: the Dickens of 1846 simply could not find a way of making public execution work, whereas the Dickens of 1849 has found a solution (or at least one that works for him). It also moves him beyond his account of capital punishment in *Oliver Twist*, which had also implied that the condemned become reborn through some form of Newgate narrative that memorialises their life (and death). Indeed, the closing lines of the novel attempt to supplant this possible resurrection by dwelling on the spirit of Oliver's mother, Agnes, when Oliver visits a church with his aunt Rose Maylie, where it is noted:

> Within the altar on the old village church there stands a white tablet, which bears as yet but one word 'AGNES'. There is no coffin in that tomb; and may it be many, many years, before another name is placed above it. But, if the spirits of the Dead ever come back to earth, to visit spots hallowed by the love – love beyond the grave – of those they knew in life, I believe that the shade of Agnes sometimes hovers round that solemn nook. I believe it none the less because that nook is in a Church, and she was weak and erring. (pp. 479–80)

The concluding lines thus emphasise a theologically legitimate resurrection associated with redemption, love and forgiveness that permits Agnes to enter the church.

In Dickens, the criminal dead must be forgotten, but the loving dead must be allowed to continue. As we shall see, this is in part due to an idea of 'home' that is central to Dickens's conceptualisation of the virtuous life. However, the type of death we have looked at concerns capital punishment as the consequence of criminal activity. Dickens addresses the issue differently when considering politically motivated executions, and the ending of *A Tale of Two Cities* is instructive in that regard.

As Sydney Carton awaits his execution he comforts the Little Seamstress, who is also awaiting execution and who regards Carton as angelic due to his support. In her eyes he becomes Christ-like through association when she claims that '"But for you, dear stranger, I should not be so composed, for I am naturally a poor thing, faint of heart; nor should I have been able to raise my thoughts to Him who was put to death, that we might have hope and comfort here to-day. I think you were sent to me by Heaven'".[27] Carton's resurrection through an afterlife is thus theologically sanctioned whereas Fagin's is not, as his fate is deserved. The final scenes of *A Tale of Two Cities* contrast the spiritual purity of the self-sacrificing Carton with the corruption of the revolutionary forces, representatives of which voyeuristically congregate to observe the executions. Here an entire regime is rendered unjust rather than unworkable (as it is in the earlier British context). Carton, as he is about to ascend the steps to the guillotine, recites the Order for the Burial of the Dead from St John's Gospel, '"I am the Resurrection and the Life, saith the Lord: he that believeth in me, though he were dead, yet shall he live: and whosoever liveth and believeth in me shall never die'" (p. 403). Revealingly, Carton's resurrection is finally played out in a closing narrative where he records ideas about his life, death and his future resurrection, all of which are manifested through the anticipated sympathetic memories of those whom he has saved. Death, conceived of in putatively political terms, is thus elided with a familiar Christian discourse about sacrifice.

Within the context of capital punishment, Dickens's account of death plays a significant role in the development of our Gothic tradition. As we saw in the letters, the public spectacle of death may well, for Dickens, awaken a death instinct in those with a certain disposition. On a criminological level, it is an act of cruelty that is psychologically reflected in the crowd that bears witness to it. At a political level, it fails because, as in the case of Carton, a spiritual narrative of honourable self-sacrifice transcends, and so resists, state power. For Dickens, the instance of capital punishment is as much metaphysical in its ramifications as it is political. It is also a process that is not immune, as we saw in Derrida's account of Nietzsche's reading of Kant, from economic considerations – which Dickens had noted in the nihilistic claim that a murderer might make about a life-for-a-life debt that is being paid off. This language of economics is directly recalled in Dickens's account of an execution (a guillotining) that he witnessed in Rome in 1845. The execution constituted a 'sickening spectacle', and Dickens recalls that 'Such a sight has one meaning and one warning. Let me not forget it. The speculators in the lottery, station themselves at favourable points for counting the gouts of blood that spirt out, here or there; and buy that number. It is pretty sure to have a run upon it'.[28] Death is shaped by an economic process that depersonalises the condemned, which demonstrates just how far things have moved beyond the discourse of sympathy suggested by Burke. Dickens tries to restore a theological significance to the idea of sacrifice that we have seen in *Oliver Twist*. The final lines of the novel suggest that the family can spiritually congregate after death, and this establishes an idea of the 'home' that is, as we shall see, culturally linked to ideas about interment procedures.

The shift towards burial practices might seem different in kind from the emphasis on capital punishment, but in reality this is all a matter of degree. The inward turn that we find in the contemplation of the psychological effects of the execution is restaged in the case of burial via a focus on family ties and the emotional disruption caused by death. Death, and its peculiar allure, becomes transferred to the home in another critique of the social contract.

The culture of the graveyard

The opening scene of *Great Expectations* (1861) sees Pip mulling over his family, who are buried in the local cemetery. He did not know his parents and tries to conjure his father from the shape of his tombstone, which suggests to Pip 'a square, stout, dark man, with curly black hair', whilst the inscription on his mother's tombstone leads him to the 'childish conclusion that my mother was freckled and sickly'.[29] He notes of his five siblings, who all died in childhood, that he believed 'that they had all been born on their backs with their hands in their trouser-pockets, and had never taken them out in this state of existence' (p. 35). All are described as lying in plots that are akin to beds. This form of country burial stood in contrast to urban burials, and the cultural context of burial practices provides another way of thinking about death in the period (Dickens was also acutely conscious of the presence of unhygienic oversubscribed graveyards in London), which is helpful to explore further.

Urban areas witnessed the establishment of large cemeteries in London that were set out in specially designed parks by private companies. Between 1832 and 1841, seven such cemeteries were established in London (Kensal Green in 1832, West Norwood in 1837, Highgate in 1839, Abney Park, Nunhead and Brompton in 1840 and Tower Hamlets in 1841), with similar ventures established in other large cities throughout Britain. It was widely believed that these developments would alleviate the unsanitary conditions that often pervaded city-centre churchyards, where graves were frequently reused and where the dead were not always properly buried due to overcrowded graveyards. In *Oliver Twist*, whilst Oliver is working for Sowerberry, the undertaker, it is noted of one attempted interment that 'It was no very difficult task; for the grave was so full, that the uppermost coffin was within a few feet of the surface. The grave-digger shovelled the earth, stamped it loosely down with his feet, shouldered his spade, and walked off' (p. 84). Pip's country churchyard has his informal family plot in it; such gatherings were not possible in the old city churchyards, of which Julia Rugg has noted their 'often chaotic nature …, where bodies were crammed rather than interred, and which lacked respect for familial affection'.[30] The ideal family plot constituted an extension of the domestic sphere in which the family would reconvene after death as a family unit. Rugg argues that 'the private grave within the cemetery became an institution: a means of organizing both nuclear and extended family members into a single cohort' (228). The irony in *Great Expectations* is, of course, that the orphaned Pip, like the orphaned Oliver Twist, does not belong to a harmonious family that is idealised by the family plot.

The issue of graveyard management in the period might seem like a highly technical matter, but it bears on our narrative about death because at its heart lies a debate about the accommodation of the family. It was an issue that was closely tied to class and economics.

We have noted how the language of money frames an idea of justice in the period. It also plays a role in how issues of burial were addressed. The key intervention during the period was Edwin Chadwick's follow-up to his *Report on the Sanitary Condition of the Labouring Population of London* (1842), which was published in 1843 as *A Supplementary Report on the Results of a Special Inquiry into the Practice of Interment in Towns.*[31]

Chadwick's 1843 enquiry centres on the disposal of the diseased body. The concern is that improper burial would lead to the spread of disease and he explores a number of circumstances in which the dead could be more hygienically disposed of, such as ensuring that the dead are not buried near running water, as this could lead to the propagation of waterborne diseases. He is also concerned about the potential of the corpse to spread disease throughout the home. Chadwick notes a class-bound narrative that needs to be addressed because:

In a large proportion of cases in the metropolis, and in some of the manufacturing districts, one room serves for one family of the labouring classes: it is their bed-room, their kitchen, their wash-house, their sitting room, their dining room; and, when they do not follow any out-door occupation, it is frequently their work room and their shop. In this one room they are born, and live, and sleep, and die amidst, the other inmates.[32]

The working-class home poses a particular problem, according to Chadwick, because of a reluctance to give up their dead in a prompt way. He also touches on issues of labour in implying that the residual structure of the old cottage industries is threatened by the retention of the potentially diseased corpse. Economic factors are never far away from Chadwick's account of how to develop healthy interment practices. Mary Elizabeth Hotz has summarised that 'In the microenvironment of the house, Chadwick wants to construct homes as spaces without dead bodies, to remove the dead quickly, efficiently, and anonymously by medical officers in order to free the home of its male occupants for work in the national economy and female occupants for work in the domestic economy.'[33] Chadwick also regards the working-class corpse as a special category because cultures of working-class mourning mean that the protracted retention of the corpse in the home leads to the potential spread of disease to all of society. He is clear that such corpses require social banishment, 'if the corpse of the poor man could be deposited at a distance ... I think it would improve the health of our large towns very much' (p. 34). Chadwick took advice from various doctors who visited homes where the dead were laid out, and one recalls: 'What I observe when I first visit the room is a degree of indifference to the presence of the corpse: the family is found eating or drinking or pursuing their usual callings, and the children playing. Amongst the middle classes, where there is an opportunity of putting the corpse by itself, there are greater marks of respect and decency' (p. 35). The working-class corpse is part of family life, whereas the middle-class corpse is not. These different engagements with the dead became inverted after death because the family plot was, due to costs, more readily available to the middle classes in the newly formed large urban cemeteries.

Dickens had commented on the moral turpitude of the crowds that gathered at public executions, and Chadwick, in a critique of funerary expenses, levels a similar accusation against professional undertakers when noting that 'The impressions created by the bearing of these coarse, unknown, unrespected, irresponsible hands, add to the revolting popular associations with death' (p. 52), in part because of their supposedly frequent drunken behaviour. Some of this is also recalled in *Oliver Twist* in the characters of Mrs Sowerberry and Noah Claypole during Oliver's employment with the undertaker, Sowerberry.

For Chadwick, as with Dickens, the dead are not treated with the appropriate respect. Sanitary reformers like Chadwick were also concerned that the dead should be buried in graves of a certain size and depth in order to ensure that any disease that may lurk within the corpse could be contained. Ultimately, a more complex understanding of the nature of disease, and the popularity of cremation towards the end of the century, would eradicate the perceived problems of the post-mortem family reunion. What is notable from Chadwick's report is that for all its focus on the idea of a loss of dignity in certain funerary practices, it is devoid of any obvious theological dimension. Given the strategic nature of the report this is not surprising, but it indicates the lack of spirituality accorded to the dead, who are here constituted as a potential health problem. Hotz notes that whilst earlier in the culture there may have existed an 'ambiguous relationship between body and soul', this has now been replaced by 'an emphasis on the centrality of the corpse' (p. 15). The culture of the laying out of the dead, however, relocates an idea from the eighteenth century when the recently deceased seemed to simultaneously occupy two places – the grave, but also a place in heaven. The former would ultimately be supplanted by the latter because, by the 1840s, this had been reworked by an alternative, more secular 'belief that the time between death and burial of a person was a time when the person was neither dead nor alive' (Hotz, p. 15), as mourning keeps them alive and retained within the domestic sphere. For Chadwick, the corpse is alive with death because of its potential to spread disease. The role of the family is central to these debates.

The growth of the large cemeteries made family plots possible and the private companies that developed these sites were in the main happy to provide such a service when it was no longer possible to accommodate families in overburdened city churchyards. Such places did not specifically prioritise sanitation (although they did address this in their burial procedures), as they were more concerned with memorialising the dead. The family home, which attempted to retain the integrity of the family unit even in death, could now be transplanted to the family plot. However, as Rugg has noted, it was typical that only middle-class families would be accorded this type of respect, and there were many scandals during the period concerning the interment of working-class families in plots that appeared to be oversubscribed and encroached upon.[34]

The dead family is thus restored to life in the grave as their collective burial suggests the importance of family togetherness. It is noteworthy in Dickens that the death of children, such as Little Nell and Paul Dombey, explores the idea of familial mourning in ways that turn the home into a symbolic mausoleum. What is striking in *Dombey and Son* (1848), however, is the suggestion that the recently deceased linger about the home. Early on, after the death of Mrs Dombey, her rooms are closed, but not thereby unoccupied:

> Odours as from vaults and damp places, came out of the chimneys. The dead and buried lady was awful in a picture-frame of ghastly bandages. Every gust of wind that rose, brought eddying round the corner from the neighbouring mews, some fragments of the straw that had been strewn before the house when she was ill, mildewed remains of which were still cleaving to the neighbourhood: and these, being always drawn by some invisible attraction to the threshold of the dirty house to let immediately opposite, addressed a dismal eloquence to Mr Dombey's windows.[35]

The house is touched by an inescapable aura of death. The dying Paul Dombey is manifested out of this as he heads towards his seemingly inevitable end. Brigid Lowe has argued that *Dombey and Son* represents Dickens's attempt to write a domestic novel, which was a genre that typically explored 'the domestic as the ambit of a range of human values increasingly marginalized in the industrialized world of capital'.[36] The house of Dombey and Son is both domestic and commercial, and the novel explores the danger of blurring these two worlds as such an elision compromises family life. The home becomes a dead place as a consequence of this economic narrative and this should be read within the context of Dickens's critique of economic metaphors in his account of capital punishment. The implication is that the very materiality of commerce replaces life with objects so that people become thing-like and so not properly alive. Paul Dombey is figuratively killed by his father's economic interests. The house is the place where death is to be found and the home is not a place of obvious security until the adult Florence is accepted by Dombey, with the suggestion that Paul lives on in some way through Florence's son, also called Paul. The house is diseased, but the disease does not emanate from the corpse (as Chadwick would have it), but from the dead world of a cold materialism. The point is to reconnect, as Scrooge would in *A Christmas Carol*, with a model of family from which money removes you. However, repeatedly there emerges the suggestion that it is in the home that death takes on a symbolic form, and within this we witness the formation of a mode of uncanniness that appears to anticipate Freud, although Dickens's reworking of a literary context complicates Freud's model – an issue that is clear from Dickens's use of doubles.

Twins and doubles

The haunted house of Dombey is self-inflicted as it is unable to cast off the gloom of the death of Mrs Dombey, which, as we saw, gathers both within and without. Dickens's interest in the self-destructive aspects of his culture is apparent not just here but also in the account of capital punishment that fosters the corruption that it is intended to eradicate. Dickens's focus on death, dying and anticipated death is used to address these social and economic concerns. However, whilst it is tempting to see this as part of an unfolding secular narrative, it is also the case that Dickens saw his views as conditioned by a New Testament ethos that emphasised redemption and forgiveness for those who were capable of acting as moral agents (which explains his tone of moral outrage at the behaviour of execution-day crowds). Dickens wants death to have meaning, but it can only be granted meaning if life has a moral dimension to it – one that is typically found within the restored family unit. The counterpoint is the isolation of those in the death cell (such as Fagin), or those whose belated conscience cannot redeem them (such as Sikes). Punishment by death can thus be self-generated in Dickens by falling out of the social contract. However, his representation of doubles both illustrates this and, in the instance of twins, complicates it.

It is important to note that an early model of the double is to be found within the *American Notes* (1842) in the account of solitary confinement at the Eastern Penitentiary in Philadelphia. Solitary confinement was discussed by Dickens for a number of years as he also witnessed its implementation at a number of prisons in Britain. Dickens's view was that protracted terms of solitary confinement would be counterproductive as they would lead to emotional and psychological instability. In the instance of the regime at the Eastern Penitentiary, he states that 'I believe it, in its effects, to be cruel and wrong'.[37] He writes of such a prisoner that 'He is a man buried alive; to be dug out in the slow round of years; and in the mean time dead to everything but torturing anxieties and horrible despair' (p. 148).[38] This sense of the corpse-like prisoner is reinforced in his account of one inmate, who is described as 'looking as wan and unearthly as if he had been summoned from the grave' (p. 150). Dickens's attempt to imaginatively engage with his plight leads to the conjecture that such a figure becomes self-haunted by a 'phantom' that follows their movements. This phantom inhabits the corner of his cell, which becomes 'every night the lurking-place of a ghost: a shadow: – a silent something, horrible to see, but whether bird, or beast, or muffled human shape, he cannot tell'

(p. 155). This figure represents a projection of what the prisoner has become as they are progressively dehumanised by solitary confinement and made animal-like or spectral.[39] This psychological projection is therefore always present, so that 'When night comes, there stands the phantom in the corner. If he have the courage to stand in its place, and drive it out (he had once: being desperate), it broods upon his bed' (p. 155). The prisoner is haunted by his double and this is reproduced through the 'live burial' that constitutes solitary confinement, which, like capital punishment, potentially touches us all. Dickens notes: 'What monstrous phantoms, bred of despondency and doubt, and born and reared in solitude, have stalked upon the earth, making creation ugly, and darkening the face of Heaven!' (p. 156). The danger is that, on completion of their sentence, such prisoners will cause harm to society because 'those who have undergone this punishment, MUST pass into society again morally unhealthy and diseased' (p. 156). Yet again an image of the self-destructive society is reflected in the creation of the destroyed self.

Susan K. Gillman and Robert L. Patten have argued that Dickens's doubles come from two sources: one source demonstrates moral polarities (which he inherited from the Bible, Hogarth and Fielding), and the other is defined by tensions based around rank, or images of innocence and experience that centre on different epistemic understandings (which is derived from the picaresque).[40] Whilst they claim that there is a shift in the 1850s, represented by *David Copperfield* (1850) and *A Tales of Two Cities*, which 'locate doubles within the protagonist' (445), the examples of the *American Notes* and Dickens's view of capital punishment demonstrate that his thinking about this new 'double' can be seen much earlier. What is interesting about Dickens is that this version of a seemingly recognisable psychology of the double exists alongside these other doubles that are derived from pre-existing non-Gothic literary and cultural sources. There are different versions of the double at work in Dickens that compete to the degree that they are defined by the level at which they engage, or refuse to engage, with the social contract.

Gillman and Patten, who do not make explicit reference to the uncanny, argue that Dickens developed a version of doubling that can be termed ontogenetic, 'in which a character lives through a variety of selves externalized as alternatives and internalized as possibilities' (446). The self is projected outwards and redirected inwards as a narrative about the self. It is in relation to death that these narratives are granted an emerging Gothic flavour. Joanna Shawn Brigid O'Leary has explored the peculiar prevalence of twins in Dickens and has argued that even images of benign doubles, such as the cheerful Cheerybles in *Nicholas Nickleby* (1839), can be read as touched by Freud's version of the uncanny but only when considered in Marxist terms. She argues that 'they represent a human version of the mass-produced material commodities they trade' because, like them, they 'are not unique ... but replicated across a series'.[41] To some degree this echoes Dickens's account of haunting in the *American Notes*, when he claims of his prisoner that 'as the darkness thickens, his Loom begins to live' (p. 155). Objects come alive with their associated labour and although there is an interesting argument about spectrality and capitalist economics that can be pursued here, it is not the case that we can plausibly perceive the Cheerybles as demonstrably Gothic.[42] They also lack the type of inwardness that Freud defines, which suggests that in this instance we need to move beyond a purely Freudian account of the uncanny.

Juliet John's critique of psychology, which was touched on earlier, argues that for Dickens the inward turn is a negative one as it indicates a refusal to participate in the wider social narratives that define us as moral agents. Indeed, figures such as Sikes and Fagin are hardly positive examples of where the inner life may lead you. This is also part of a condemnation of solitary confinement because it takes the prisoner out of society and makes them unfit to return to the social world. However, the conscience defines a key aspect of this inner life, although increasingly in Dickens the focus shifts to what happens when the conscience fails, and on what replaces it.

The inward turn is a disturbing one in Dickens and is linked to ideas of death and what such ideas might inspire. As we saw in the example of capital punishment, images of death might awaken murderous desires, which Dickens saw as a fundamentally metaphysical problem. This model of the troubled inner life and its Gothic associations brings back into focus a discourse relating to creativity that has run throughout this account of the Gothic from the eighteenth century. Death and creativity have been related to each other in complex ways in the Gothic tradition explored here, and whilst Dickens might seem to be far removed from such matters as his work appears to be so obviously indebted to pre-existing narrative modes, his writings are increasingly defined by such considerations. Gillman and Patten have noted an impulse in Dickens that links 'creativity and murder' (448) because his work is informed by 'the contemporary lay and scientific image of the unconscious as criminal, immoral, uncivilized' (457). Dickens is thus writing before 'turn-of-the-century psychology both reflects and corrects' this anxiety 'by stressing the positive and, primal energies of the unconscious' (457). The seemingly transgressive potential of the unconscious can be seen in how Dickens's accounts of dreams articulate concerns about a loss of agency that is related to both destruction and to the possibilities of the creative imagination.

Dreams, death and the imagination

On 8 March 1851, Dickens published 'Dreams' in *Household Words*. The article appears to have been inspired following correspondence with one Dr Stone, who had earlier submitted an article on dreams that Dickens did not publish, feeling that it was an unoriginal synthesis of current ideas on the topic. Dickens's account of dreams is marked by typical rhetorical slips between comedy, pathos and melodrama, and it is clear that he is uncertain about what we are to make of dreams. However, he is interested in the type of visions that are conjured and whether they have any moral significance. He notes that in dreams, 'the mind may not be wholly under eclipse; for, although some of its faculties – such as perception, comparison, judgement, and especially the will, may be suspended – others, (for example, Memory and Imagination), are often more active in the waking state'.[43] For this reason, the dreamer may observe 'The events of his whole life ... hurry past him in dim obscurity; he may be revisited by the dead' (p. 566). Dream narratives may be shaped by external noises and Dickens recalls a dream in Italy that was influenced by 'the noise of people in the streets, on All Souls'-night, invoking the alms of the dead' (p. 567). These external factors cannot be controlled and Dickens provides a series of anecdotes (including one about an army officer who, whilst asleep, was induced to carry out various acts by his mischievous brother officers) that illustrate this loss of agency. He is, however, initially reassured by the idea that when we dream we dream of recognisable versions of ourselves and that this ensures that we behave in accordance with our true moral character. This even extends to dreams about being dead, because 'we have heard of persons who have dreamt they were dead, and in a spiritual state; but the spirit was still their own – they maintained their identity' (p. 568). He also asserts that the dreamer would not commit acts that went against their conscience because 'we cannot believe that the identity of moral goodness can be so perverted in the dreaming state', and although he admits that dreams may often be unsettling, that is attributed to '[a] guilty conscience' (p. 568). In an article on insomnia titled 'Lying Awake', published in *Household Words* on 30 October 1852, he revised this view in an account of himself, Queen Victoria and a fictitious vagrant he calls Winking Charley and their dream world, in which he claims that within them 'It is probable that we have all three committed murders and hidden bodies'.[44] A less troubling version of the dream is explored in 'Dreams', where he argues that the often frivolous nature of dreams suggests that we should not see them as spiritual, or as aspects of our soul, because 'Surely it is absurd to suppose that the soul, which we invest with such high and perfect attributes, should commit such frivolous and irrational acts' (p. 569). The article is ultimately unclear about whether dreams are secular visions, which may be meaninglessly prompted by outside noises. Whilst there is a possible commonplace cause to a dream, they can also possess an imaginative dimension, with Dickens recalling Coleridge's claim that 'Kubla Khan' was composed in a dream.

If dreams might be creative, and possibly devoid of spirituality (influenced by noises), this is in part because the dream takes us out of the social world and so denies us the possibility of acting as moral agents. Dreams act upon us and not vice versa. Their visions cannot be explained, but they are granted a problematic metaphysical status that relates to memory. He claims that in dreams, 'The faculty of Memory appears to be praeternaturally exalted' (p. 570), as we can recall instances from our early lives that we have consciously forgotten. He claims that such visions are found not just in dreams but also 'sometimes in hanging' (p. 570), as if the beginning of our life is recapitulated at its end. This unusual turn towards capital punishment is further elaborated in the following passage, which refers to the murders carried out by Burke and Hare. Dickens claims that:

> We had ourselves an interview with Burke, after his condemnation, when he told us that Many months before he was apprehended and convicted, he used to dream that the murders he committed had been discovered, then he imagined himself going to be executed, and his chief anxiety was how he should comport himself on the scaffold before the assembled multitude, whose faces he beheld gazing up and fixed upon him. (p. 571)

This claim is unlikely given that Dickens was aged seventeen at the time of Burke's execution.[45] What is revealing about Burke's projected dream is the sense that some limited form of moral conscience is manifested in the desire to behave with composure on the scaffold, but it is not significant enough to restrain him from murder. Death begets death in this version of Burke, which is in keeping with the narrative about self-destruction that governs Dickens's views on capital punishment.

Dickens explores the nature of the inner life in 'Dreams' and he seems unclear about the moral status of the dream. The dream takes away our conscious agency and yet it retains a potent sense of who we really are, and at the end of the article he urges 'all persons to study, whether waking or dreaming, the phenomena of their own minds' (p. 572). Dickens's account of hanging and Burke in 'Dreams' is reworked in 'Lying Awake', where quasi-oneiric contemplation of the popular display of ballooning in Cremorne Gardens leads him into a dream of the Mannings' execution in which he sees a vision: 'a limp loose suit of clothes, as if the man had gone out of them; the woman's, a fine shape, so elaborately corseted and artfully dressed, that it was quite unchanged in its trim appearance as it slowly swung from side to side' (p. 92). This image haunts him until he revisits the gaol and can see that the bodies have been removed. Later in the article he returns to the dead in a reference to the Paris morgue, where he contemplates a body that resembles 'a heap of crushed over-ripe figs' (p. 94). In the end he cannot fall asleep, noting, 'I found that I had been lying awake so long that the very dead began to wake too, and to crowd into my thoughts most sorrowfully' (pp. 94–5). In an earlier review of Catherine Crowe's *The Night Side of Nature; or, Ghosts and Ghost Seers* (1848), a book that tried to gather evidence of post-mortem existence, he had suggested that tales about death and dying may have their origin in a state somewhere between sleeping and waking, which frustrates our attempt at analysis.[46] However, he asserts one explanation for their origin when he claims that we all share 'that instinctive avoidance of death, which is one of the hardest conditions on which we hold our being – that attraction to repulsion to the awful veil that hangs so heavily over the grave' (p. 84). As we saw in the previous chapter, this was a veil that Eliot would be happy to try to lift. Dickens restates the view about capital punishment when referring to the 'attraction to repulsion', which implicates a fascination with death more widely, although one that is just beyond the reach of explanation.

In his account of dreams he makes the consistent, if implicit, claim that fantasies of death are central to understanding psychology. Such a topic is clearly beyond the requirements posed by the social contract, but as the beginning of *Great Expectations* illustrates, chance encounters in graveyards may lead to social advancement. Catherine A. Bernard has noted that Dickens's library contained many books on dreams published in the 1840s and that the recurring discussion in such texts centred on whether the subject lost their moral character in the dream, with such falling away from morality often being ascribed 'to physiological, not psychological causes' and so attributed to atypical states such as physical illness.[47] However, a view began to emerge outside physiology in the emerging discourse of neuroscience, as practised by Thomas Laycock in the 1870s, who claimed 'that during sleep the higher or moral instincts remained passive, giving rein to the lower or sensual ones' (p. 200).[48] Dreams became increasingly subject to scientific scrutiny in the period, which required the dream to be opened up to interpretation, and Dickens would, as Bernard notes, ask his readers to relate their psychological experiences to their dreams in 'Doctor Marigold's Prescriptions', published in *All the Year Round* on 7 December 1865. Bernard also claims that in the later novels such as *Great Expectations* and *Our Mutual Friend*, dreams frequently 'reveal egotistic impulses and wishes that permit the dreamer to satisfy in hallucinatory fashion what he or she cannot state consciously' (207). Dreams, in other words, gain meaning, but through associations with death that also have links to creativity.

Leon Litvack has noted that Dickens frequently indicated in his correspondence that when writing, his characters seemed to take on a life of their own and drove the plot forward in ways that Dickens seems to have had little conscious control over, leading Dickens to claim that he records their actions rather than creates them. Litvack asserts that in most aspects of his life Dickens was very much in control both personally and professionally, but that in the instance of writing 'the novelist continually recalls the passive/receptive mode of creation: characters suddenly appear before him, and he acts as reporter, recording what he sees as it is presented to him in vivid detail'.[49] Creativity occupies the same place as the dream for Dickens as it sits beyond any conscious control. This loss of agency is represented in anxious terms in relation to both creativity and dreams because, as we have seen, dreams often centre on the dead. These links are given a specific turn in arguably the most Gothic of his novels, which he was working on at the time of his death, *The Mystery of Edwin Drood*.

Drood: decoding death

The mystery of Edwin's Drood's demise is probably not so mysterious given that Dickens made it clear to a number of his contemporaries that John Jasper was the murderer and that the plot was going to focus on Jasper's agonised realisation that he had not needed to murder Drood. If we agree with this then the plot can be read as being about death and self-destruction, themes that we have seen elsewhere in Dickens's work.

Edwin Drood is notable for its use of doubling and divided selves. Not only is John Jasper divided between outer respectability and inner turmoil, other characters such as Miss Twinkleton are also represented as having conflicted inner selves. Simon J. James has also noted how 'The presence of two twins in Cloisterham, of different gender but impossibly near-identical, unsettles the security of the self still further'.[50] Jasper tells Drood, his nephew, about the dreary life he follows as the choirmaster of the cathedral city of Cloisterham: '"No wretched monk who droned his life away in the gloomy place, before me, can have been more tired of it than I am. He could take for relief (and did take) to carving demons out of the stalls and seats and desks. What shall I do?"'[51] Cloisterham is closely associated with death; it is a place without transcendence because it is devoid of any obvious spirituality. The visions in the novel are fundamentally secular, as registered at the start with Jasper regaining consciousness after his opium-induced sleep when his 'scattered consciousness' is 'fantastically pieced ... together' (p. 37). The problem of the inner life is one of recognition in which the self denies that which haunts it. This is made clear in Rosa's account of being pursued by Jasper, which reworks Sikes's haunting by the eyes of Nancy, when Rosa recalls to Helena the disturbing way that Jasper looks at her:

> 'I avoid his eyes, but he forces me to see them without looking at them. Even when a glaze comes over them (which is sometimes the case), and he seems to wander away into a frightful sort of dream in which he threatens most, he obliges me to know it, and to know that he is sitting close at my side, more terrible to me then than ever.' (p. 95)

Rosa, however, is more trapped by Jasper than she is prepared to acknowledge. Later she reflects on this confession to Helena, where she senses the ambivalent need 'to keep out his ghostly following of her – that no reasoning of her own could calm her terrors. The fascination of repulsion had been upon her so long, and now culminated so darkly, that she felt as if he had the power to bind her by a spell' (pp. 233–4). Rosa wants to ignore Jasper's desires for her, and yet it is the presence of desire (and her desire to explore it) that is registered in these moments which she is not prepared to interrogate, but flee from. Allan Lloyd Smith has argued that 'Rosa cannot afford to see what her unconscious knows'.[52] Lloyd Smith's argument is that the novel can be read via Abraham and Torok's theory of cryptonymy, in which the traumas of a text are so deeply embedded that they structure the narrative, even whilst the reasons for that structure have become so dispersed that they are difficult to recover. Whilst this is based upon a theory of influence in which the subject becomes defined by anxieties that do not immediately belong to them (inherited from a parent, for example, with whom they are more properly associated), they help explain why the pervasive presence of the crypt in *Edwin Drood* is related to death, memory and a failure of language.[53]

Throughout the novel there is an emphasis on 'blindness or lack of self-knowledge' (Lloyd Smith, 297), which seemingly touches all. This 'fascination of repulsion' is an issue that we have seen in Dickens's account of capital punishment and in his account of death in 'Dreams'. Rosa is fascinated by the repulsive Jasper, who is described as both spectral and corpse-like. He is buried in Cloisterham and sees his life as a type of living death. As Lloyd Smith notes, 'Cloisterham is ... a city of death' (300). Durdles, the stonemason, is the character who knows most about the graveyard and the crypts and is described as 'always prowling among old graves and ruins like a Ghoule' as he gives Jasper a tour of the cathedral's crypt (p. 151). The graveyard is allegedly haunted by 'a mysterious lady, with a child in her arms and a rope dangling from her neck' (p. 153), and it is unclear if this is a suicide or an image of the executed. The graveyard is haunted not just by images but also by noises, as Durdles relates to Jasper that on the previous Christmas Eve he was awoken by '"The ghost of a cry. The ghost of one terrific shriek"' (p. 155). The novel repeatedly centres on an atmosphere of death and decay and Dickens uses this to define the fragmented, incomplete and dislocated lives of Cloisterham's residents. The plot, centring on the murder of Drood, refocuses this idea of death and demonstrates its inescapability, which is in keeping with Dickens's plan for Jasper's intended self-destruction and self-incrimination.

Charles Mitchell has noted how the novel repeatedly uses dreams to show characters as estranged from reality, as closer to death than life. Such figures are lost in 'the fantastical creations of [their] own imagination'.[54] They, as in Litvack's account of creativity, are subject to forces that are beyond their conscious control. For Dickens, the dictates of the conscience demonstrate the existence of our spiritual self. In *Edwin Drood*, however, the cathedral is simply stone and the city a necropolis. The consistently bleak tones of the novel register the absence of moral choice. They also indicate the difficulty in finding a new language in which to account for this apparent Gothic emptiness. Mitchell claims that Grewgious, Rosa's guardian, appears to have no inner self, but, whereas other characters such as Sapsea and Durdles lead 'dead lives', he represents 'a dead man coming to life' (237). Grewgious discusses love with Edwin and verbally sketches a portrait of an ideal lover. His speech touches on doubles and the failure of language:

> 'my picture does represent the true lover as having no existence separable from that of the beloved object of his affections, and as living at once a doubled and a halved life. And if I do not clearly express what I mean by that,

it is either for the reason that having no conversational powers, I cannot express what I mean, or that having no meaning, I do not mean what I fail to express.' (p. 142)

Lovers are lost in the other, their lives doubled and divided, and how to explain this escapes Grewgious (as meaning also eludes any model of uncanniness that could be identified as such in the 1870s). The novel makes an unconscious link to Young's *Night Thoughts* when later we see Grewgious looking at the stars for a possible source of comprehension. He examines the stars 'as if he would have read in them something that was hidden from him. Many of us would, if we could; but none of us so much as know our letters in the stars yet – or seem likely to, in this state of existence – and few languages can be read until their alphabets are mastered' (p. 216). The coming back to life of Grewgious represents a desire to return to the past, to an idea of the cosmos that has meaning. The fact that his language repeatedly disintegrates demonstrates the problem of reconstituting meaning in a world that seems to consist of fragments that, as in the image of Jasper with which the novel opens, need to be 'fantastically pieced ... together'. The inward turn is now truly Gothic and the cultural imperative from here is how to find the language that will make sense of what this new discourse about death entails.

This chapter has charted the different ways Dickens explored death. Death in Dickens subtly moves towards the secular bleakness of *Edwin Drood* in a journey that sees Dickens repeatedly explore the moral significance of death. The instance of capital punishment is key in this as it shows how Dickens began to conceive of such issues in metaphysical and psychological terms centring on the attraction of repulsion. In Dickens we see a Gothic uncanny emerge, although one that is not straightforwardly Freudian. Grewgious's speech about love and doubling is revealing in this context as it, paradoxically, suggests that love is both uncanny *and* relieves the very anxieties produced by Gothic uncanniness. The next chapter will explore how love and death are related in Rider Haggard's *She* (1887) and its sequels, Stoker's *The Jewel of Seven Stars* (1903, revised 1912) and *The Lady of the Shroud* (1909) and Wilde's *The Picture of Dorian Gray* (1891). The problem of interpretation that we find in *Edwin Drood* is restated through models of love. At the *fin de siècle*, love grants a post-mortem existence that keeps the dead emotionally alive. We are, seemingly, no longer solely redeemed by the love of God, but also by the love for another as we see Gothic novels attempt to move beyond a Gothic terror of death by exploring new reconfigurations of empathy.

Notes

1. Robert Mighall, 'Dickens and the Gothic', in David Paroissien (ed.), *A Companion to Dickens* (Oxford: Blackwell, 2008), pp. 81–96, p. 82. All subsequent references are to this edition and are given in the text.
2. Mighall discusses the issue of a Gothic London in Dickens in his critically canonical *A Geography of Victorian Gothic: Mapping History's Nightmares* (Oxford: Oxford University Press, 1999).
3. Mary-Catherine Harrison, 'The Paradox of Fiction and the Ethics of Empathy: Reconceiving Dickens's Realism', *Narrative*, 16:3 (October 2008), 256–78, 263. All subsequent references are to this edition and are given in the text.
4. George Eliot, 'The Natural History of German Life', in *Essays of George Eliot*, ed. Thomas Pinney (New York: Columbia University Press, 1963), pp. 266–99, p. 271.
5. William M. Thackeray, 'On Going to See a Man Hanged', *Fraser's Magazine*, 22 (August 1840), 150–8.
6. Charles Dickens, 'Capital Punishment', *The Daily News* (28 February 1846), p. 6.
7. Edmund Burke, *A Philosophical Enquiry into the Origins of Our Ideas of the Sublime and Beautiful*, ed. Adam Phillips (Oxford: Oxford University Press, 1998), p. 43. All subsequent references are to this edition and are given in the text.
8. Charles Dickens, 'Capital Punishment', *The Daily News* (28 February 1846), p. 6.
9. Ibid.
10. Ibid.
11. Ibid.
12. Charles Dickens, 'Capital Punishment', *The Daily News* (13 March 1846), p. 5.
13. Jacques Derrida, *The Death Penalty*, ed. Geoffrey Bennington, Marc Crépon and Thomas Dutoit, trans. Peggy Kamuf (Chicago and London: University of Chicago Press, 2014), vol. I, p. 152. All subsequent references are to this edition and are given in the text.
14. Charles Dickens, 'Capital Punishment', *The Daily News* (9 March 1846), p. 5.
15. See Claire Wood's *Dickens and the Business of Death* (Cambridge: Cambridge University Press, 2015) for an account of how Dickens explores a business of death consisting of, amongst other things, undertakers, joint-stock cemeteries and body-snatching.
16. Charles Dickens, 'Capital Punishment', *The Daily News* (16 March 1846), p. 5.
17. Charles Dickens, letter titled 'Mr Charles Dickens and the Execution of the Mannings', *The Times* (13 November 1849).
18. Ibid.

19 Juliet John, *Dickens's Villains: Melodrama, Character, Popular Culture* (Oxford: Oxford University Press, 2003), pp. 3–5.
20 Charles Dickens, *Oliver Twist* (Harmondsworth: Penguin, 1985), p. 33. All subsequent references are to this edition and are given in the text.
21 See Edgar Allan Poe's 'William Wilson' (1839) for a tale that is about doubling and the killing of one's conscience.
22 Valentine Cunningham, 'Dickens and Christianity', in David Paroissien (ed.), *A Companion to Dickens* (Oxford: Blackwell, 2008), pp. 255–76, p. 268. All subsequent references are to this edition and are given in the text.
23 Weidmann murdered six people in 1937 with the motivation of robbing them.
24 Charles Dickens, letter to *The Times* (19 November 1849).
25 Ibid.
26 Ibid.
27 Charles Dickens, *A Tale of Two Cities*, ed. George Woodcock (Harmondsworth: Penguin, 1989), p. 402. All subsequent references are to this edition and are given in the text.
28 Charles Dickens, *Pictures from Italy*, ed. Kate Flint (Harmondsworth: Penguin, 1998), p. 144. The murderer had robbed and killed Anna Katin, a Bavarian countess who was on a pilgrimage.
29 Charles Dickens, *Great Expectations*, ed. Angus Calder (Harmondsworth: Penguin, 1986), p. 35. All subsequent references are to this edition and are given in the text.
30 Julie Rugg, 'Lawn Cemeteries: The Emergence of a New Landscape of Death', *Urban History*, 33:2 (August 2006), 213–33, 228. All subsequent references are to this edition and are given in the text. I am indebted to Val Derbyshire for the reference to Rugg, which she made in her MA essay on '"Holmes and the Adventure of the London Burial Grounds": Discourses of Death in the Fin-de-Siècle' (University of Sheffield, 2014).
31 Dickens was critical of Chadwick and mocks his views on austere school food provisions in 'A Sleep to Startle Us', *Household Words* (13 March 1852), pp. 577–80.
32 Edwin Chadwick, *A Supplementary Report on the Results of a Special Inquiry into the Practice of Interment in Towns* (London: Clowes and Sons, 1843), p. 31. All subsequent references are to this edition and are given in the text.
33 Mary Elizabeth Hotz, *Literary Remains: Representations of Death and Burial in Victorian England* (Albany, NY: State University of New York, 2009), p. 22. All subsequent references are to this edition and are given in the text.
34 Julie Rugg, 'Constructing the Grave: Competing Burial Ideals in Nineteenth-Century England', *Social History*, 38:3 (2013), 328–45, see 340–1.
35 Charles Dickens, *Dombey and Son*, ed. Peter Fairclough (Harmondsworth: Penguin, 1975), p. 75. All subsequent references are to this edition and are given in the text.

36 Bridgid Lowe, 'Dombey and Son', in David Paroissien (ed.), *A Companion to Dickens* (Oxford: Blackwell, 2008), pp. 358-68, p. 368.

37 Charles Dickens, *American Notes for General Circulation*, ed. John S. Whitely and Arnold Goldman (Harmondsworth: Penguin, 1985), p. 146. All subsequent references are to this edition and are given in the text.

38 It has been noted that Dickens had this experience in mind when describing the eighteen-year solitary confinement of Dr Manette in *A Tale of Two Cities*. See editorial commentary on this in *American Notes*, p. 345.

39 See my extended reading of spectrality in the American Notes in 'Colonial Ghosts: Mimicking Dickens in America', in Avril Horner and Sue Zlosnik (eds), *Le Gothic* (Basingstoke: Palgrave, 2008), pp. 185-200.

40 Susan K. Gillman and Robert L. Patten, 'Dickens: Doubles: Twain: Twins', *Nineteenth-Century Fiction*, 39:4 (March 1985), 441-58, 442. All subsequent references are to this edition and are given in the text.

41 Joanna Shawn Brigid O'Leary, 'Two for the Price of One?: Twins and the Anxieties of (Re)production in Dickens', *English: Journal of the English Association*, 62:238 (2013), 275-93, 279.

42 See Tricia Lootens, 'Fear of Furniture: Commodity Gothicism and the Teaching of Victorian Literature', in Diane Long Hoeveler and Tamar Heller (eds), *Gothic Fiction: The British and American Traditions* (New York: MLA, 2003), pp. 148-53, for an interesting account for how we might relate commodities to spectrality. See also my chapter on 'See the Spectre: An Economic Theory of the Ghost Story', in *The Ghost Story 1840-1920: A Cultural History* (Manchester: Manchester University Press, 2010), pp. 10-31.

43 Charles Dickens, 'Dreams', *Household Words* (8 March 1851), pp. 566-72, p. 566. All subsequent references are to this edition and are given in the text.

44 Charles Dickens, 'Lying Awake', in *Household Words* (30 October 1852), in *'Gone Astray' and Other Papers from Household Words*, ed. Michael Slater (London: J. M. Dent, 1998), pp. 88-95, p. 91. All subsequent references are to this edition and are given in the text.

45 He may have in mind a piece by Christopher North (real name John Wilson, one of the founders of *Blackwood's Magazine*) that appeared in *Blackwood's Magazine* in March 1829, where there is a brief reference to Burke's likely dreams before a character portrait of both Burke and Hare, whom he had visited in their cells.

46 Charles Dickens, '*Review*: The Night Side of Nature', in *The Examiner* (26 February 1848), in *Dickens' Journalism*, ed. Michael Slater (London: J. M. Dent, 1996), pp. 80-9, p. 83. All subsequent references are to this edition and are given in the text.

47 Catherine A. Bernard, 'Dickens and Victorian Dream Theory', *Annals of the New York Academy of Sciences*, 360 (April 1981), special issue on 'Victorian Science and Victorian Values: Literary Perspectives', 197-216, 200. All subsequent references are to this edition and are given in the text.

48 See Thomas Laycock, *A Chapter on Some Organic Laws of Personal and Ancestral Memory* (Lewes: George P. Bacon: Steam Printing Offices, 1875).
49 Leon Litvack, '*Dickens's Dream* and the Conception of Character', *The Dickensian*, 103:1 (Spring 2007), 5–36, 28.
50 Simon J. James, 'The Mystery of Edwin Drood', in David Paroissien (ed.), *A Companion to Dickens* (Oxford: Blackwell, 2008), pp. 444–51, p. 448.
51 Charles Dickens, *The Mystery of Edwin Drood*, ed. Arthur J. Cox (Harmondsworth: Penguin, 1974), p. 48. All subsequent references are to this edition and are given in the text.
52 Allan Lloyd Smith, 'The Phantoms of *Drood* and *Rebecca*: The Uncanny Reencountered through Abraham and Torok's "Cryptonymy"', *Poetics Today*, 13:2 (Summer 1992), 285–308, 297. All subsequent references are to this edition and are given in the text.
53 See Nicholas Abraham and Maria Torok, *The Wolf Man's Magic Word: A Cryptonymy* (Minneapolis: University of Minneapolis Press, 1986 [1976]).
54 Charles Mitchell, '*The Mystery of Edwin Drood*: The Interior and Exterior of Self', *ELH*, 33:2 (June 1966), 228–46, 242. All subsequent references are to this edition and are given in the text.

5

Loving the undead: Haggard, Stoker and Wilde

This book has concentrated on the complex relationships that existed during the period between death, creativity and forms of interpretation. Whilst the emotional and social consequences of capital punishment were considered in the previous chapter, we also saw how death in Dickens is linked to social, political and psychological analysis. *The Mystery of Edwin Drood* (1870) is a hybrid Gothic and detective novel and Dickens focuses on dreams and opium-induced reveries as the places where the truth, about the subject, can be found. How to read critically represents a significant shift in the literary culture as it casts off the older Romantic emphasis on the creative imagination. This development is also bound up with questions of epistemology. How to create is progressively replaced by acts of knowing, and whilst this has points of contact with a scientific mindset of the late nineteenth century (which will be discussed in the following chapter), it is still one that, in the Gothic, cannot be isolated from more febrile emotional experiences. This chapter explores how models of romantic love were used in the *fin de siècle* Gothic as a means of knowing the Other. That Other frequently represents another culture, place or time, and 'love' evidences a complex *fin de siècle* Orientalism. What is revealing is how these engagements are repeatedly played out in relation to the dead. Loving the dead is one way of resurrecting the past as a means of understanding it, and Vernon Lee, the ghost story writer and historian, developed the idea that empathy enables an embracing of the past which reflects this. In her essay, 'Faustus and Helena: Notes on the Supernatural in Art' (1880), Lee outlines a theory of ghosting in which art quasi-numinously relocates the feelings of its age. There she records how 'the scent of mouldering plaster and mouldering bones from beneath the broken pavement' is spectrally brought back to life by an image of the ghost, which enables us to understand 'the imaginative power of the past'.[1] Whilst for her this represents a model of the supernatural that replaces divine intervention, it is couched in an argument that weighs the demands of a religious culture against a secular age. The paradox, for her, is that a secular culture reads older religious beliefs (and she has in mind ancient Egypt but also early Christian-dominated periods) through an emotional, rather than scriptural, engagement. This type of engagement also shapes the work of Haggard and Stoker, whose excavations of the past explore whether these older systems of belief still speak to us. Their approach examines how love reanimates history, which, to a significant degree, both literalises and erotically overshoots Lee's sense of an empathetic archaeology.

Haggard: love and death in *She*

She employs death in both imperial and emotional terms. The past seems to be symbolically alive as the lost imperial city of Kôr, which once ruled the world through its navy, appears as a gloss on Britain's imperialism. Ayesha sees herself as a queen who could oust Queen Victoria if she so chose (much to the horror of our narrator, Holly). The novel, however, centres on Holly's lovelorn feelings for her, but before Holly encounters Ayesha we witness him grappling with ethical issues that are closely tied to religious principles. Holly, who has taken quinine to ward off a tropical illness, contemplates the night-time sky, which leads him to conclude that we can never truly discover God's presence through our powers of observation alone because:

> Such things are not for us to know. Knowledge is to the strong, and we are weak … For what is the first result of man's increased knowledge interpreted from Nature's book by persistent effort of his purblind observation? Is it not but too often to make him question the existence of his Maker, or indeed any intelligent purpose beyond his own? Full knowledge is not for man as man is here.[2]

Holly's view of the stars is quite different from what we witnessed in Young's *Night Thoughts*. Here the stars are drawn from 'Nature's book', which invites an epistemic rather than spiritual interpretation that makes the secular observers overlook the type of religious questions that Holly wants to raise.

Holly is repeatedly defined by his interest in moral systems, which enables him to redeem the ostensibly savage Amahagger because of the presence of socially binding ceremonial rituals that, for Holly, indicates the presence 'of morality' (p. 60) and social values. His first sight of Ayesha, however, is a morally baffled but erotically charged one:

> a tall figure stood before us. I say a figure, for not only the body, but also the face was wrapped in a soft gauzy material in such a way as at first sight to remind me most forcibly of a corpse in its grave-clothes ... I could clearly distinguish, however, that the swathed mummy-like form before me was that of a tall and lovely woman, instinct with beauty in every part, and also with a certain snake-like grace which I had never seen anything to equal before. (p. 106)

Holly also notes 'the gleam of the pink flesh', which is thinly disguised by the material. Ayesha is both alive and dead, an object of veneration and fear. Her 'snake-like' movements suggest that she does not quite belong to the human world, and Holly is at a loss to categorise her. His protracted beguilement by Ayesha is in part tempered by an attempt to gauge her moral status. However, it is in Ayesha's beauty that we see the aesthetic considerations about the relationship between death and creativity being reworked.

Ayesha describes herself as possessing '"more than the loveliness of that Grecian Helen, of whom they used to sing"' (p. 112), which is combined with a wisdom that is '"wider, ay, far more wide and deep than the wisdom of Solomon the Wise"' (p. 112) because she knows the secrets of life and death. Ayesha disguises her beauty by wearing a veil, and Holly's consideration of her beauty is, typically, a moral one, although paradoxically tinged by erotic factors. He notes after this early encounter, 'I have heard of the beauty of celestial beings, now I saw it; only this beauty, with all its awful loveliness and purity, was evil – or rather, at the time it struck me as evil' (p. 116). Holly finds her beauty terrifying and overwhelming. She is a beautiful corpse, which means that the potentially degraded status of the dead is replaced by an aesthetics of beauty that Holly cannot quite trust even whilst he feels 'Drawn by some magnetic force which I could not resist' (p. 117). Ayesha is aware of this destructive, indeed deathly, force of her beauty: '"Beauty is like the lightening; it is lovely but it destroys"' (p. 117). For Holly, Ayesha's shroud suggests a spirituality that her physical form contests and in the end he tells her that he 'would give my immortal soul to marry her' (p. 143), as if he were aware of the blasphemy of his erotic gaze. She is, of course, intended for Leo Vincey who, as the embodiment of the resurrected Kallikrates (whom she had killed in a fit of jealousy), represents the return of her lost love from 2,000 years before.

Love stories unite and divide all of the principal characters in *She*. Ayesha had loved Kallikrates, and observes his reincarnation in Leo.

Leo will come to love Ayesha but only after she has killed Ustane, who has fallen in love with him. Holly loves Ayesha and is also homosocially bound to Leo. What constitutes love is, however, subject to some debate. Holly questions Ayesha's claim that immortality leads to perfection; her response is that "'With love shall life roll on gloriously from year to year'" (p. 189). Holly counters that love can be a curse if it is unrequited and that one needs to distinguish between physical and spiritual love, with the latter only possible after death when "'shall the spirit shine forth clad in the brightness of eternal good'". Ayesha responds, "'thou dreamest that thou shalt clasp the star. I believe it not, and I name thee fool'" (p. 190). Privately, Holly acknowledges that he rebuts Ayesha's position because 'I had no wish to prolong an existence which must always be haunted and tortured by her memory, and by the last bitterness of unsatisfied love' (p. 190). The sense of an 'unsatisfied love' is not unique to Holly, however, because Ayesha tells Leo that "'I may not mate with thee, for thou and I are different, and the very brightness of my being would burn thee up, and perchance destroy thee'" (p. 188). Ultimately, love seems to be largely theoretical but it is also the point of entry into knowledge as Holly's fascination with Ayesha initiates a series of debates about life, death and morality.

Ayesha is a chemist who has discovered how to eugenically create different races. Her encounter with the flame of life has seemingly made her immortal. Her triumph over death represents for Holly a victory that makes her almost divine. She seems to be able to exercise control over life, but Holly is appalled by her stark Darwinian perspective in which she claims: "'day by day we destroy that we may live, since in this world none save the strongest can endure. Those who are weak must perish'" (p. 153). Holly considers 'what may not be possible to a being unshackled by a moral sense of right and wrong' (p. 153), as he progressively casts her as a femme fatale. The key issue is reincarnation, which suggests that time is circular and as such prone to the type of repetitions that work against the model of moral progress that Holly is searching for.[3] This idea of recycling the past is emphasised when the embalmed (and therefore highly flammable) corpses of the denizens of Kôr are used to illuminate a dance. Holly recounts that 'There was something very terrible, and yet most fascinating, about the employment of the remote dead to illumine the orgies of the living; in itself the thing was a satire, both on the living and the dead' (p. 164). This recycling has been linked by Barri J. Gold to a process of story-telling within *She* in which the dead become important because of the narratives they inspire.

In his tour of Kôr, Holly discovers an embalmed dead mother and her baby, which leads him to speculate on how the pathos of death speaks to the present, as it indicates 'a forgotten human history speaking more eloquently to the heart than could any written record of their lives' (p. 138). He later discovers the corpses of a young man and women who are clasped together, having been stabbed; nearby is a motto that indicated that they had been *'Wedded in Death'* (p. 139, italics in original), which leads him to speculate on the circumstances of their demise. Earlier Billali had told Holly about a woman's foot that he used to play with as a child; Billali discovers it in its original place and hands it to Holly, which leads Holly to think about how 'it had upborne through the pomp and pageantry of a forgotten civilisation – first as a merry child's, then as a blushing maid's, and lastly as a prefect woman's' (p. 82). This echoes Vernon Lee's notion of empathy (although here tempered by eroticism), and Barri J. Gold's claims that 'For Holly ... the attraction of the dead is that they are available for reprocessing, specifically into narrative – erotic fancies, romantic tales, invested with hope'.[4] Indeed, scenes of death in childhood and murdered lovers do not appal Holly, but rather move him by their human dramas. Holly's self-conscious reflection on these narratives suggest that 'interpretation [is] an imaginative act' (Gold, 319), which illustrates this slip from the creative to the interpretive that we have witnessed from the mid nineteenth century onwards. However, this also raises questions about how such acts can be linked to Holly's moral quest.

At the centre of the necropolis that is Kôr, Holly describes a statue of a beautiful winged woman, with her face veiled, positioned on a globe. For Holly, it was 'perhaps the grandest allegorical work of Art that the genius of her children has ever given to the world' (p. 199). Ayesha explains that the figure represents Truth and that it is only in death that truth will be found. The figure is thus both angelic and a femme fatale whose veiled face echoes that of Ayesha. For Bradley Deane, such imagery should be seen within the context of Victorian perceptions of Egypt in which Ayesha functions as a mummy-like figure. Deane notes that whereas the Orient was represented at the time as backward and culturally alien, 'Pharaonic Egypt represented greatness so permanent, so exempt from the usual standards of historical development, that it could be more properly regarded with a feeling of awe',[5] which explains why at the sight of the statue Holly records that 'my breath stood still, and for an instant my heart ceased its beating' (p. 200). The feelings of unrequited love in *She* are also a feature of tales about Egypt from the period, and Ailise Bulfin has noted that 'none of the romances ever produce satisfactory or sustainable unions',[6] which can in part be attributed to an ambivalent response to the 'Egyptian Question' during a period when the British established a veiled Protectorate (to help protect British ownership of the Suez Canal) that resulted in a 'blurring of colonizers and colonized' in which 'the operation of imperial influence was imagined as a sort of partnership of Egyptians and their British advisors' (Deane, 392). This is reworked in *She* around images of the corpse, and Gold has referred to it as 'a novel truly fascinated with the corpse, yet horrified by its own fascination' (305). Ayesha symbolically represents an ambivalent British attitude towards Egypt that is worked out as an engagement with ancient Egypt, during a period in which there were many tomb excavations.[7]

In *She*, the dead are blurred with the living and the West with the East, and yet Holly is in pursuit of an historical, national and cultural narrative of morality. His inclination to projectively reconstruct the lives of the dead is intended to incorporate such figures, and their plights, into recognisable patterns of (Western) human behaviour. His pursuit of ethics is clearly linked to a religious sensibility even whilst he sees Ayesha, disappointingly, as representing a moral vacuum. David Gange has noted that from the 1870s onwards, European explorers of Egypt were not in the main motivated by quasi-scientific principles of archaeological examination. Instead they were specifically looking for evidence of how Christianity could have influenced the ancient Egyptians and so prove that the Old Testament was historical fact. This would lead to such claims that Rameses II was in fact the pharaoh referred to in Exodus.[8] Such a biblically conditioned way of reading ancient Egypt was thus intended as a rebuttal of evolutionary and geological theories that indicated that the earth, and the people on it, pre-dated Genesis (1,089). Ayesha's Darwinian views are characterised by an ethical poverty, which suggests that Holly should be seen, if only implicitly, as on the side of the biblical scholars. In death he is looking for the presence of a spirituality that Ayesha repeatedly denies. However, this is the position of the 1880s and, as Gange notes, this shifted in the 1890s as 'late Victorian Egyptologists, painfully aware of the challenges facing contemporary religion, held up [some] aspect of ancient Egyptian culture as an ideal for Victorian Britain to aspire to, emphasizing faith, steadfastness, and tolerance' (1,092). The picture would also become blurred through claims that Christianity should be seen as an historical offshoot of the cult of Mithras combined with the idolisation of Isis, which suggested that Christianity represented a latter-day religious belief (1,098). *She* thus represents an early form of Egyptian Gothic that focuses on the relationships between the living and the dead as a way of exploring how a clash of cultures might be putatively resolved by Holly and Leo becoming more like Ayesha (by stepping into the flame of life) and Ayesha more like them – by becoming 'humanised' through love. Many of these ideas also anticipate a Freudian view of love.

Freud kept a range of original ancient Egyptian artefacts on his desk, some of which are incomplete, which demonstrated both their authenticity and the passing of time. The collection reflects Freud's idea that one needs to reassemble the fragments of the subject's past in order to make the unconscious surrender its secrets.[9] Freud was also interested in *She*, and in *The Interpretation of Dreams* (1900) he recounts how in a dream he recommends the book as one that is 'full of hidden meaning' about 'the eternal feminine, the immortality of our emotions'.[10] Freud, in the first of his three essays on the psychology of love, explores the reason why men are attracted to unattainable women (as Holly is to Ayesha). Freud argues that this represents the inability to retain the mother, but that whilst this appears in neurotics (such as the Wolf Man, for example), it can also be seen 'in people of average health or even in those with outstanding qualities'.[11] In *She*, love provides a way of engaging with the past, which can seemingly, in the instance of Kallikrates, restore the corpse to life. Love thus functions as an epistemology that promises to break down the boundaries between self and Other and so lead to a new understanding. However, the problems of love (its tendency to neurosis) can also form part of the problem, and this is an issue that Stoker addresses in *The Jewel of Seven Stars* (1903, revised 1912), which should be seen as an explicit commentary on *She*.

Love and understanding in *The Jewel of Seven Stars*

There are many clear comparisons between *Jewel* and *She*, and in turn Stoker's novel influenced *Ayesha: The Return of She* (1905), which will be discussed below. In *Jewel*, Tera is a femme fatale queen who, like Ayesha, is associated with the various scientific advancements of her age. Towards the end of the novel she appears to psychically take over Margaret Trelawney, with whom the narrator, Malcolm Ross, is in love. The concluding attempt to resurrect Tera ends in disaster in the 1903 ending as she kills all except Ross, but in triumph in the 1912 ending where there is a romantically happy ending for Margaret and Ross. However, love is a problem in the novel because it is associated with emotional instability.[12]

The novel begins with Ross's dream of Margaret in which he acknowledges a loss of self that is conditioned by his feelings for her so that he 'only just obeyed imperative orders'.[13] This loss is emphasised throughout the novel and is the cause of his inability to clearly interpret the changes in Margaret, as she becomes influenced by Tera. The idea that love is an idealised dream is later restated by Margaret when she contemplates Tera's life and reads it in romantic terms when asserting that during Tera's wait for resurrection, she must have been subject to 'The dream of a love that she felt she might, even under new conditions, herself evoke', and that this is 'the dream of every woman's life; of the Old and of the New; Pagan or Christian' (pp. 152–3). Love is thus truly transcendent in this romantic vision, albeit in a novel that suggests that love interferes with interpretation. Indeed, the novel represents a tension between a type of regressive subjectivity associated with love and a world of objects represented by the Egyptian paraphernalia employed in the resurrection of Tera. Margaret's father is a collector of such artefacts, which populate his rooms in London and which need to be assembled in a particular order to effect the resurrection. Indeed, the wider emphasis in the text is in turning Tera from an object (an embalmed mummy) into a subject, which depends upon a process of textual exegesis that is typical in the representation of death in the Gothic of the time.

Many of the objects collected by Trelawney are covered in hieroglyphics, with Tera's sarcophagus 'wrought with hundreds, perhaps thousands, of minute hieroglyphics, seemingly in an endless series' (p. 79). It is also noted that on one side of the sarcophagus was a table, 'exquisitely chased with symbolic figures of gods and the signs of the zodiac', on which sits a case 'beautifully engraved with hieroglyphics' (p. 81). The account, from 1650, of the discovery of Tera's tomb also emphasises the presence of cryptic signs and symbols that are written on stone near the entrance of the tomb as 'cabalistic signs … and many quaint symbols' (pp. 96–7). In the Mummy Pit of the tomb, 'All the walls of the chamber and the passage were carved with strange writings in the uncanny form mentioned' (p. 98). Whilst Holly is confronted by an allegory about truth and the world, the characters in *Jewel* are tested by more complex forms of textual interpretation. Mr Corbeck, an archaeologist who accompanied Trelawney in his excavation of Tera's tomb, explains that the hieroglyphics outside the tomb were written by priests to warn any tomb raiders of the danger of disturbing the 'Nameless One' (p. 107), who has been deserted by the gods because the gods had been insulted. Corbeck was able to decipher the other hieroglyphics, which identified Tera as an Egyptian queen with an impressive list of achievements. For Corbeck, 'To us was given to read this message from the dead' (p. 110), as they begin their excavation. Their ability to decode signs and symbols means that they do not work in ignorance, unlike the earlier explorers, and many of these texts were produced by Tera 'in hieroglyphic writing of great beauty' (p. 111). The hiding of her name bars her from entry into the Egyptian afterlife, so she seeks resurrection. The procedure for the resurrection is to be found through analysis of texts centred on a non-Christian discourse of spirituality.

Knowledge of Egypt includes discovering an encounter with a possible model of resurrection in which 'What changes might happen, did men know that the portals of the House of Death were not in very truth eternally fixed; and that the Dead could come forth again!' (p. 158). This leads Ross into an account of religion that is informed by contemporary issues relating to the Bible and what the gods of ancient Egypt symbolise. He contemplates a version of the universe that encompasses a diverse range of religious beliefs that includes old and new faiths, though does not unite them: 'Was there room in the Universe for opposing Gods; or if such there were, would the stronger allow manifestations of power on the part of the opposing Force which would tend to the weakening of His own teaching and designs?' (p. 159). It is tempting to read this as a gloss on British political influence in Egypt at the time, but it is also an attempt to align different faiths around an idea of 'the Mid-Region', which is 'the home of the Gods' and which Ross claims Milton may have seen 'in the rays of poetic light falling between him and Heaven' (p. 159). This spirit world may be different from 'the tangible world of facts' that governs the physical world, but the reference to 'rays' suggests a scientific engagement that is subsequently developed in reference to 'The Röntgen Ray' (p. 160), which identified the presence of electromagnetic radiation in X-rays (by Wilhelm Röntgen in 1895). This invites an inference about the forces of nature in which the light emitted by stars (in reference to the seven stars that symbolically help in the resurrection) might lead to a time 'when Astrology shall be accepted on a scientific basis' (p. 160). Such speculation links the old and new worlds with reference made to the discovery of radium (in 1898) and the suggestion that the ancient Egyptians may have been aware of its properties, given its likely presence in the geology of Egypt. The existence of radium is also addressed in Haggard's *Ayesha: The Return of She*, which indicates a dialogue across these novels.

That *Jewel* is centred on models of knowing is also indicated by the presence of Sergeant Daw, who is investigating the attacks on Trelawney but who withdraws with evident relief when the attacks cease, because, as he tells Ross, '"I verily believe I was beginning to get dotty over it all. There were too many mysteries, that aren't in my line, for me to be really satisfied as to either facts or the causes of them"' (p. 135). The mysterious influence of Tera defies a narrow procedural investigation, and order is restored through narrative construction rather than police deduction, with Corbeck noting that the scattered textual references relating to Tera can be combined to form a complete narrative in which 'Isolated facts, doubts, suspicions, conjectures, give way to a homogeneity which is convincing' (p. 93). *Jewel* explores different interpretations of what Tera represents. Textual analysis suggests the presence of a pattern that leads to the type of knowledge that is required to effect her resurrection; as in *She*, however, there is also a narrative that is about morality and what one might gain from the Egyptian spirit world.

The links between the old and new world are, as we have seen, highly tentative because they are highly speculative. In *She*, Holly is looking for an abstract ethical presence that unites the past with the present – only, in the end, to Other Ayesha as amoral. In *Jewel* there appears to be greater ethical flexibility as Tera (like Ayesha) promises a liberation from conventional moral constraints. Ross notes of their impending resurrection of Tera that 'The question of the moral aspect of the case, which involved the religious belief in which I had been reared, was not one to trouble me; for the issues, and the causes that lay behind them, were not within my power even to comprehend' (p. 175). Ross sets aside his Christian beliefs when confronted by the possibility of raising the dead. The old knowledges from the past work their way into the present even as Tera appears to take up temporary occupancy of Margaret, in which the latter was 'at times in a sort of negative condition as though her mind – her very being – was not present' (p. 176). The figure that inhabits her possesses an 'intellectual aloofness' that, whilst typical of Stoker's hostility to the new woman, also emphasises that this is a mental as well as an epistemological battle.[14]

Jewel can be read as a critique of *She*. Ross is a version of Holly, although neither a scholar nor a man of action. His first sight of Tera, as she is unveiled, echoes Holly's first sight of Ayesha: 'the white wonder of that beautiful form was something to dream of. It was not like death at all; it was like a statue carven in ivory by the hand of Praxiteles' (p. 203). In *Jewel*, however, Tera is a different type of femme fatale who, in the 1903 ending, leaves only Ross alive at the end.

In *Jewel*, the past haunts the present. A genealogy is established that implies various scientific and religious convergences between modern-day Britain and ancient Egypt. Love appears to be the force that will reach out and bridge these worlds, but the end of the 1903 edition suggests that this has been a lie, that Tera has manipulated rather than enlightened them. The past is ultimately made Other, dangerous, strange and deadly because the corpse represents the embodiment of a certain history and ethos that is hostile to the middle-class world of Stoker's Egyptologists. The main sacrilege has been the raising of the dead. Tera, however, is allowed to triumph in the end and the world that she represents is granted a form of power that defeats that of modern-day Britain, and this contrasts with *She* where Ayesha is seemingly defeated. Haggard, however, is conscious that he cannot leave the story at Ayesha's apparent demise after she had entered the flame of life for the second time, and he produced three sequels to the novel.[15] His *Ayesha: The Return of She* should be seen as a riposte to the type of moral uncertainties that Stoker had been prepared to entertain in *Jewel*.

Ayesha: The Return of She and dialogues with the dead

In *She*, Holly's pursuit of a moral vision can be read within the context of the influence that the Bible had on the Egyptian excavations of the 1880s. Stoker's *Jewel* can also be seen as a product of its time as it too explores debates about Egyptology, but now from the more religiously complicated position that emerged in the 1890s. In *Ayesha: The Return of She*, Haggard returns to Holly's quest as we see him and Leo, some twenty years after the events recorded in *She*, discovering the reincarnated Ayesha. For the past twenty years they have been looking for her and spent much time in 'Thibet' (as the novel refers to Tibet), where they have engaged with various non-Christian spiritual practices. The novel is a retrospective account written by the now dying Holly, and at the beginning he emphasises that his journey has been a spiritual one: 'My death is very near me, and of this I am glad, for I desire to pursue the quest in other realms, as it has been promised to me that I shall do. I desire to learn the beginning and the end of the spiritual drama of which it has been my strange lot to read some pages upon earth.'[16] Holly and Leo spend some time as residents in a Buddhist monastery where Leo is scornful of what he sees as nihilist beliefs in which people at the end head towards '"the void"', whereas Holly takes a more liberal view in suggesting that '"we have no choice; we follow our fate"' (p. 34), although whether this is one ordained by a Christian God is not clear at this point. These quite specifically Buddhist-inflected discussions about death and spirituality can be also be contextualised to the period as they gained currency in Britain from the 1880s onwards. J. Jeffrey Franklin has explored how such considerations were linked to images of race at the time. He articulates two key questions that were repeatedly discussed: 'did Buddhism influence the origins of Christianity, and is India the geographical and genetic point of origin for the European Aryan race?'[17] Whilst Buddhism's lack of a concept of a divine creator combined with the idea of reincarnation and the apparent 'void' of nirvana made it unattractive to many, there were others who asserted spiritual similarities between Buddha and Jesus (Franklin, 22). A chief concern in such debates was whether Buddhism pre-dated Christianity, alongside other anxieties that ancient Egyptian notions of the spirit world may have helped to shape Christianity and not vice versa. Franklin has noted that Haggard's novel explicitly reworks these debates by centring them on Buddhist doctrine that identified a conflict between love (which is about active desire) and the 'law of necessity' (which is about denying desire in the pursuit of nirvana) (32).

Holly's quest for spiritual enlightenment is dramatised in a series of encounters that force him to address spiritual concerns. At one level the novel glories in a masculine ethic of activity, adventure and heroism, whilst at another level (typically when Holly and Leo are recovering from the wounds inflicted during their various adventures) a spiritual world is advanced. The priest Oros tells the recuperating Holly that he needs to look within because '"Man is more than flesh and blood. He is mind and spirit as well, and these can be injured also"' (p. 149). Religious conflict becomes asserted through Leo, who is critical of both Buddhist and Egyptian beliefs. As part of his marriage ceremony with Ayesha he is required to wear formal clothes and to carry a sceptre. Holly identifies the crook-shaped sceptre as symbolically associated with Osiris, which leads Leo to proclaim, '"I don't want to impersonate any Egyptian god, or to be mixed up in their heathen idolatries"', even whilst Holly takes a pragmatic line: '"Better go through with it ... probably only something symbolical"' (p. 204). Holly, however, also approvingly notes that Leo 'retained the religious principles in which I had educated him' (p. 204). Leo later casts off these trappings and tells Ayesha, '"Thy religion I do not understand, but I understand my own, and not even for thy sake will I take part in what I hold to be idolatry"'; however, Ayesha counters this, arguing that Leo needs to understand that '"all great Faiths are the same, changed a little to suit the needs of passing times and peoples ... hidden in a multitude of manifestations, one Power great and good, rules all the universes: that the holy shall inherit a life eternal and the vile, eternal death"' (p. 213). As in *She*, it is Ayesha's associations with death that are crucial here. Holly notes that within her sanctuary she sat in a 'death-like majesty' (p. 211), in which 'She seemed a Queen of Death receiving homage from the dead. More, she was receiving homage from dead or living – I know not which – for, as I thought it, a shadowy Shape before the throne bent the knee to her, then another, and another, and another' (p. 211). The indication of Holly's ignorance, about what he might not 'know', becomes crucial in interpreting whether Ayesha represents power over life and death or whether she is conjured up by a human need to try to understand what death signifies. She reveals to Leo that:

> 'I, Ayesha, am but a magic wraith, foul when thou seest me foul, fair when thou seest me fair; a spirit-bubble reflecting a thousand lights in the sunshine of thy smile, grey as dust and gone in the shadow of thy frown. Think of the throned Queen before whom the shadowy Powers bowed and worship, for that is I. Think of the hideous withered Thing thou sawest naked on the rock, and flee away, for that is I. Or keep me lovely, and adore, knowing all evil centred in my spirit, for that is I. Now, Leo thou hast the truth.' (p. 216)

Ayesha seems more like a subjective need than an objective presence. The divisions between self and Other are blurred at this point as the novel returns to some quasi-Buddhist precepts in which the binary differences of self and Other, subject and object and life and death are erased. For Holly, this means that Ayesha poses a problem for interpretation, a fact that Ayesha is also aware of when she responds to his questions with '"cease to question me, for there are things of which I can but speak to thee in figures and in parables not to mock and bewilder thee, but because I must. Interpret them as thou wilt"' (p. 224). This leads Holly to conclude 'that to this hour I do not know whether Ayesha is spirit or woman, or, as I suspect, a blend of both' (p. 225). Ayesha is, of course, not only a 'Queen of Death', she is also a love object, and underpinning the narrative is the return of the love story involving Kallikrates and Amenartas, Leo and Ustane, and now Leo and Atene. When Ayesha unveils, Leo has to choose between her and Atene. Ayesha is revealed as old and shrivelled, but still inspiring love in Leo, who kisses her on the forehead and comments '"love is immortal"' (p. 192), and love appears to bestow some form of redemption in which 'Ayesha grew human' again (p. 286). As in *She*, however, theirs is a relationship that cannot be consummated and after they kiss, 'there, withered in Ayesha's kiss, slain by the fire of her love, Leo lay dead' (p. 289). Tellingly, his corpse falls across the dead body of Atene, which suggests that she would have been, physically speaking, a more appropriate love object. In the end Ayesha dies, consumed again by a flame. The priest Oros notes, however, that Ayesha '"never dies. She changes, that is all"' (p. 300).

The moral and subjective status of Ayesha appears, initially, to be unclear. Holly recalls how Ayesha showed them images in a flame to demonstrate her awareness of Holly and Leo's adventures in their quest. For Holly, 'They were but reflections of scenes familiar to the mind of Ayesha, or perhaps not so much as that. Perhaps they were only phantasms called up in our minds by her mesmeric force' (pp. 193-4). Later, Holly will question her about the shadowy forms that had paid homage to her in the 'hall of Shades' (p. 211). She replies: "'Perchance they were ancient companions and servitors of mine come to greet me once again and to hear my tidings. Or perchance they were but shadows of thy brain, pictures like those upon the fire, that it pleased me to summon to thy sight, to try thy strength and constancy'" (p. 215). Later she tells Holly, "'Perchance my face is but as thy heart fashions it'" (p. 260). Ayesha is caught somewhere between an objective presence and a subjective projection. She belongs to a liminal realm that Ross in *Jewel* had perceived to be the place where the spirits dwell. The suggestion that she may be conjured out of some emotional need appears to compromise Holly's continued pursuit of moral certainty. In the battle between the armies of Atene and Ayesha, Holly sees the clash of forces taking place on 'the darkling, sunburnt plain' (p. 273), which evokes Thucydides's description of the Athenian invasion of Sicily in his account of the Peloponnesian War, but also that battle's reworking by Matthew Arnold in 'Dover Beach' (1867), where Arnold refers to being 'here as on a darkling plain' (l. 35) in a poem that focuses on the apparent waning of 'The Sea of faith' (l. 21).[18] Attitudes to love are key to resolving this issue, as it is clear that Holly's feelings for Ayesha are now spiritual rather than physical. There is a moment when she kisses his brow and he recalls that 'all I felt for her was a love divine into which no human passion entered' (p. 197). His love is pure, whereas Leo's is carnal, which is why he dies. Ultimately, the novel represents the triumph of the spirit over the body as the spiritual world enables the casting off of bodily desires to embrace the precepts of nirvana, which are translated into Christian principles centred on images of the afterlife.

Holly's theology seems to be more flexible than Leo's, but the chief difference is that he is less doctrinaire. Holly can see past the symbols of religions, as in Osiris's crook, for example, in order to engage with the spiritual essence of a particular belief. His critique of Ayesha in *She* is that she has no associations with spirituality; however, she is cast in a different mould in the sequel. Holly's feelings for her are no longer physical as he looks beneath the surface for signs of spiritual presence. Ayesha reflects this back by suggesting to Holly that perhaps these views are projections, with the implication that he would find spirituality within himself. Holly thus retains an optimism that contrasts with the type of nihilism we find in *Jewel*, where love and spiritual beliefs generate delusion. At the end of *Ayesha: The Return of She* the dying Holly returns to the Buddhist monastery, where a head monk reflects on Holly's tale and contemplates whether Holly, Leo and Ayesha (because the dead are not dead for him, merely waiting reincarnation) are accumulating enough spiritual merit to gain nirvana (and so in the end avoid reincarnation), concluding that '"doubtless you are all winning merit, but, if I may venture to say so, you are winning it very slowly"' (p. 301). In the novel, death becomes meaningful as a way of making life meaningful. The inward turn that Ayesha suggests indicates that a level of self-analysis is possible, one that is beyond the lovelorn Ross in *Jewel*. The idea that death may not be the end, however, was explored further by Stoker in *The Lady of the Shroud* (1909), which should be seen as a response to the issues raised by Haggard in *Ayesha: The Return of She*.

Raising the dead: *The Lady of the Shroud*

Ayesha: The Return of She explores the tribal tensions that spill over into war between the armies controlled by Atene and Ayesha. Ayesha is figured as a war-like imperial monarch who is not at peace either personally or politically, until the final battles are won, but even then she will ultimately lose Leo. *The Lady of the Shroud* also engages with political and personal dramas as its seven-foot-high hero, Rupert Sent Leger, following the bequest of his uncle's will, helps to arm and lead the inhabitants of the Land of the Blue Mountains against Turkish aggression (in what is a gloss on the Balkan crisis of the period). Rupert prosecutes war to create peace, and that he is also looking for personal peace is reflected in his pursuit of a love object. As we have seen in the earlier texts, love becomes the means through which one might gain a problematic, because partial, sense of the Other. Whilst in *Jewel*, love functions as a type of delusion that hinders any epistemic insight, love in *The Lady of the Shroud* provides a way for apparent opposites to be reconciled. Love initially appears in Rupert's reflections on his dead mother, whom he cannot regard as dead because 'I love my mother so much'.[19] The dead are really alive and this is a theme that is developed in relation to Teuta (a princess who will inherit the throne of the Blue Mountains), who masquerades as a living corpse (a vampire) in order to deter would-be Turkish kidnappers. Rupert becomes aware of sightings of an apparent corpse in a boat and writes to his aunt that he walks 'about sometimes aimlessly, and find my thoughts drifting in such an odd way. If I didn't know better, I might begin to think that I was in love!', even though 'There is no one here to be in love with' (p. 51). In part Rupert is in love with the beauty of the place, in which 'I keep finding out new beauties ... Broadly speaking, it *is all* beautiful' (p. 57, italics in original). Rupert's journey into the Blue Mountains is not imaged as a journey into an unknown terrain as it is in the *She* series, because for him 'it seems to me that to get here again is like coming home', and he notes of the Blue Mountaineers that they resemble 'Highlanders' (p. 59). He recounts to his aunt that 'I love them already for their splendid qualities, and I am prepared to love them for themselves. I feel, too, that they will love me (and incidentally they are sure to love you)' (p. 60). This repeated emphasis on love heralds the appearance of Teuta, whom he first encounters peering into his rooms late at night. The description echoes that of Holly's first sight of Ayesha in *She*:

> There, outside on the balcony, in the now brilliant moonlight, stood a woman, wrapped in white grave-clothes saturated with water, which dripped on the marble floor, making a pool which trickled slowly down the wet steps. Attitude and dress and circumstance all conveyed the idea that, though she moved and spoke she was not quick but dead. She was young and beautiful, but pale, like the grey pallor of death. Through the still white of her face, which made her look as cold as the wet marble she stood on, her dark eyes seemed to gleam with a strange but enticing lustre. (p. 69)

She appears to be physically dead, but obviously alive. She is part erotic spectacle, but also part object of pity because, unlike Ayesha, she is seemingly not a figure of authority. It is her very vulnerability that awakens compassion in Rupert, who is quick to set aside any reservations he may have about her being seemingly dead. He grants her access to his room and is prepared to assist her because 'she was a woman, and in some dreadful trouble; that was enough' (p. 70). She also, however, like Ayesha, indicates that her behaviour should not be circumscribed by convention. When Rupert hints at the seeming impropriety of her presence in his rooms at night, she asserts:

> 'What are convenances or conventions to me! If you only knew where I have come from – the existence (if it can be called so) which I have had – the loneliness – the horror! And besides, it is for me to make conventions, not to yield my personal freedom of action to them. Even as I am – even here and in this garb – I am above convention.' (pp. 72–3)

Rupert does not realise it at this point, because he cannot decide whether 'it was a living woman who had held my hand, or a dead body reanimated' (pp. 74–5), but Teuta is referring to her status as a princess who is therefore able to wield some political authority. His misreading of her leads him to pursue a supernatural line of enquiry that is supported by his reading of the occult books sent to him by his aunt. The vampire seems to correspond most closely to Teuta, which leads to the rejection of ethical considerations. Rupert notes that to think of Teuta as a supernatural being means that 'I came to think that I must reconstruct my self-values, and begin a fresh understanding of ethical beliefs' (p. 77). Also, because he realises that 'I have fallen in love with her' (p. 78), he is prepared to set aside his qualms in ways that echo the loss of selfhood experienced by Ross in *Jewel* when Rupert recounts, 'Somehow I seemed to lose sight of my identity' (p. 83), as he is prepared to consider that she may come from 'Heaven or Hell' (p. 86). Indeed, Rupert goes so far as to suggest that the power of love can affect the resurrection of the dead when claiming that 'There is not one of us but has wished at some time to bring back the dead. Ay, and who has not felt that in himself or herself was power in the deep love of our dead to make them quick again, did we but know the secret of how it was to be done?' (p. 95). These considerations appear to place the novel consciously beyond any conventional, or putatively Christian, morality. Christopher Herbert's reading of *Dracula* (1897), however, bears some relevance here. According to Herbert, the figure of the vampire can be read as an 'uncanny manifestation' of Christian belief because the emphasis on blood and flesh has links to Christ, as does the idea of resurrecting the dead.[20] Rupert's sense that his love for Teuta can restore her to life is given a religious inflection when he discovers her asleep in the crypt of St Sava, and he gains confidence that she is alive because 'How could anyone believe for a moment that such sweet breath could come from the lips of the dead[?]' (p. 103). This discovery leads to a telling shift in his language. It is notable that shortly afterwards there is repeated use of 'rapture' to describe his feelings on seeing the crypt with 'its strangeness and its stranger rapture', and he states that he was possessed by 'the rapture' of being 'her lover' (p. 110). He speaks to her in 'that breathless softness which is a lover's rapture of speech' (p. 111). He recalls that 'she stood in a glorious rapture like a white spirit in the moonlight' (p. 112). He anticipates meeting her with a 'longing rapture' (p. 119). After his marriage to her, 'I was rapt into a heaven of delight' (p. 150). David Punter, in his study of rapture, has noted the religious connotations of the word, which refers to 'the act of conveying a person from one place to another, especially to heaven'.[21] Rupert's feelings of rapture are because he knows that Teuta can be saved, and in this salvation a religious principle is at work. He sees her in a glass tomb in St Sava, which is actually her hiding place (and not a vampire's den), and he subsequently marries her in the church and ponders on her position as 'a Christian woman' who is threatened by the non-Christian Turks. Her apparent resurrection is seemingly both a personal one and a religious one, which is asserted against the presence of a threatening non-Christian nation. In this context her shroud takes on greater symbolic significance. We noted in the previous chapter that Derrida had, via Genet, discussed how the wrapped body creates a symbolic connection to Christ, and Punter too explores a homonym between 'rapt' and 'wrapped' that can be linked to the shroud worn by Teuta. In *The Lady of the Shroud*, Teuta's restoration to life is not without its dangers as the Turks kidnap her, but after her rescue her shroud is granted political significance when, at the end (and after the Blue Mountaineers have triumphed over the Turks), Rupert tells Teuta that her shroud has been '"adopted ... as a national emblem – our emblem of courage and devotion and patriotism, which will always, I hope, be treasured beyond price"' (p. 248), and Teuta agrees to wear it at the ceremony at which they are crowned king and queen.

These forms of rapture are also implicit in Holly's response to Ayesha, and Punter notes that such images typically appear in moments that bridge the gap between self and Other, and the living and the dead. Such a space appears in *Jewel* as 'the Mid-Region' where the gods might reside, but also where spirits could be united, so that rapture is 'the liminal realm' where 'distinction ceases to operate' (Punter, p. 159). Personal triumphs in *The Lady of the Shroud* are secured through the erasure of social, national and metaphysical distinctions, whereas on a political level these distinctions are asserted. Stoker's novel picks up where Haggard's had left off as the symbolic triumph over death in Stoker's novel completes Holly's quest. *The Lady of the Shroud* is a doubled narrative, with the first part focused on the metaphysical uncertainties that surround Teuta, which, when resolved, lead into the second part that focuses on national concerns. This transforms Teuta from corpse to political leader, moving her from absence to presence – a metamorphosis that pivots on Rupert's feelings of rapture. These movements are not without epistemic considerations.

Rupert's early attempts to decode Teuta rely on a number of texts relating to the occult that outline the characteristics of various non-human entities, such as the vampire and the werewolf. Teuta is thus read through Gothic texts that seem to confirm that she is a vampire. The prefatory narrative purports to be an eye-witness account of seeing a female corpse-like figure (obviously Teuta) in a boat, published in 'The Journal of Occultism'. Such an account is intended to correspond to the type of documents submitted for scientific scrutiny to the Society for Psychical Research (founded in 1882). The novel thus entertains the possibility that 'truth' requires new ways of thinking as the world contains within it a spiritual presence that can be read in secular, rather than strictly theological, terms. Rupert's occult readings have led him to read Teuta metaphysically rather than politically. What appear as metaphysical questions are thus bogus, and although Rupert asks the type of questions that Holly puts to Ayesha, they are the wrong ones to ask. *The Lady of the Shroud* is thus conceptually doubled, however, because on a purely psychological and emotional level Rupert does indeed work through the types of questions, fears and desires that are entertained by Holly. Teuta is brought to life in these terms and Rupert's expressions of rapture indicate the genuine power of this transformation. On a more pragmatic level, the novel exposes these spiritual dramas as resting on a performance of them as the novel quickly heads towards addressing a political crisis involving the Turks in which Rupert can play a heroic role. The novel moves from superstition to political reality and marginalises the type of spiritual narrative that Haggard had so doggedly pursued. In Stoker's novel, spirituality fulfils an emotional need, but it does not stand up to scientific scrutiny. In the end the dead (as in the plight of the crew of a Turkish warship) stay dead and any resurrection is a purely political one as the shroud moves from a sign of death to a symbol of national triumph. Death seems to serve a merely symbolic function in what is a faux-vampire story, about forms of symbolism and occult accounts of them, that produces no real knowledge except a secondary understanding concerning the emotional needs of the lovelorn self. This is not to say that the novel mocks occult understandings by parodying the earnestness of the vampire story. Rather the knowledge that the occult produces is about an emotional need to reconcile oneself to the dead as love repeatedly functions as a means of keeping the dead alive – as Rupert's comments about his deceased mother make clear. An epistemology of the self becomes shaped in such moments, which explains how love functions as a way of reading, and so engaging, with the Other. Rupert moves through rapture to set aside the personal narrative when the battle against the Turks takes over. Ross in *Jewel* has no such moment of transformation as he becomes trapped by his love for Margaret, which makes him unable to decode what Tera really represents. For Holly, one needs to discriminate between physical and spiritual love, and Haggard suggests that it is by setting aside the desires of the flesh that a purely spiritual love becomes attainable. The quest in Haggard is for spiritual enlightenment – one that might flirt with other faiths but which ultimately celebrates Christian values about love, self-sacrifice and service, values that Stoker morphs into political principles that underpin his model of heroism in *The Lady of the Shroud*.

This chapter has focused on the different ways in which love is represented in relation to the dead. Love provides a way of reading death in the Gothic as love searches for an inner spiritual presence that appears to unite subjects. Haggard and Stoker stage a dialogue about these points of contact across the four novels discussed here. Their work also, of course, celebrates the principles of masculinity articulated in archaeological investigations, warfare and the pursuit of women. This strictly heterosexual (although interestingly homosocial) model of love can be usefully counterpointed with that of Oscar Wilde, whose discussions about art, death and the imagination provide an alternative way of thinking about love in the period. The following brief discussion of *The Picture of Dorian Gray* also helps to situate the novel within a scientific context that will be addressed further in the following chapter.

Dorian Gray and the imagination

The Picture of Dorian Gray (1891) might seem to address significantly different concerns than the novels discussed so far in this chapter. The inner life of Dorian is a highly troubled one, and although he has various artistic and intellectual pursuits they do not constitute spiritual quests. The novel is also, of course, far removed from the type of masculine adventure story plotted by Haggard and Stoker. Catherine Wynne's reading of *The Lady of the Shroud*, however, does suggest points of contact with Wilde by addressing the shared theatrical background of Stoker and Wilde. Wynne connects *The Lady of the Shroud*'s dedication to the actress Geneviève Ward to the type of theatricality that Stoker explores in the novel. Teuta is an actress of sorts who plays the role of a vampire until she is able to resume her position as a princess. Such a transformation in reality requires a different type of public acting, which in part requires her to reprise her now exposed role as a vampire on state occasions. Ward's life was more radically complex in gender terms than that of Teuta, who in the end relinquishes her authority as queen in order to pass on the role of national leader to Rupert. As Wynne notes, 'Teuta appreciates the power of performance but by the novel's close she is content to rock the cradle, abdicate the responsibility of rule to her foreign husband, and retire from performing the role of the female lead'.[22] In *Dorian Gray*, acting is explicitly associated with Sybil Vane, who becomes unable to perform as a romantic lead once she has fallen in love with Dorian. Love gives her away, but it also, so Lord Henry suggests and Dorian feels, leads to bad art. Acting and camp have some points of contact here. Thomas A. King has argued that camp challenges bourgeois notions of presence and authenticity by drawing attention to the ideological staging of class-bound gender scripts.[23] Moe Meyer has further developed this line of enquiry by arguing that Wilde encountered a form of theatrical training whilst in America in 1882 that emphasised 'the causal correspondence between exterior signification and essential interiority', in a new style of acting that was quite different from the hyperbolic gestures of melodrama.[24] For Meyer, such acting enabled Wilde to fashion a camp performance that would be visible to a gay culture but invisible to a heterosexual one. In the novel, this idea of a discreet gay presence is referenced in Basil Hallward's concern that his painting of Dorian has given away his feelings for him because "'I know that as I worked it, every flake and film of colour seemed to me to reveal my secret'".[25] Such considerations require that culturally tabooed desire must necessarily remain hidden so that the truth is concealed by a wider idea of performance – which is why Sybil is criticised for becoming bad art, because in doing so she gives herself away.

These artistic concerns may seem to raise questions that are beyond those discussed in Haggard and Stoker, but Wilde's novel also addresses the idea of a possible epistemology of the self that can be read within an historically available scientific context that bridges art and science, whilst also relating to a model of the 'soul', which Dorian has seemingly sold in order to gain immortality. Dorian may ostensibly seem superficial, but this is at odds with a level of self-reflection that comes from reading the unidentified novel Lord Henry has lent him.[26] He relates to the novel's hero, seeing in him that 'the romantic and scientific temperaments were so strangely blended [which] became to him a kind of prefiguring of himself' (p. 141). Lord Henry also has an enthusiasm for 'the methods of natural science' (p. 64) and regards influencing Dorian as a type of experiment, which leads Lord Henry to surmise, 'Soul and body, body and soul – how mysterious they were! There was animalism in the soul, and the body had its moments of spirituality' (p. 65), an observation that has much in keeping with Holly's view of Ayesha. He also notes, in what can be read as a direction to the reader, that 'It was clear to him that the experimental method was the only method by which one could arrive at any scientific analysis of the passions; and certainly Dorian Gray was a subject made to his hand, and seemed to promise rich and fruitful results' (p. 66). Indeed, the novel explores the relationship between the soul and the body in terms that are familiar from our discussion of Haggard and Stoker. Elana Gomel has argued that whilst one can argue that after Dorian's Faustian pact the painting takes on the burdens of corporeality as Dorian wrestles with his soul, a more nuanced position is available in which the novel 'points not at the Cartesian duality but at a more complex model of subjectivity, in which the portrait represents Dorian's corporeal self, mind and body together, influencing and influenced by each other'.[27] How to decode this self invites an investigation about where the self is located, a theme the novel self-consciously addresses when Dorian develops an interest in 'the Darwinisimus movement in Germany, [through which he] found a curious pleasure in tracing the thoughts and passions of men to some pearly cell in the brain, or some white nerve in the body, delighting in the conception of the absolute dependence of the spirit on certain physical conditions, morbid or healthy, normal or diseased' (p. 147). Dorian's investigations might be more evolutionary than spiritual, and although ultimately they seem to represent a half-hearted attempt to gain an understanding of the self, it is also because to him 'no theory of life seemed ... to be of any importance compared to life itself' (p. 147). His other studies include an exploration of unusual musical instruments from South America in which 'he felt a curious delight in the thought that Art, like Nature, has her monsters, things of bestial shape and with hideous voices' (p. 149), an apparently flippant remark that the novel takes quite seriously.

After Sybil's suicide, Dorian contemplates whether there might be a scientific explanation for how he has seemingly swapped places with his portrait. He works through a series of questions that leads to a conclusion which is couched in a scientific discourse relating to atoms:

> Had it indeed been prayer that had produced the substitution? Might there not be some curious scientific reason for it all? If thought could exercise its influence upon a living organism, might not thought exercise an influence upon dead and inorganic things? Nay, without thought or conscious desire, might not things external to ourselves vibrate in unison with our moods and passions, atom calling to atom in secret love of strange affinity? (p. 118)

Dorian's theory suggests that the inanimate and animate world are molecularly conjoined at an atomic level. Thought might have an influence over the dead as dead things may actually contain within them a kind of life. According to Michael Davis, this focus on atoms links Dorian to the painting because it indicates 'the materiality of both'.[28] Davis develops this argument in relation to theories of the mind championed by W. K. Clifford, James Sully and William James. Davis's account of Wilde's commonplace book, which Wilde kept whilst a student at Oxford, demonstrates that Wilde was aware of such accounts of the mind that suggested a possible reciprocal influence between mind and matter that, building on the work of Huxley, blurred 'the distinction between organic and inorganic matter' (549). Such considerations enable a revision of ideas about creativity that, as we have seen throughout the earlier parts of this book, were emphasised in the Romantic Gothic. Whilst Huxley might have suggested the presence of materialism, the mathematician and philosopher W. K. Clifford claimed in his essay 'The Philosophy of the Pure Sciences' (1876) that the presence of the creative imagination indicated that the mind may have the capacity to transcend the material nature of the body. Davis notes that Wilde comments on Clifford's essay in his commonplace book, and there is an argument to be made that Wilde's manifesto for the unshackled creative imagination in 'The Soul of Man under Socialism' (1891) reworks this transcendent version of the creative artist. *Dorian Gray* should be read as an interrogation of these ideas: an interrogation that raises questions about the relationship between creativity and death which suggest that art (the now restored painting at the end of the novel) grants a form of immortality that is familiar from both earlier Romantic considerations *and* these later scientific contexts.

The issue of love is played out differently in Wilde than it is in Haggard and Stoker. The cultural pressure for discretion displaces emotional revelation onto art and away from the explicitly anxious soul-searching of Holly, Ross and Rupert Sent Leger. Art becomes the place where sexual politics are debated, whilst discussions about the soul are shaped by scientific ideas of the self. The analytical inclinations of Lord Henry and Dorian represent a subtext in the novel about issues of interpretation that we have witnessed elsewhere in the late-nineteenth-century Gothic. Love has played a role in many of these interpretations as it provides a model of empathy that is advanced, often unsuccessfully (as in *Jewel*), as a way of understanding the self and the Other. In *Dorian*, art becomes the space where this empathetic engagement is developed, but as Hallward notes, artistic procedures need to be internally policed as desire is hidden within an aesthetic that strives to impersonally support ideal models of beauty. Beauty becomes a mask in Wilde's aesthetic, whereas in Haggard beauty represents a potentially destructive (because soul-destroying) force.[29] The terms are the same across these texts, but in Wilde's queer aesthetic they are reconfigured as Dorian becomes increasingly loveless. The issue of the scientific context, however, brings these texts together.

Wilde's commonplace book reveals an interest in attempting to bridge the gap between mind and body, art and nature and self and Other through engaging with contemporary scientific debates, which are also introduced into *Dorian*. In *Ayesha: The Return of She*, Ayesha is described by Holly as 'a true chemist, the very greatest, I suppose, who ever lived' (p. 250), and a eugenicist who can manufacture races, as she does in *She*. The discovery of the physics that explained X-rays which is mentioned in *Jewel* is also developed in an editorial footnote in *Ayesha: The Return of She*, which states that the 'Fire of Life', which seems to grant Ayesha immortality, can be attributed to 'emanations from radium ... of which our chemists and scientific men have, at present, but explored the fringe' (p. 251).[30] These scientific engagements indicate the presence of an alternative way of decoding death (and indeed life) as they examine the relationship between the dead and the living in both molecular (materialist) and psychological terms. How issues of interpretation and quasi-scientific analysis are linked to ideas of reading is discussed further in the following chapter on Arthur Machen and Bram Stoker. Love provides one way of making sense of death, but reading death in ostensibly scientific terms is another aspect of the *fin de siècle* Gothic that we need to address.

Notes

1 Vernon Lee, 'Faustus and Helena: Notes on the Supernatural in Art' (1880), in *Hauntings and Other Fantastic Tales*, ed. Catherine Maxwell and Patricia Pulham (Peterborough: Broadview Press, 2006), pp. 291–319, pp. 310, 309.
2 Henry Rider Haggard, *She* (Ware: Wordsworth Editions, 1995), p. 86. All subsequent references are to this edition and are given in the text.
3 Reincarnation also invites consideration of time as circular, which was discussed briefly in Chapter 1 in a discussion of Pfau's analysis of the Romantic elegy as providing a secular repudiation of a Christian tradition of the eternal, because repeated, life. In part, this would explain Holly's religious deliberations when confronted by Ayesha and her ideas.
4 Barri J. Gold, 'Embracing the Corpse: Discursive Recycling in H. Rider Haggard's *She*', *English Literature in Transition, 1880–1920*, 38:3 (January 1995), 305–27, 319. All subsequent references are to this edition and are given in the text.
5 Bradley Deane, 'Mummy Fiction and the Occupation of Egypt: Imperial Striptease', *English Literature in Transition, 1880–1920*, 51:4 (2008), 381–410, 395. All subsequent references are to this edition and are given in the text.
6 Ailise Bulfin, 'The Fiction of Gothic Egypt and British Imperial Paranoia: The Curse of the Suez Canal', *English Literature in Transition, 1880–1920*, 54:4 (2011), 411–43, 420–1.
7 Haggard was, of course, also interested in excavations and visited the Valley of the Kings on several occasions.
8 David Gange, 'Religion and Science in Late Nineteenth-Century British Egyptology', *The Historical Journal*, 49:4 (December 2006), 1,083–103, 1,088. All subsequent references are to this edition and are given in the text.

9 This was an observation made by Jonathan Sawday in answering questions after his keynote speech, 'On Rochester's Sex Machine' at the 'Pathologies' conference hosted by the Research Centre for Literature, Arts and Science at the University of Glamorgan, 20–21 August 2007.
10 Sigmund Freud, *The Interpretation of Dreams*, The Penguin Freud Library, vol. IV, ed. James Strachey (Harmondsworth: Penguin, 1991).
11 Sigmund Freud, 'A Special Type of Choice of Object Made by Men (Contributions to the Psychology of Love I)', in *On Sexuality*, The Penguin Freud Library, vol. VII, ed. Angela Richards and Albert Dickson (Harmondsworth: Penguin, 1991), pp. 227–42, p. 232.
12 I discuss some of these ideas specifically in relation to the 'female Gothic' in 'Love, Freud, and the Female Gothic: Bram Stoker's The Jewel of Seven Stars', *Gothic Studies*, 6:1 (May 2004), special issue on 'Female Gothic', ed. Andrew Smith and Diana Wallace, 80–9.
13 Bram Stoker, *The Jewel of Seven Stars*, Introd. David Glover (Oxford: Oxford University Press, 1996), p. 5. All subsequent references are to this edition and are given in the text.
14 I am thinking of Mina Harker's representation of the new woman in *Dracula* as another example of this.
15 The sequels are *Ayesha: The Return of She* (1905), *She and Allan* (1921) and *Wisdom's Daughter* (1923). I discuss these texts in a postcolonial context that is also related to images of death in 'Beyond Colonialism: Death and the Body in H. Rider Haggard', in Andrew Smith and William Hughes (eds), *Empire and the Gothic: The Politics of Genre* (Basingstoke: Palgrave, 2003), pp. 103–17.
16 Henry Rider Haggard, *Ayesha: The Return of She* (Polegate: Pulp Publications, 1998), p. 1. All subsequent references are to this edition and are given in the text.
17 J. Jeffrey Franklin, 'The Counter-Invasion of Britain by Buddhism in Marie Corelli's *A Romance of Two Worlds* and H. Rider Haggard's *Ayesha: The Return of She*', *Victorian Literature and Culture*, 31:1 (2003), 19–42, 23–4.
18 Matthew Arnold, 'Dover Beach', in *The Norton Anthology of English Literature: The Victorian Age*, ed. Catherine Robson and Carol T. Christ (New York and London: W. W. Norton, 2012), pp. 1387–8.
19 Bram Stoker, *The Lady of the Shroud*, Introd. Ruth Robbins (Stroud: Sutton, 1994), p. 42. All subsequent references are to this edition and are given in the text.
20 Christopher Herbert, 'Vampire Religion', *Representations*, 79:1 (Summer 2002), 100–21, 113.
21 David Punter, *Rapture: Literature, Addiction, Secrecy* (Brighton: Sussex Academic Press, 2009), p. 20. All subsequent references are to this edition and are given in the text.

22 Catherine Wynne, 'Bram Stoker, Geneviève Ward and *The Lady of the Shroud*: Gothic Weddings and Performing Vampires', *English Literature in Transition, 1880–1920*, 49:3 (2006), 251–71, 268.
23 Thomas A. King, 'Performing "Akimbo": Queer Pride and Epistemological Prejudice', in Moe Meyer (ed.), *The Politics and Poetics of Camp* (London: Routledge, 1994), pp. 23–50. I also discuss these ideas in *Victorian Demons: Medicine, Masculinity and the Gothic at the Fin de Siècle* (Manchester: Manchester University Press, 2004), see ch. 6 on 'Performing Masculinity: Wilde's Art', pp. 150–76.
24 Moe Meyer, 'Under the Sign of Wilde: An Archaeology of Posing', in Moe Meyer (ed.), *The Politics and Poetics of Camp* (London: Routledge, 1994), pp. 75–109, p. 80.
25 Oscar Wilde, *The Picture of Dorian Gray*, ed. Peter Ackroyd (Penguin: Harmondsworth, 1985), p. 127. All subsequent references are to this edition and are given in the text.
26 The novel is widely assumed to be *À rebours* (1884) by Joris-Karl Huysmans.
27 Elana Gomel, 'Oscar Wilde, *The Picture of Dorian Gray*, and the (Un)death of the Author', *Narrative*, 12:1 (January 2004), 74–92, 82–3.
28 Michael Davis, 'Mind and Matter in *The Picture of Dorian Gray*', *Victorian Literature and Culture*, 41 (2013), 547–60, 547. All subsequent references are to this edition and are given in the text.
29 In this respect, Wilde's essay on 'The Truth of Masks', first published as 'Shakespeare and Stage Costume' (1885), is relevant.
30 Radium also plays in a key role in *The Lady of the Shroud* as a type of energy that can be harnessed in the development of machines of war.

6

Decoding the dying: Machen and Stoker

This book has explored the transition from writer to reader and how this underpins models of death and dying in the period. As we saw in Chapter 3, the mid nineteenth century represents the moment when this shift to the reader gains cultural visibility. In part this can be attributed to a post-Romantic critical view of notions of creativity, one that no longer emphasises the importance of the creative imagination. However, as we have also seen, the movement from writer to reader is a matter of emphasis, because acts of interpretation also require creative acts of reading. This particular development is addressed in this second chapter on the *fin de siècle* Gothic.

The focus here is on why epistemological issues are repeatedly foregrounded in texts such as Arthur Machen's *The Great God Pan* (1894) and *The Three Impostors* (1895) as well as Bram Stoker's *Dracula* (1897). As we shall see, epistemological enquiry and acts of writing are difficult to disentangle due to an elision between quasi-scientific modes of decryption and acts of detection. How to read the dead constitutes a problem for both knowledge and scientific method at the *fin de siècle* and these concerns cannot be separated from the narrative issues that we have explored throughout the period. We will also observe how these issues were addressed in Henry Drummond's best-selling *Natural Law in the Spiritual World* (1883) and F. W. H. Myers's *Human Personality and Its Survival of Bodily Death* (1903, revised 1907), as they develop a way of reading post-mortem existence that has clear cultural echoes with how death was addressed in the Gothic.

Although this chapter does not focus on spiritualism to any great extent, such issues do occasionally intersect with the epistemological concerns addressed here. Arthur Conan Doyle, in the second volume of his *History of Spiritualism* (1926), records his frustration with cross-correspondences, when a spirit message sent in fragments via a number of mediums would require textual reassembly. He notes how, between March and April 1907, a series of fragmented references to Euripides were channelled through three mediums, Mrs Piper, Mrs Verrall and Mrs Holland ('Mrs Holland' was Rudyard Kipling's sister, Alice MacDonald Fleming). Doyle recalls that each of the mediums subsequently received messages about death and dying that culminated in Mrs Verrall writing 'a script wholly occupied with the idea of Death, with quotations from Lander, Shakespeare, Virgil and Horace, all involving the idea of Death'.[1] Such messages were often highly cryptic and were delivered only in this format in order to demonstrate how the spirit world could utilise seemingly unrelated mediums. It is telling that such messages frequently involved the transmission of literary references that spiritualists had to decipher. The spirit text makes sense because of the skills of the reader, despite Doyle's evident exasperation with messages that were intended to convince unbelievers, whereas 'To the ordinary Spiritualist they seem an exceedingly roundabout method of demonstrating that which can be proved by easier and more convincing methods' (p. 42). This idea of 'method' will be addressed in the early sections of this chapter, because how to write about the spiritual world in relation to the natural world raised concerns about methodology that have clear implications for an epistemology of death.

The science of spirits: Henry Drummond

Henry Drummond's *Natural Law in the Spiritual World* was something of a publishing phenomenon, selling around 1,000 copies a month in the first year of publication.[2] Drummond's background was in Scottish evangelism and he sought to outline how the natural world and the spiritual world were conditioned by similar laws of continuity. For Drummond, the spiritual was natural and nature was spiritual and the convergences between these two worlds could be witnessed through empirical observation. Indeed, he was eager to set aside any theological tendencies that might result in the projection of a spiritual discourse onto the natural world. For Drummond, what united the spiritual and the natural was 'Revelation', and he argued that an unbiased observation of what was revealed constituted his 'method'.[3] Science might relate to a tangible world of objects, but Drummond was also struck by 'the integrity of the scientific method' as it was one that could also be applied to spiritual revelation. His ambition therefore was 'not to "reconcile" Nature and Religion, but to exhibit Nature in Religion' (p. xxii). He also claimed that the application of scientific principles could purify religion by ridding it of ideas about the spontaneous acquisition of faith because faith, in keeping with accounts of evolution, was part of an ongoing spiritual process. For Drummond, natural laws and spiritual laws are identical and the relationship between them is elaborated not through 'a mere image or emblem' (p. 27), but through a shared process focused on life, death and evolution. Crucially for Drummond, in both the natural and the spiritual realms 'the same processes of growth go on' (p. 27), and what we can see with our physical eye is matched by what can be seen by 'the mental eye' (p. 33), which observes our true moral character.

Drummond applies a series of scientific claims to the spiritual world in order to outline a version of the subject whose spiritual life (and possible moral death) is echoed in their physical life. Drummond argues that death in nature 'has an acknowledged spiritual equivalent' (p. 144), one that the modern world, with its fashionable cynicism, has lost sight of. Drummond notes of death that 'The word has grown weak. Ignorance has robbed the Grave of all is terror, and platitude despoil Death of its sting. Death itself is ethically dead' (p. 144). How to turn death into an epistemology requires us to see our physical health as dependent upon a model of spiritual well-being. In his chapter on 'Death', Drummond explains that science sees death as the result of our inability to adapt to changes in our physical environment. Herbert Spencer clearly informs this view (Darwin is not explicitly mentioned by Drummond), which prompts Drummond to argue that alienation is a consequence of our failure to address, or maintain correspondence with, our spiritual needs. For Drummond, 'Spiritual Death is a want of correspondence between the organism and the spiritual environment' (p. 152). As the physical body would die for want of food, so the spirit atrophies due to a lack of ethical nourishment. However, Drummond also asserts that, spiritually considered, 'Death is a relative term' (p. 152), because the subject may have some, limited, engagement with a spiritual world that makes them at least partially alive. This is reflected in nature, for Drummond, by lower life forms such as animals that are not as physically, intellectually and spiritually complex as humans and so are less alive to their environment. Drummond summarises that 'Those who are in communion with God live, those who are not are dead' (p. 158). To live completely we need to develop our full spiritual potential and to fail in this task makes us unnatural. He supports Spencer's claim in *The Data of Ethics* (1879) that we have an evolutionary obligation to both physically and ethically advance, which leads Drummond to conclude that 'To refuse to cultivate the religious relation is to deny to the soul its highest right – the right to a further evolution' (p. 172). This model of the self-aware, Christian subject depends upon what H. G. Wells would refer to as an 'Excelsior biology', which moves the subject through increasing levels of refinement. Whilst Wells's pithy comment about an evolutionary ladder was intended as a critique of Edwin Lankester's supposed misreading of Darwin, it also applies to Drummond.[4] Drummond might, via Spencer, replace Darwin's idea of adaptability with 'correspondence', but this is to overlook the central place that adaptability has in Darwin's theory of evolutionary change. Drummond sidesteps Darwin on this point because he is looking to protect a notion of religious authority that seems to be, for him, under threat at the *fin de siècle* in which 'It has been indicated that the authority of Authority is waning' (p. 29), although it can be reasserted through firm religious guidance.

In essence, Drummond's theory of spiritual life and ethical evolution is a response to the anomie that he regards as prevalent at the time. The image of a fragmented world that Drummond addresses is important in this context as it is one that, as we shall see, appears repeatedly in the Gothic. As noted in the brief outline of the cross-correspondences above, a theory that unites fragments into a coherent whole is one way in which to make sense of a world 'in a transition period like the present' (Drummond, p. 30). This means that for Drummond, 'Perfect life is not merely the possessing of perfect functions, but of perfect functions perfectly adjusted to each other and all conspiring to a single result, the prefect working of the whole organism' (p. 129). Drummond is conscious that there is still work to be done on this, but claims that science confirms that spiritual evolution is a necessary element of human evolution. Drummond is ultimately led to what is for him a rhetorical question, 'Is Evolution to stop with the organic?' (p. 244), which at this advanced point in his treatise invites an emphatic 'no' from the reader. It is also a theory of evolution that accords death a particular significance because 'the condition of … further Evolution is that the spiritual be released from the natural' (p. 249), which means that 'Death, being the final sifting of all the correspondences, is the indispensible factor of the higher Life' (p. 249). In death we gain ultimate perfection, which corrects the subject's 'sicklier symptom of his incompleteness, his want of spiritual energy' (p. 269). Indeed, death appears to usher in a utopia in evolution because it grants us access to a new vitality that heralds an 'Embryology of the New Life' (p. 295), through which we are effectively born again because 'the goal of Evolution is Jesus Christ' (p. 314). This spiritual dimension means that Christianity plays an important role in enriching the prevailing model of evolution by transposing biological principles to the spiritual realm, so that 'What we are reaching …

is nothing less than the *evolution of Evolution*' (p. 407, italics in original). Death is not the end and our post-mortem existence is assured so long as we embrace an evolving spiritual world during our terrestrial life. We come to life before we die in such moments, which prepares us to take forward this new discourse of ethical evolution that has been transferred from the spiritual world.

Drummond's treatise about how science could be applied to spiritual matters gained cultural importance at the time and he would develop his theories further in *The Ascent of Man* (1894). What is telling about *Natural Law in the Spiritual World* is the emphasis given to method as a means of ensuring proof. His book is far removed from the occult interests of spiritualists as it reaffirms an evangelical Christian vision (and is scathing about other claims made on faith, such as Buddhism and Roman Catholicism). His thesis, however, emphasises that spirituality depends upon a scientific reading of the natural world. His focus on method is closely allied to issues of epistemology because the 'method' seeks to overcome the model of the fragmented self that Drummond saw as prevalent at the *fin de siècle*. This model of the fragmented subject would reappear in the Gothic as it too worked through ideas about death and knowledge of the afterlife, but it would also appear in spiritualist ideas and in psychological theories that attempted to account for what seemed to be a new inward turn at the end of the century. To some degree, such matters informed the religious contexts discussed in the previous chapter, but it is the emphasis on method, as a way of reading, that is explored here. Religion, science, death and the self would play an important role in shaping F. W. H. Myers's view of the subject – a subject that has more in keeping with Drummond's position on the Christian self than it first appears, and one that is culturally shaped by a model of the subject that also appears in the Gothic.

Myers and the subliminal self

Alex Owen has argued that medical psychology at the *fin de siècle* modelled a version of the self that was far removed from a Lockean tradition of self-reflection and which is also clearly at odds with Drummond's notion of the spiritual subject. This new version of the self is unsure of its place in the world and seemingly has little capacity for self-knowledge. Owen summarises that at the end of the century:

> Gone was the sense of the self as a transcendental entity, a single applied consciousness conceived in the tradition of affective individualism but with an everlasting aspect – the soul. In its place was a variously conceived but

invariably fragmented or multiple self, formulated through complex processes of remembering and forgetting, and one in which the conscious 'I' of the moment is inherently unreliable or unstable – certainly one in which the geography of the self is shifted dramatically as attention was redirected from a higher, timeless, or divine aspect to the subterranean, temporal, and mundane foundations of human personality.[5]

This version of the self feels more recognisably Gothic than Drummond's. It was this type of instability that Drummond sought to challenge, although it required a reworking of the principles of natural science, rather than other scientific claims that specifically centred on the mind. Drummond's move from body to spirit effectively omits discussion about the mind. His response could be seen as an attempt to impose moral order on an otherwise chaotic, and putatively Gothic, version of the self. It is, however, around the issue of method that certain similarities can be observed. The unstable self mapped by Owen gains focus when subjected to particular types of scientific scrutiny. This is clear from the methods used by spiritualists, for example, who attempted to conduct seances as if they were like scientific experiments because, as Owen notes, 'Spiritualists considered that they employed scientific and empirical methods in their own séances' (p. 36). The issue of science is a broad one and it is important to distinguish between different branches, even though the principle of objectivity ostensibly unites them in matters of formal enquiry. Richard Noakes, for example, has explored the links between experimental physics and psychical research during the period and has noted that these two very different fields of investigation were bridged by 'a genuine conviction that these apparently divergent areas of enquiry shared many experimental problems and might share solutions'.[6] This contrasts with the concerns of the 1870s when scientists kept their distance by asserting, according to S. E. D. Shortt, 'a point of epistemology' that sought to consign psychical investigations to sub-scientific metaphysical speculation.[7] Shortt also claims that 'The empiricism championed by the neuroscientists of the 1870s had, in less than a decade, stripped spiritualism of the supernatural to create the nascent but scientifically legitimate field of abnormal psychology' (354). Whilst this might be true of the very specific field of American neuroscience, it did not banish such occult considerations from theories of psychology that were discussed in Britain. Indeed, when in 1898 the physicist, chemist and spiritualist William Crookes gave an address to the British Association for the Advancement of Science, he declared that 'Experimental Psychology … unites the difficulties inherent in all experimentation connected with mind, with tangled human temperaments and with observations dependent less on automatic record than on personal testimony'.[8] Drummond too had claimed that it was through observation that we would discern (via the mind's eye) the presence of an evolving spiritual world. That the issue was one centred on methodology was also asserted by Edmund Gurney (the co-founder of the Society for Psychical Research), who claimed in 1884 that investigations into psychical research used broader principles than those employed in other scientific disciplines, noting that 'The method is wider but less precise, more various but less technical; and the application of it demands disengagedness rather than any specialised aptitude'.[9] In fact it represented the application of pure science, abstractly considered.

These approaches also represent an optimistic view of experience that is quite different from that found in theories of degeneration. Instead of being defined by their potential for reversion, the subject is associated with a capacity for positive development. Roger Luckhurst in *The Invention of Telepathy* (2002) noted that investigations into the paranormal tended to 'situate themselves on the edge of a utopian future in technology, science, and human sensitivity'[10] that was far removed from the ontological gloom found in theories of degeneration. As we have seen throughout, the dead are repeatedly referenced in broadly positive ways as they elicit our sympathy and empathy, and death at the *fin de siècle* also has a progressive function as it enables us to access our true spiritual natures.

Owen has noted that Myers's version of the self contrasts with that found in psychological theories that claimed that the self was created out of negative drives, as in Freud, for example. In its place Myers asserted the existence of a subliminal realm that was beyond our conscious (or supraliminal) control. This functions like the unconscious, but it is 'positive and integrative' (Owen, p. 175) rather than disruptive. In this realm we discover an indwelling soul that can communicate with other souls (or spirits) via subliminal messages. This means that we are able to commune with the dead and, astrally, with other 'live' souls. Myers, a Cambridge-educated classical scholar, founded the Society for Psychical Research in 1882 (and became its president in 1900). He presided over an association of scientifically trained investigators and contributed to the two-volume *Phantasms of the Living* (edited with Edmund Gurney and Frank Podmore in 1886), which influenced his *Human Personality and Its Survival of Bodily Death*. In *Human Personality* Myers raises issues about scientific method that are similar to Drummond's concerns, although the importance he accords to analogies and symbols is different in kind from Drummond's assertion that the natural (and therefore spiritual) law works directly upon us.

Myers, however, also addresses ideas about evolution and creativity and indicates that death should be seen as part of an unfolding spiritual narrative in which our disembodiment grants access to a realm of creativity, one that we are dimly aware of in our dreams.

For Myers, the 'entirely dispassionate' principles of modern scientific method need to be applied to the 'problem of ... the destiny of the human soul',[11] because human life includes within it a version of all human history in which 'we retraverse, from the embryo to the corpse, the history of life on earth for millions of years' (p. 17). This is a view of life (and indeed death) that was, as we shall see, foreshadowed in Machen's *The Great God Pan*. However, gaining access to this occluded knowledge is problematic because our conscious selves divert attention away from it, so that 'Our retrogressions seem often a recovery of isolated fragments of thought and feeling' (p. 23). His overall ambition is to overcome this image of *fin de siècle* fragmentation by claiming that an emerging principle of spiritual evolution will enable us to defeat the 'dissolutive' feelings of modern subjectivity. For this reason, according to Myers, the hysteric may seem to be a figure who is peculiarly susceptible to psychic fragmentation but in reality they can be made whole again once we understand the reasons for their psychosis, which lurks within the 'dreamlike or hypnotic stratum of the subliminal self' (p. 38). The subliminal thus makes us whole again and is also the realm where creative inspiration is generated.

Myers is clear that he is looking for moments that define the subject in all their potential completeness and argues that even psychosis merely represents a temporary falling away from a state of integration. He makes reference to Freud and Breuer's account of hysteria, but pursues a different line of enquiry: 'We are looking for integrations in lieu of disintegrations; for intensifications of control, widening of faculty, instead of relaxation, scattering or decay' (p. 53). The problem he confronts is an epistemic one, as the evidence for this 'widening of faculty' is to be found in dreams, creative inspiration and textual analogies – all areas he mines for factual evidence for the existence of the subliminal realm. The problem, according to Myers, is that in creative acts subliminal messages seem to come through in fragments because they are interfered with by 'middle-level subliminal centres' rather than guided by higher, and therefore more authentic, subliminal drivers. This can lead to 'half-insanities' (p. 58) rather than coherence, prompting him to conclude, using the example of Blake, that 'Throughout all the work of William Blake ... we see the subliminal self flashing for moments into unity, then smouldering again in a lurid and scattered glow' (p. 58). The post-mortem self can, for Myers, be discerned in romanticism (he also refers to Wordsworth and Coleridge) but only in flickering visions that are now becoming clearer at the *fin de siècle* as this post-dead self comes into evolutionary existence. Myers accords a chapter to 'Genius', and its emphasis on originality has much in common with Young's 'Conjectures on Original Composition' (1759); however, one telling difference is that Myers also marks out an important role for the reader, which is a further example of this shift from writer to reader that we have witnessed throughout the period.[12] Myers claims that 'What the poet feels while he writes *his* poem is the psychological fact in his history; what his friends feel while they read it may be a psychological fact in *their* history, but does not alter the poet's creative effort' (p. 60). The subliminal mind is present in acts of original creation but also in reading. This relationship glosses Myers's claim that spirits speak to each other in the subliminal realm, which means that writing may also be inspired by ideas impressed upon us by the dead or even by God. The fact that we are now in a position to observe these changes also indicates an advancement in our evolution, because 'The higher gifts of genius – poetry, the plastic arts, music, philosophy, pure mathematics [are] in the central stream of evolution' (p. 76). Our intellectual evolution is matched by an evolution of the spirit, and Myers can be regarded as inheriting Drummond's model of spiritual evolution even as he adapts it beyond an orthodox Christian framework by suggesting that the dead can commune with our subliminal inner ghost.[13] The precise point of inspiration might sit within the subliminal realm but we can never be sure who it is that has been speaking to that inner self.

The guarantee that the flickering presence of the subliminal appears in creative acts ultimately lies with the reader (or analyst) who can decode its presence in ways that elude the author. The problem is that these texts represent 'fragments of a knowledge which no ordinary thought could attain' (p. 169), so that rather like the assembled spirit messages sent as cross-correspondences, the emphasis is placed on the reader.[14] This is also because 'subliminal symbolism ... meets us at each point of our enquiry' (p. 202). He also argues (in ways that Drummond would emphatically not) that 'one must question, on general idealistic principles, whether there be ... any real distinction between symbolism and reality' (p. 203). By decoding this symbolism, we enter into the world of the dead, the spiritual realm, 'And the prospect thus opened to human knowledge, in this or other worlds, would be limitless indeed' (p. 253). For Myers, we read this symbolism by interpreting the analogies through which the subliminal world manifests itself, and these analogies provide the bridge between physical and spiritual worlds. This means that literary texts (and other creative acts, such as spirit messages) need to be read for the symbolic presence of the dead, which appears in cryptic symbolic forms that place demands upon our interpretive skills. The chief demand is because our physical world possesses a mode of symbolism that is specific to it, so that 'the highest task of science must be to link and co-ordinate the symbols appropriate to our terrene state with the symbols appropriate to the state immediately above us' (p. 338), which a reading of analogy permits. For Myers, we need to develop a new way of looking at the world in order to subject these analogies to scientific analysis. His view is that we are, at the *fin de siècle*, being granted this as we become confronted by the presence of an evolving spirit world – one that confirms a developing moral sensibility that touches us all.

Luckhurst has claimed that Myers's investigations were influenced by the Gothic (Myers corresponded with Stevenson about *Jekyll and Hyde*, and *Human Personality* includes Stevenson's account of the double in the appendices) and helped to shape the *fin de siècle* Gothic, so that 'Psychology and Gothic fiction informed each other' (Luckhurst, p. 195). This is a position that can be demonstrated through a reading of Machen, which explores how ideas of creativity and reading are linked to these models of death and spirituality.

Machen's Gothic fragments

Arthur Machen's views on writings are to be found in the eccentric *Hieroglyphics* (1902). The book is structured as a series of encounters between the narrator and an unnamed friend, with the former recording the latter's views on literature. The friend's central claim is that the true passion of ecstasy demarcates original literature from more formulaic kinds. The issue of fragments that underpins both Drummond and Myers's view of the subject is also echoed in the narrator's 'fragmentary notes' that constitute the narrative.[15] However, these fragments can, in keeping with the strategies employed by Myers, reveal the truth, so that 'these fragments ... are evidence' of 'the truth' (p. 10) sought by 'the obscure literary hermit' (p. 5), whose narrative the narrator records. The author is in pursuit of the signs of ecstasy and rapture that condition original writing. Tellingly, they regard Poe as analogously supplying the means by which one attempts to recover this presence, because 'the detective is the symbol of the mystagogue' (p. 25). They state that in the figure of Dupin:

> I find a faint suggestion of the under-consciousness or other-consciousness of man, a mere hint, not, I think, expressed in so many words, rather latent than patent, that if you would thoroughly understand the rational man you

must have sounded the irrational man, the mysterious companion that walks besides each one of us on the earthly journey. (pp. 25–6)

In Chapter 3 we witnessed how Poe's detective stories can be read as accounts of narrative composition in which the dead inspire the creative disentangling of the causes of death. In *Hieroglyphics*, the issue of detection is granted a metaphysical status, but it is related to how narratives need to be decoded in order to surrender this 'mysterious companion'. The problem is one of epistemology because this spiritual presence is a 'shadowy, unknown, or half-known Companion' (p. 31). The problem is further compounded because 'Everything terrestrial is so composite … one is confronted by an almost endless task of distinguishing matter from form, and body from spirits' (p. 65). This can, however, be overcome by reading in a symbolic way for moments of spiritual presence. Decoding the 'hieroglyphics' of the text requires the reader to act like a detective who can spot the creative within the formulaic. Like Myers, Machen indicates that such creative visions come to us in dreams, in that 'dream that came to the author from the other world' (p. 69), which emphasises that what is important is the moment of transition between the physical and the spiritual, which is why *Jekyll and Hyde* comes in for criticism because 'The transformation of Jekyll into Hyde is solely material as you read it, without artistic significance; it is simply an astounding incident, and not an outward sign of an inward mystery' (p. 73). Machen's preferred texts are ones that, revealingly, centre on the dead, as he extols the pre-eminent virtues of both Milton's *Lycidas* (1638) and Wordsworth's 'Intimations of Immortality' (1807). Machen's positive view of artistic inspiration is couched in a language of love that would be echoed in Myers's claim that spiritual love would in the future bind us all together. Machen asserts that 'Art, you may feel quite assured, proceeds always from love and rapture, never from hatred and disdain' (p. 95), and, like Myers, he claims that 'all the quintessence of art is distilled from the subconscious and not from the conscious self' (p. 108). Like Myers, Machen associates the genesis of this literature with romanticism in references to Wordsworth, Coleridge and Keats. He characterises romanticism with an artlessness that celebrated the importance of the 'untaught man' (p. 119), who nevertheless provides a conduit to a world of 'myths and symbols' that the cultured reader could interpret. It is as if the middle-subliminal realm identified by Myers functions in the educated reader to distort the purity of a naturally creative process. However, if creativity is natural reading is not, as it needs to be tutored into what to look for. The assertion is made that it is

Catholicism that provides the requisite skill in symbolic reading that enables us to understand 'that man is not the creature of the drawing-room and the Stock Exchange, but a lonely awful soul confronted by the Source of all Souls' (p. 163). Machen thus shifts the emphasis to a reader who can recode the dead as alive. Machen's links to mysticism are well known and his membership of the Hermetic Order of the Gold Dawn suggests associations that developed in *Hieroglyphics*. The possible links between death, creation and the reader were also clear from his earlier Gothic fiction, which can be demonstrated by a reading of *The Great God Pan* and *The Three Impostors*.

Images of fragments occur repeatedly in Machen's work and they are often used to emphasise the alienated experience of modern urban life. His long short story 'A Fragment of Life' (1899–1904) centres on the disjunction between middle-class respectability and the desire for an experience of life that is more paganistic and so more natural. Tellingly, the tale finishes on a book written by Edward Darnell, the story's main focaliser, that consists of seemingly inexplicable jottings about the pagan world.[16] It represents a moment in which an experience of 'Otherness' can be given a voice and indicates that Machen emphasised that knowledge and narrative are intimately linked. How to read texts (and how to read hieroglyphics) plays a central role in establishing an epistemic basis for his neo-pagan Celtic cosmology. Darryl Jones has noted of Machen that:

> Throughout his writings, the ancient Celtic and Romano-British legacies of spiritualism and the occult, and the permeable borderland between the two worlds of spirit and matter, are all imaged forth in geographical terms on the Welsh border of Caerleon, and in the occult investigations of seedy men of letters, theosophists and scientists, working in exile, obscurity and poverty in the secret labyrinths of the shabby outer suburbs of West London.[17]

It is the transitions between these worlds that are important to Machen as he explores the tensions between the modern and the ancient, the physical and the spiritual and the living and the dead. In *The Great God Pan*, science is given particular scrutiny as it provides access to an otherwise hidden world, whilst also functioning as an agent of destruction because science can breach the barriers between worlds that seemingly need to be kept apart. At one level the novella explores the apparent moral poverty of scientists such as Dr Raymond, whose opening experiment appears to unleash ancient malevolent forces. At another level Machen suggests that new scientific understandings have enabled us to see the world in a different way, and that this radically unsettles our conventional moral systems.

At the beginning Raymond tells Clarke that he practises 'transcendental medicine', a phrase drawn from *Jekyll and Hyde* and intended to indicate his ability to look beyond the purely physical world in order to see through '"the shadows that hide the real world from our eyes"'.[18] It is tempting to read this model of the otherworld as corresponding, at least conceptually, with spiritualist beliefs and debates about the soul that are familiar from Drummond. The chief question is, what does this otherworld generate? So far we have seen that the writings of Drummond and Myers indicate optimism about the possibility of evolutionary change. Myers was also interested in the idea that primitive cultures contained a lost knowledge of spirituality that was only now being reconnected to. The overlooked past thus generates a model for future development. Similarly for Machen, the way forward is the way back but this has consequences for the soul.

Raymond's experiment on Mary (a seventeen-year-old that Raymond had rescued from poverty some years before) results in her giving birth nine months later to Helen, who, it is suggested, is the daughter of Pan. Helen brings together the human and the non-human just as the brain experiment promises to bridge 'the world of matter and the world of spirit' (p. 7). For Drummond, death is not just physical, it is also spiritual, and it is noted that during the experiment on Mary 'the soul seemed struggling and shuddering within the house of flesh' (p. 13). Later we witness an encounter between two former Oxford friends in London; Villiers is wealthy and successful but Herbert is destitute, and he explains that this was a result of marrying Helen Vaughan (Mary and Pan's daughter), who, Herbert claims, '"corrupted my soul"' so that he became '"a ruined man, in body and soul – in body and soul"' (p. 26), as Helen proceeds to provoke a series of men into committing suicide.

The destruction of the 'soul' is clearly intended as a Christian concept that is at odds with a pagan world but which is referenced, if obliquely, in Clarke's arrangement of narrative testimony about the occult that he titles 'Memoirs to Prove the Existence of the Devil' (p. 15). More widely, the problem of 'souls' becomes reconstituted as an epistemic one and the emphasis on science privileges method above morality. At one level Helen is a classic *fin de siècle* femme fatale, but she brings more than just death into the world; she also destabilises social and ontological categories and so raises issues concerning epistemology. Christine Ferguson has noted of Helen that her 'ultimate refutation of the imperative to be semantically stable and socially useful – to, above all else, mean something – comes, ironically, when she confronts the greatest of all limitations placed on the subject: death'.[19] Villiers discusses Helen with a friend, Austin, who had visited a now vacated property that Helen had once inhabited. He tells Villiers that, as he approached one room, "'I was racked from head to foot, my eyes began to grow dim; it was like the entrance of death'" (p. 42). After the death of Helen, Clarke returns to rural Caermaen (based on Caerleon in South Wales) and writes to Raymond, describing his visit to an area associated with the young Helen where he noted the presence of 'the faint sweet scent of wild roses [that] came to me on the wind and mixed with the heavy perfume of the elder, whose mingled odour is like the odour of the room of the dead, a vapour of incense and corruption' (pp. 72–3). Helen is confronted with her crimes and persuaded to commit suicide. Her death is recounted by a Dr Robert Matheson, who records that he witnessed "'some internal force, of which I knew nothing, that caused dissolution and change'" (p. 70). He also notes that:

> 'Here too was all the work by which man has been made repeated before my eyes. I saw the form waver from sex to sex, dividing itself from itself, and then again reunited. Then I saw the body descend to the beasts whence it ascended, and that which was on the heights go down to the depths, even to the abyss of being. The principle of life, which makes organism, always remained, while the outward form changed.' (p. 70)

The dissolution of Helen thus recapitulates a narrative of evolutionary change. The issue, however, is one of epistemic evaluation, which reasserts the significance of reading. Helen's death is recounted in a chapter titled 'The Fragments', and whilst at one level this refers to her dissolution, it also refers to the fragmentary nature of the written evidence. It is noted that Matheson's account consisted of 'a leaf of manuscript paper ... covered with pencil jottings. These notes were in Latin, much abbreviated, and had evidently been made in great haste. The MS was only deciphered with great difficulty' (pp. 68–9). Indeed, the MS is acknowledged to be 'a translation' (p. 69), which invites questions over its accuracy. The text also generates a link between narrative and bodily instability when it records Matheson's perception of Helen as 'lying there black like ink, transformed before my eyes' (p. 69). Here she is imaged as a writerly text whose instabilities are echoed in the structure of both the novella (as a series of documents) and in Clarke's 'Memoirs to Prove the Existence of the Devil', which he keeps in a bureau where the 'pigeonholes and drawers teemed with documents on the most morbid subjects, and in the well reposed a large manuscript volume, in which he had painfully entered the gems of his collection' (p. 14). Clarke is a bricoleur with an eye to arranging the material to tell a story: 'It was one of his humours to pride himself on a certain literary ability: he thought well of his style, and took pains in arranging the circumstances in dramatic order' (p. 15). Matheson's baffled gaze is the problem because although it records the dissolution of Helen (who throughout the novella is only made present via the texts of others), he is not sure what any of it means. As Ferguson has noted, Helen is required to 'mean something' and this desire for meaning is where interpretation and reading gain significance.

Machen focuses on how we can bring together the fragments to form a narrative (an enterprise that Clarke shares with the narrator of *Hieroglyphics*). In the discussion between Villiers and Austin there emerges a view that in order to understand Helen's tale it would need to be read symbolically. Villiers states: 'those who are wise know that all symbols are symbols of something, not nothing. It was, indeed, an exquisite symbol beneath which men long ago veiled their knowledge of the most awful, most secret forces which lie at the heart of all things' (p. 65). In *Hieroglyphics*, Machen had argued that in order to create and to read literature it is necessary to be 'subconsciously Catholic' (p. 163), because Catholic symbolism provides the closest analogue for a method of reading that is 'merely the witness, under a special symbolism, of the enduring facts of human nature and the universe' (p. 163). Villiers claims that these occulted forces and revelations about 'human nature' 'cannot be named, cannot be spoken, cannot be imagined except under a veil and a symbol' (p. 65). It is a veil that science cannot properly penetrate, which suggests that a new way of reading is required in order to make sense of the symbolic forms that, in *The Great God Pan*, repeatedly relate to death and the blurring between the living and the dead – which was also the principal epistemic focus of both Drummond and Myers. For Myers, literature functioned as a symbolic encoding of the subliminal realm, but also constituted a problem for interpretation. Spirit messages sent as cross-correspondences also reflect this paradoxical hesitancy about reading, even whilst such messages were regarded as demonstrating a proof for the existence of spirits. Where Machen stands on these issues may seem to be unclear. Helen is, at a conventional level, a demonised figure, but at another level this is because she has not been properly decoded. She represents the presence of a type of knowledge that can be intimated but not properly read, with a quasi-Catholic form of interpretation coming closest to providing a model of understanding, although one that in this instance fails to force Helen into meaning. Machen's emphasis on ways of reading indicates a desire to make sense of the fragments whilst also embracing the positive radical potential that those fragments pose for conventional ways of reading, such as that associated with Matheson's medical science. Matheson's failure to 'read' therefore produces a positive secondary knowledge about the limitations of medical interpretation. One way to contextualise these issues is by reference to the decadent culture.

Machen's work was associated with *fin de siècle* decadence because of the prevalence of amoral characters in his work, such as Raymond and Clarke. At the end of the previous chapter, we briefly explored how Wilde could be related to the scientific ideas of the period and these links can also be applied to Machen. Christine Ferguson has argued that naturalism and decadence were united because the amorality associated with the decadent artist represented a way of looking at disease that was also referenced in medical science. Both positions dehumanise the subject and as a consequence generate no real knowledge of subjectivity – only surfaces, manifested as bodies or in models of beauty (467). Also, decadence is characterised by its pursuit of forbidden knowledge and this leads to fragmentation: as Ferguson suggests, 'the most forbidden knowledge of all was that which had no clear use or moral purpose, that which, far from fixing and stabilizing identity, functioned to dissolve the way the subject had been envisioned, to seek the truth behind the self, regardless of the costs of this unveiling' (470). This new 'truth' represents one aspect of the decadent culture's 'obsessive epistemiphilia' (470), which demonstrates the presence of an instrumentalist desire for knowledge that was more properly associated with the dominant scientific paradigms. However, as we have seen in the case of Myers, scientific principles could be redirected towards ostensibly metaphysical ends in an attempt to overcome the epistemic fragmentation produced by death and to interpret the intimations of a subliminal realm that suggested the possibility of a post-mortem existence. Science can take us into the unknown because it is able to extend the principles of evolution to it. Decadence suggests new ways of thinking that require an alternative approach in which 'decadent disintegration [constituted] not an ethic of futility and waste but the fulfilment of a particular kind of epistemological idealism' (476). The apparent Gothic pessimism of Machen is in reality optimism about a deferred principle of idealism that will, at some point, enable us to read the ineffable. As we have seen, these reading practices are closely focused on how to read the dead, which appears to be especially problematic at a time when the dead do not die but pass over.

It is on the threshold between the physical and the spiritual and the living and the dead that the work of Machen should be situated. He privileges fiction as *the* symbolic mode that grants access to this world, and

Nicholas Freeman has noted that Machen 'sought an alternative way of viewing the world, one steeped in mystical and occult tradition and within which the artist played a central role'.[20] This is clear from Machen's *The Hill of Dreams* (1907), which centres on the apparent mental disintegration of Lucian Taylor as he attempts to develop as a writer, even whilst that disintegration appears to lead to some privileged insights.[21] The issue of textual construction was also central to Myers's account of how messages could be sent telepathically but become complicated because they can be constructed through many minds, so that a text becomes multi-authored, a position that is echoed in the multi-textual structure of *The Great God Pan* and *Dracula*. Charles Ko, in an article on James Joyce, has acknowledged these echoes within the Modernist text, arguing that the 'unconscious' in Myers 'is unsealed, operating not only intrapersonally but also *interpersonally* as a kind of vast, decentralised, open-ended, palimpsestic writing machine linking one porous mind to another, continually rereading and rewriting itself as multiple messages intersect and overlap, circulate and re-circulate'.[22] Ko also argues that Myers's evocation of the 'soul' should be regarded as a Romantic legacy as it evokes a discourse of sympathy (associated with Smith and Burke), although one that Myers unwittingly transgresses because, despite his model of the integrative subliminal realm, his account of telepathy implies the presence of fragmentation rather than unity (Ko, 747). If Myers appears to uphold the principles of science and Machen those of mysticism, we can also see that Machen was self-conscious about the possible tensions between these different cultures as he scrutinises them in *The Three Impostors*, a narrative that centres on a death but which is also self-reflexive about narrative construction.

The novel opens with Dyson's account to his friend Phillips about an incident that occurred one evening whilst he was in an area near Tottenham Court Road in London when he saw one man chasing another. The first man, in a hurry to make good his escape, threw a coin in Dyson's direction, which Dyson picked up, unobserved by the chasing man. He shows the gold coin to Phillips, who explains its history. The coin features the emperor Tiberius and was minted to 'commemorate an infamous excess', but was the only one of the batch to survive an accident that saw the rest of the coins destroyed in a melting pot.[23] It transpires that the man who was being chased, Joseph Walters, had fallen under the spell of one Dr Lipsius, who had introduced him to the activities of a group who were apparently interested in the occult (and, it is suggested, orgies) and who also murder people for pleasure and gain. One such unfortunate, Mr Headley, who was murdered by Dr Lipsius for the coin, sparks Walters's conscience, prompting him to steal the coin. Three friends of Dr Lipsius who are trying to find Walters and get the coin back variously approach Dyson, and then Phillips when they observe a connection between them. They pose as characters in some desperation but who in reality are trying to see if Dyson or Phillips know of Walters's whereabouts. Their tales make up much of the novel and this emphasises the idea of narrative, detection and interpretation that runs throughout. How their narratives, which centre on the dead and the missing, are interpreted is in part determined by the contrasting temperaments of Dyson and Phillips.

Dyson is a writer who believes that story-telling provides a way of getting at the truth, whereas Phillips, 'a gentleman of pronounced scientific tastes' (p. 37), regards not only 'truth' as subject to scientific principles but also literature. This means that between them 'There was a constant jarring of literary formulas, Dyson exalting the claims of the pure imagination; while Phillips ... insisted that all literature ought to have a scientific basis' (p. 8). Much of the early scenes of the novel focus on their different perspectives on writing, with Dyson emphasising the importance of 'the Marvellous' (p. 9), which contrasts with Phillips's 'firm dependence on the natural order of things' (p. 14). However, the novel suggests that their differences are more due to an adherence to particular forms of discourse (the literary versus the scientific) than to any disagreement about possible occult experiences. It is noted of Phillips that, 'Flattering himself with the title of materialist, he was in truth one of the most credulous of men, but he required a marvel to be neatly draped in the robes of Science before he would give it any credit, and the wildest dreams took shape to him only if the nomenclature were severe and irreproachable' (p. 37). Phillips does not see wonder as wonder unless it is reflected in the language of materialism, so that 'He laughed at the witch, but quailed before the powers of the hypnotist, lifting his eyebrows when Christianity was mentioned, but adoring protyle and ether' (p. 37). Dyson, however, tells Phillips that he regards him as a '"visionary"' because '"your scepticism has defeated itself and become a monstrous credulity"' (p. 38). The scientific imagination can be tricked, according to Dyson, whereas the literary imagination understands, and can decode, the world's underlying symbolic forms. These tensions inform the first interpolated narrative when Phillips shares a bench with a tearful woman in Leicester Square, who tells him that she is trying to find her missing brother (whose physical description matches that of Dyson's account of the running man), with whom, she claims, she has been in occasional telepathic contact.

The woman, 'Miss Lally', tells Phillips about her employment as governess to the two children of Professor Gregg, an eminent ethnologist whose work Phillips is aware of, referring to Gregg as "'one of our most acute and clear-headed observers'" (p. 45). Miss Lally's tale casts Gregg as an anti-materialist, who informed her that "'Life, believe me, is no simple thing, no mass of grey matter and congeries of veins and muscles to be laid naked by the surgeon's knife; man is the secret which I am about to explore'" (p. 51). He shows her a drawer containing annotated scraps of paper, a black stone and jottings clipped from various journals, which Miss Lally refers to as an 'eccentric odds and ends of evidence' that leaves her confused as to 'what theory could be founded on the fragments that had been placed before me' (p. 53). The issue of textual assembly and interpretation hinges on the analysis of a cryptic message that has sixty characters in it and which appears on a stone that 'has a secret unspeakable name on it: Ixaxar' (p. 58). Decoding the mystery will lead Gregg to the occulted Celtic figures who inhabit the area (again, in South Wales) where he lives. Gregg employs a local boy, Jervase Cradock, to help with menial tasks. Jervase is prone to fits in which he speaks 'an infamous jargon, with words, or what seemed words, that might have belonged to a tongue dead since untold ages' (p. 64), which for Miss Lally "'is the very speech of hell'" (p. 64), whereas for Gregg it is a language that "'belongs to … the fairies'" (p. 66) that he is looking for. Landmarks also possess a symbolic import when Gregg notes of the designs on a bridge that "'I confess it seems to me symbolic; it should illustrate a mystical allegory of the passage from one world to another'" (p. 67), and because of the cryptic nature of such signs they form "'a problem in the Manner of the inimitable Holmes'" (p. 69). Gregg goes to find these strange beings and leaves behind a narrative explanation with Miss Lilly, which she opens when he fails to return (he is never seen again). In it he discloses that the figures he intends to meet possess secrets about the world that reveal 'how man can be reduced to the slime from which he came, and be forced to put on the flesh of the reptile and the snake' (p. 82). Phillips is convinced by her account of Gregg's research and asserts that "'The most extraordinary circumstances in your account are in perfect harmony with the latest scientific theories'" (p. 84), and he urges her to write an account of it to submit to Oliver Lodge, a spiritualist and scientist who would become president of the Society for Psychical Research in 1901.

Stefania Forlini has noted that Machen's novel owes a debt to R. L. Stevenson and Fanny De Grift Stevenson's *The Dynamiter* (1885), which focuses on three amateur detectives and their attempt to thwart a secret society whose members use narratives to disguise themselves. For Forlini, Tiberius's coin represents a fetish that demonstrates 'how Machen builds an object-driven narrative that literalizes the scientific practice of building developmental narratives based on found objects'.[24] The ethos of the detective story is applied to narratives centred upon scientific decryption, but crucially, given that the narratives are told by impostors, the novel 'call[s] attention to the act of fabricating narratives' (485). The novel is therefore about writing, but it is a form of writing that is also about acts of interpretation. Phillips thus adjudicates Miss Lally's narrative in terms of its claims to truth, noting that her '"narrative puts the whole matter out of the range of mere hypothesis"' (p. 84), even whilst he overlooks the fact that the tale is merely iterated in order for the impostor to discover whether Phillips knows the whereabouts of Miss Lally's brother, in reality the running man seen by Dyson. A later narrative, titled the 'Novel of the White Powder', begins with Dyson listening to a tale by a 'Miss Leicester' that recounts her brother's physical dissolution after he had taken some tainted medicine that reduced him to 'a dark and putrid mass, seething with corruption and hideous rottenness' (p. 122). The mixture is sent by a Dr Harberden to one Dr Chambers for chemical analysis, and Chambers's response outlines an anti-materialist stance in which 'The whole universe … is a tremendous sacrament; a mystic, ineffable force and energy, veiled by an outward form of matter' (p. 124). The new sciences have enabled this shift so that 'you must not, it is true, believe in witchcraft, but you may credit hypnotism; ghosts are out of date, but there is a good deal to be said for the theory of telepathy' (p. 125). Dyson realises that 'Miss Leicester' has merely told the tale in order to see if he has seen someone who resembles the running man and this realisation introduces a different order of mystery into the narrative.

Dyson enters a public house and sees the running man accosted at the bar by one of the story-tellers that he had earlier encountered; Dyson 'divined that all unconscious and unheeding he had been privileged to see the shadows of hidden forms, chasing and hurrying, and grasping and vanishing across the bright curtain of common life, soundless and silent, or only babbling fables and pretences' (p. 134).

As we have seen, many of the narratives told by the impostors are about hidden metaphysical realities that suggest epistemic changes. But these tales are told simply to elicit information about the running man, not to enlighten Dyson and Phillips. Within the narrative there is another narrative that is about Walters, who is finally discovered in the pub. However, although the narratives told by the impostors are a ruse to gain information, it does not negate their discussions about science. The emphasis on evidence within their narratives echoes the form of the detective story, as Dyson and Phillips try to discover the meaning of Walters's story. The novel can therefore be read as a tale of detection and as about scientific procedures that build 'truth' through narrative formations, which is why Forlini regards the novel as 'a text thoroughly implicated in a particular scientific discourse and its practice of narrative building' (487). Tellingly, it is important that at this stage Dyson, the author, becomes turned into a reader. As Walters is led out of the pub he drops 'a little old-fashioned notebook, bound in faded green morocco' (p. 135), and one of the first revelations is that Walters is a figure in pursuit of knowledge – an ambition that emphasises reading:

> I chose the glorious career of scholar in its ancient sense; I longed to possess encyclopaedic learning, to grow old amongst books, to distil day by day, and year after year, the inmost sweetness of all worthy writing. I was not rich enough to collect a library, and I was therefore forced to betake myself to the Reading-Room of the British Museum. (p. 136)

The Reading Room becomes a place of death for Walters, who refers to it as 'O dome, tomb of the quick! surely in thy galleries, where no reverberant voice can call, sighs whisper ever, and mutterings of dead hopes; and there men's souls mount like moths towards the flame, and fall blackened beneath thee' (pp. 136–7). It is whilst in the Reading Room that he encounters Dr Lipsius, who introduces him to an alternative world of forbidden knowledge that seemingly centres on the type of pre-Christian pleasures that we have witnessed elsewhere in Machen. This is a decadent world in which amorality leads to death and Walters plays a key role in leading Mr Headley, the owner of the coin, to Dr Lipsius, who murders him and then disguises the body as an Egyptian mummy that he intends to sell to the British Museum. The pleasures Walters had been introduced to are transformed into images of death that are reflected on a faded ceiling painting in a deserted old house that Dyson and Phillips discover on one of their rambles, a house Dyson describes as being '"as moral as a graveyard"' (p. 152). On entering the house they are struck by the images on the ceiling in which they note the presence of 'all gay colours and light fancies of cupids in a career [which] disfigured with sores of dampness, seemed transmuted into other work' (p. 152). The time-corrupted images of pleasure represent a clear symbol of how desire can lead to death, and Dyson and Phillips observe how the painting illustrates a tale in which 'Love had become a Dance of Death; black pustules and festering sores swelled and clustered on fair limbs and smiling faces showed corruption, and the fairy blood had boiled with the germs of foul disease; it was a parable of the leaven working, and worms devouring for a banquet the heart of a rose' (p. 152). The reference to the parable of the leaven suggests that a divine plan, centring on punishment, is being worked out in response to the pagan pleasures enjoyed by Walters. In the house they find the naked corpse of Walters, who had been bound, tortured and burnt to death. In the end a type of amorality, rather than a divine plan, seems to triumph, which makes sense of the Prologue where the three followers of Dr Lipsius discuss the killing of Walters and their story-telling. The nameless woman, who appeared as Miss Lally and Miss Leicester, says '"Farewell to all occult adventure; the farce is played"' (p. 4), which reflects on the construction of the supernatural narratives that populate the novel.

The Three Impostors is both about occluded knowledge centring on a possible spirit world and a detective story concerning the moral characters of the three impostors. The novel foregrounds a shift to readers and away from writers, a conversion that is familiar from these *fin de siècle* Gothic narratives. Forlini has noted the new demands that Machen imposes on readers of his novel (and not just on Dyson and Phillips) when noting that the 'readers are left to contemplate the artifice of the whole and to glimpse not the transcendent meaning of the text and the events it depicts so much as its constructed material form' (490). The text invites the reader to attempt an interpretation so that 'The world of the text ... overspills its bounds into the reader's world' (494). The process of interpretation and its links to the spiritual world are clear in Machen and the notion that a spirit world attempts some form of communication with us can be found in other writings such as 'The Inmost Light' (1894) and 'The Shining Pyramid' (1895), both of which cast Dyson as a detective-like figure, and 'The White People' (1904) (to name only a few).

The issue of reading for spiritual presence in such a way that a new epistemology is developed unites the disparate cultures inhabited by Drummond, Myers and Machen. These cultural links indicate that reading the dead is problematic, in part because the dead are, in reality, alive in some other form. Writing about the dead does not creatively reanimate them, as it did in the eighteenth century and the later Romantic culture, because now the dead are there for us to touch and speak to (as a seance might stage it). How to write about these new formations of the subject requires a shift from writer to reader and this is also clear from Stoker's *Dracula*, whose subtitle of 'the dead undead' implicates the vampire (and indeed the vampire hunters) in a discourse of liminality that raises epistemic questions about how we gain knowledge about the dead.

Dracula: writers, readers, editors

The scientific engagements of *Dracula* have been well noted and theories of degeneration, models of psychology and accounts of hypnotism have now become critically commonplace contexts in which to situate the novel. *Dracula* can, however, also be read as an exercise in scientific method in which textual assembly constitutes 'a process analogous to that of scientific investigation'.[25] This is clear from the epistemic failures of Harker's opening journal where Harker repeatedly notes the limitations of his Western, legal, fact-based perspective when confronted by the seemingly supernatural Count. Harker is also unsure about the type of narrative form he has adopted in his journal, recalling at one point that 'the diary seems horribly like the beginning of the "Arabian Nights"'.[26] This entry is immediately followed by one for 12 May beginning, 'Let me begin with facts – bare, meagre facts, verified by books and figures, and of which there can be no doubt' (p. 31). This abrupt transition from the fantastical to the factual represents a textual instability in Harker's journal as he struggles to find a way to both read and write the Count. Harker is simply unable to find an epistemology that will work and he lapses into a series of horrified observations that are in part a consequence of not knowing what the Count is. The issue of writing is picked up by Mina immediately after the conclusion of Harker's journal when she writes to Lucy about learning to use the typewriter and creating her own journal, in which 'I shall try to do what lady journalists do: interviewing and writing descriptions and trying to remember conversations' (p. 53). The means of keeping record are emphasised throughout the novel as the text becomes constituted through journals, newspaper clippings, stenograph recordings and letters. How to create a coherent text from such diversity requires the multiple authors to work in a co-operative way and it is Mina who places the documents into a chronological order so that 'they will be able to show a whole connected narrative' (p. 210). The anonymous prefatory note claims that a key feature of the text concerns its construction: 'How these papers have been placed in sequence will be made clear in the reading of them. All needless matters have been eliminated, so that a history almost at variance with the possibility of latter-day belief may stand forth as simple fact' (p. 4). The telling of the tale is thus part of an epistemic process that reflects scientific procedure. Seward, seemingly baffled by Renfield's behaviour, applies these narrative principles to Renfield's likes and aversions and sets 'them in proper order' to reveal the underlying 'story' (p. 253). To decode the Count it is necessary to force him into a pattern of narrative coherence that will make sense of what he is. The problem for epistemology posed by the Count is clear from his arrival in Whitby, which forges a close symbolic link with death.

In the novel Whitby has narrative associations that grant it a quasi-unreality, as when Mina records that Whitby Abbey was referenced in Scott's *Marmion* (1808). She also notes that she is writing her journal in the 'big graveyard, full of tombstones', which, because of the view it affords of the town and the harbour, 'is, to my mind, the nicest spot in Whitby' (p. 61).[27] Mina befriends three old men who spend much of their time in the graveyard and is subjected to a protracted lecture from one of them, a Mr Swales, concerning the narrative of tombstones. Swales's own associations with narrative are suggested in Mina's claim that his speeches make him resemble 'Sir Oracle' from *The Merchant of Venice* (1600). Mina, situated in the graveyard and listening to tales about the dead, becomes a death-writer who records the disjunction between narrative presence and deathly absence. Swales points out that many of the graves are those of sailors lost at sea and that the repeated claim of '"Here lies the body"' (p. 63) is untrue. The dead are elsewhere, or misremembered, and Swales's narrative suggests that death is subject to conventions of memorialisation that fail to connect with the dead. This type of graveyard is different from the graveyard found in the Graveyard poetry of the eighteenth century, or the urban graveyards discussed in Chapter 4. Swales is cynical about what the graves represent as they misremember the lives of their occupants (with those that have them), and so the dead are placed beyond conventional discourses of sympathy or empathy. How to write about this model of the graveyard, and the version of death with which it is associated, requires a new idiom that is glossed in how Mina maintains her journal in shorthand because of its use of 'symbols that makes it different from writing' (p. 69). The writing on the graves has failed to recall the dead and a new way of writing about that is required – a thematic issue that is addressed throughout the novel. All of this is in preparation for the arrival of the Count who symbolises death. Swales, ever alert to the presence (and indeed absence) of death, claims: '"There's something in that wind and in the hoast beyont that sounds, and looks, and tastes, and smells like death. It's in the air; I feel it comin'"' (p. 72). The arrival of the *Demeter* is recalled in a cutting from the fictitious *Dailygraph* that Mina pastes into her journal. The reporter references *The Rime of the Ancient Mariner* (1798) in their description of the ship, which turns out to be appropriate given that the crew are dead. The ship is enclosed in an oddly clinging mist, which leads the reporter to reflect that 'it needed but little imagination to think that the spirits of those lost at sea were touching their living brethren with the clammy hands of death' (p. 74). Later, Swales is found dead in the graveyard with his neck broken, apparently as though he had fallen back in his seat cowering from something that scared him because, as Mina records, 'there was a look of fear and horror on his face that the men said made them shudder' (p. 83). This leads Mina to wonder, 'Perhaps he had seen Death with his dying eyes!' (pp. 83–4). Van Helsing later makes clear these associations with death when he says of the Count that 'he have still the aids of necromancy ... and all the dead that he can come nigh to are for him to command' (p. 221). The smell of death that is associated with the Count (which makes Harker shrink from him at Castle Dracula) is also clear from the coffins that the Count distributes amongst his numerous lairs. The smell is difficult to describe, as Harker records: 'It was not alone that it was composed of all the ills of mortality and with the pungent, acrid smell of blood, but it seemed as though corruption had become itself corrupt' (p. 233), a description that echoes that of the house once occupied by Helen Vaughan in *The Great God Pan*, discussed earlier. For Van Helsing, to understand how death might not die we need to know something about the Count's studies.

Van Helsing notes of the Count that 'he was in life a most wonderful man. Soldier, statesman, and alchemist – which latter was the highest development of the science knowledge of the time. He had a mighty brain, a learning beyond compare, and a heart that knew no fear and no remorse' (p. 280). The Count's occult knowledge was garnered during his attendance at the Scholomance, and Van Helsing is clear that the Count should be seen as applying a scientific understanding to their world when asserting that '"this monster has been creeping into knowledge experimentally"' (p. 281). This 'creep' is also linked to a discourse of evolution when Van Helsing claims of the Count that '"In him some vital principle have in strange way found their utmost; and as his body keep strong and grow and thrive, so his brain grow too"' (p. 297). The Count has learnt how to adapt to their environment: '"He study new tongues. He learn new social life; new environment of old ways, the politic, the law, the finance, the science, the habit of a new land"' (p. 298). The problem is that, although '"In some faculties of mind he has been, and is, only a child; but he is growing and some things that were childish at the first are now of man's stature"' (p. 280). The hope is '"that our man-brains ... will come higher than his child-brain"' (p. 315). Ultimately they need to stop him before he usurps their world and becomes '"the father or furtherer of a new order of beings, whose road must lead through Death, not Life"' (p. 280). That the Count is both dead and alive is also established by Mina when she is placed in a hypnotic trance as a means of psychically communicating with the Count whilst he is asleep; she, like Vankirk in Poe's 'Mesmeric Revelation', notes that "'It is like death!'" (p. 290). For Myers, such a condition is indeed like death as it enables the spirit to escape from bodily constraints and so anticipates the freeing of the spirit in death. Death constitutes a new life, but this is exactly the problem that Van Helsing wishes to police. Later, when she considers her infected condition, Mina states: "'I am deeper in death at this moment than if the weight of an earthly grave lay heavy upon me!'" (p. 308). These considerations of death are also closely tied to ideas about narrative.

Seward refers to Renfield as 'a sort of index to the coming and going of the Count' (p. 210), and later Harker refers to Renfield as "'mixed up with the Count in an indexy way'" (p. 231). The Count is repeatedly associated with ideas about writing, with Van Helsing referring to him as "'the author of all this our sorrow'" (p. 203) and later noting that the Count is vulnerable when "'He is confined within the limitations of his earthly envelope'" (p. 271), which also has spiritual connotations. That the Count represents a threat to textuality is also clear from his destruction of one of the copies of their manuscript. He also appears to influence the infected Lucy when, whilst asleep, she retrieves her recent account 'from her breast and tore it in two' (p. 143), before Van Helsing intervenes and takes the pieces from her. Throughout the novel the Count is represented as a mystery that needs to be deciphered, and the process of reading is repeatedly implicated in ideas about narrative construction. The Count represents death in the novel and these acts of reading should be seen in the light of other, quasi-scientific attempts at decoding death. Clearly the Count is not a spiritual entity and is different in kind from the occulted figures we see in Machen (and indeed in Drummond and Myers), but he does function as an image of a living corpse that suggests that death is not quite the end.

The vampire represents in negative form a version of death that is unacceptable to a conventional Judeo-Christian culture, and in part this is because of the Count's corpse-like ambience that obviates any spiritual presence (although arguably this is also echoed in Swales's account of the graveyard). *Dracula* represents one way in which a culture tried to make sense of the apparent permeability between the living and the dead, and there are other examples of this such as Richard Marsh's *The Beetle* (1897), which narrates an engagement with a figure of death through many narrative perspectives.[28] Kipling, in 'Wireless' (1902), would use a comatose consumptive chemist to channel 'The Eve of St. Agnes' (1820) from Keats (another consumptive chemist) whilst a radio experiment is taking place in an adjacent room.[29] Voices are subject to channelling, but such tales also repeatedly emphasise that an understanding of narrative form is an essential aspect of the process of interpretation. Death is no longer inhabited from within, but subject to an external verification that can turn death into an epistemology. This is why at the end of *Dracula* there appears to be a credibility issue because, as Harker states in the final 'Note', 'in all the mass of material of which the record is composed, there is hardly one authentic document! ... We could hardly ask anyone, even did we wish to, to accept the proofs of so wild a story' (p. 351). An 'authentic document' would be an independent one, and although they have followed Van Helsing's scientific approach, this represents a triumph of method over content as no externally verifiable epistemology of life beyond death is produced.[30]

Ultimately, the *fin de siècle* Gothic reveals that death requires narrative form. To write about death is to embark upon a process of interpretation. Writers become readers as the world of the dead takes on a shifting narrative shape. A new type of writing emerges from this: Modernism, which will be briefly touched upon in the concluding chapter.

Notes

1 Arthur Conan Doyle, *The History of Spiritualism*, 2 vols (Teddington: The Echo Library, 2006 [1926]), vol. II, p. 41. All subsequent references are to this edition and are given in the text. I discuss the issue of the literary provenance of spirit messages in some depth in my *The Ghost Story 1840–1920: A Cultural History* (Manchester: Manchester University Press, 2010), see ch. 5, 'Reading Ghosts and Reading Texts: Spiritualism', pp. 97–119.

2 Anne Scott, '"Visible Incarnations of the Unseen": Henry Drummond and the Practice of Typological Exegesis', *The British Journal for the History of Science*, 37:4 (December 2004), 435–54, 435. Scott also notes that it was still 'selling at a phenomenal rate twenty years later' (435).

3 Henry Drummond, *Natural Law in the Spiritual World* (London: Hodder & Stoughton, 1884), p. xi. All subsequent references are to this edition and are given in the text.

4 H. G. Wells, 'Zoological Retrogression', *Gentleman's Magazine*, 271 (1891), 246–53, 248. Wells's critique is of Edwin Lankester's *Degeneration: A Chapter in Darwinism* (London: Macmillan, 1880).

5 Alex Owen, *The Place of Enchantment: British Occultism and the Culture of the Modern* (Chicago: University of Chicago Press, 2004), p. 115. All subsequent references are to this edition and are given in the text.

6 Richard Noakes, 'Haunted Thoughts of the Careful Experimentalist: Psychical Research and the Troubles of Experimental Physics', *Studies in History and Philosophy of Biological and Biomedical Sciences*, 48 (2014), 46–56, 47. For a broad overview of the often troubled relationship between science and spiritualism, see Noakes's 'Spiritualism, Science and the Supernatural in Mid-Victorian Britain', in Nicola Brown, Carolyn Burdett and Pamela Thurschwell (eds), *The Victorian Supernatural* (Cambridge: Cambridge University Press, 2004), pp. 23–43.
7 S. E. D. Shortt, 'Physicians and Psychics: The Anglo-American Medical Response to Spiritualism, 1870–1890', *Journal of the History of Medicine*, 39 (July 1984), 339–55, 350. All subsequent references are to this edition and are given in the text.
8 William Crookes, 'Address', in *Report of the Sixty-Eighth Meeting of the British Association for the Advancement of Science, Held in Bristol in September 1898* (London: John Murray, 1899), pp. 3–33.
9 Edmund Gurney, 'The Nature of Evidence in Matters Extraordinary', *National Review*, 22 (1884), 472–91, 472.
10 Roger Luckhurst, *The Invention of Telepathy 1870–1901* (Oxford: Oxford University Press, 2002), p. 5. All subsequent references are to this edition and are given in the text.
11 Frederic W. H. Myers, *Human Personality and Its Survival of Bodily Death* (London: Longmans, 1907), p. 1. All subsequent references are to this edition and are given in the text. I have cited the single-volume 1907 edition that omits many of the appendicised examples of texts submitted to the Society of Psychical Research, but which retains Myers's overall thesis.
12 For an account of Myers and his relationship to the literary culture of the time, see Hilary Grimes's *The Late Victorian Gothic: Mental Science, the Uncanny and Scenes of Writing* (Farnham: Ashgate, 2010). See her ch. 6, 'Balancing the Wires', pp. 137–60, for an account of automatic writing and women's writing during the period.
13 Although Myers may have a different scientific schema than that of Drummond, he is also clearly working within a Christian framework. See his 'Epilogue', pp. 340–55, where he discusses in depth how his discoveries are linked to Christian ideas.
14 It should be noted that whilst Myers had an interest in spiritualism, he is not making direct reference to cross-correspondence.
15 Arthur Machen, *Hieroglyphics: A Note upon Ecstasy in Literature* (London: Martin Secker, 1902), p. 8. All subsequent references are to this edition and are given in the text.
16 Arthur Machen, 'A Fragment of Life', in *The White People and Other Stories*, ed. S. T. Joshi (Hayward: Chaosium, 2003), pp. 99–174.
17 Darryl Jones, 'Borderlands: Spiritualism and the Occult in *Fin de Siècle* and Edwardian Welsh and Irish Horror', *Irish Studies Review*, 17:1 (2009), 31–44, 36.

18 Arthur Machen, *The Great God Pan* in *The Great God Pan, The Shining Pyramid, The White People* (Cardigan: Parthian, 2010), pp. 1–76, p. 4. All subsequent references are to this edition and are given in the text.
19 Christine Ferguson, 'Decadence as Scientific Fulfilment', *PMLA*, 117:3 (2002), 465–78, 475. All subsequent references are to this edition and are given in the text.
20 Nicholas Freeman, 'Arthur Machen: Ecstasy and Epiphany', *Literature & Theology*, 24:3 (September 2010), 242–55, 243.
21 Arthur Machen, *The Hill of Dreams* (Cardigan: Parthian, 2010).
22 Charles Ko, 'Subliminal Consciousness', *The Review of English Studies*, 59:242 (2007), 740–65, 747. Italics in original. All subsequent references are to this edition and are given in the text.
23 Arthur Machen, *The Three Impostors* (New York: Dover, 2007), p. 12. All subsequent references are to this edition and are given in the text.
24 Stefania Forlini, 'Modern Narratives and Decadent Things in Arthur Machen's *The Three Impostors*', *English Literature in Transition, 1880–1920*, 55:4 (2012), 479–98, 485. All subsequent references are to this edition and are given in the text.
25 Philip Holden, 'Castle, Coffin, Stomach: *Dracula* and the Banality of the Occult', *Victorian Literature and Culture*, 29:2 (2001), 469–85, 471.
26 Bram Stoker, *Dracula*, ed. and Introd. Roger Luckhurst (Oxford: Oxford University Press, 2011), p. 31. All subsequent references are to this edition and are given in the text.
27 Whitby was also famous for its production of jet during the period, which was used in mourning jewellery and thus creates a symbolic association between the town and death.
28 Richard Marsh, *The Beetle*, ed. Julian Wolfreys (Peterborough: Broadview, 2004).
29 Rudyard Kipling, 'Wireless', in *Traffics and Discoveries* (London: Pocket Macmillan Edition, 1904), pp. 213–39.
30 In this context their documents can be read as a gloss on the numerous eye-witness accounts submitted to the Society for Psychical Research that Stoker would parody at the beginning of *The Lady of the Shroud* (1909).

Conclusion

This study has explored the various ways in which the dead and dying have been represented in Gothic texts from the mid eighteenth century to the early twentieth century. The history explored here began by looking at how Graveyard poetry functioned as a precursor to the Gothic. As we have seen, critical discussion about death, spirituality and creativity was established in the context of the elegy. For Edward Young, the true imagination is inspired by what it discerns within a divinely ordained nature. Fears about death are the product of a disordered imagination that has failed to grasp that death is merely the threshold to an entry into an everlasting world of spirituality. The false imagination is alienated from nature because, for Young, it copies literary, and so inauthentic, models of inspiration. However, by the end of the eighteenth century there emerged an alternative perception of these apparently fanciful Gothic images, which led Nathan Drake to claim that they should be seen as hitherto-overlooked elements of the natural world. These emerging Gothic images also demonstrated the range of the imagination by indicating the breadth of our creative capacities. Death was also construed in non-Gothic terms at this time, with both Adam Smith and Edmund Burke claiming that the dead awaken our empathy rather than evoke disgust. This image of death reappears within the Gothic as the existence of spirits suggests the possibility of communicating with the dead. Our ability to imaginatively conjure such a spirit world means that the imagination is metaphysically in tune with it. Death and the imagination became aligned, but the introduction of aesthetic factors increasingly compromised the possibility of representing the genuine feelings of loss provoked by death.

That the creative evocation of the dead foregrounded issues of aesthetic construction was seen in Charlotte Smith, Ann Radcliffe and Mary Shelley, all of whom, at different levels of explicitness, wrestle with the tension between natural states of feeling (such as grief and melancholy) and the rhetorical construction of emotion in an emerging Gothic aesthetic.

The Romantic Gothic explores the role of the writer in this Gothic discourse about death that, in its establishment of a Gothic iconography, also reaches out to an implied reader who can interpret the type of codes and symbols that characterise this discourse. The dead also occupy an unusual space in the Gothic because they repeatedly fail to function as sources of horror. By looking at these images, we see how they decentre our way of thinking about the Gothic by challenging any simple consideration of 'good' and 'evil' (which also has implications for the Freudian uncanny). How to write about death becomes progressively replaced by an emphasis on the reader, who appears within the text as an interpreter of the Gothic events with which they are confronted. This is clear in Poe, who uses his narrators, as in 'Mesmeric Revelation' (1844) and 'The Facts in the Case of M. Valdemar' (1845), as figures who initiate a quasi-scientific enquiry. How to write about death becomes supplanted by how to read and interpret the signs of death, and such issues had, as we have seen, ramifications for future forms of Gothic writing. Eliot's 'The Lifted Veil' (1859) illustrates this shift within the Gothic culture as we witness a would-be writer, the dying Latimer, becoming turned into a reader who knows how his story will end.

Dickens to a significant degree both develops and complicates the narrative about death during the period. For Dickens, a death wish is generated by scenes of public execution, and this is a genuinely metaphysical plight rather than a rhetorically produced one. The model of trauma developed by Dickens is further reflected in domestic spaces that become reconstituted in the graveyard family plot, where the post-mortem family is reunited. Dickens's view of death is framed by religious concerns about the illegitimate resurrection of the criminal dead through media accounts of their last words and execution, when it should be the loving dead that are memorialised. Dickens brings these issues together in his accounts of the dream when arguing that it is in the unconscious that we potentially discover our criminal propensities (the death wish) but also our capacity to create. Ultimately, Dickens also emphasises the problem of decoding dreams and their images of death and creativity, and we see these issues coming together in *The Mystery of Edwin Drood* (1870), where death, dreams and self-incrimination suggest that the social contract lies in fragments. The novel also highlights the importance of forms of knowing, which anticipates the models of epistemic enquiry that characterise a strand of the *fin de siècle* Gothic.

Ways of knowing the dead through love reworks an idea of empathy as a mode of engaging with the Other. Love, however, as we saw in Haggard and Stoker, can be a troubling emotion as it can confuse (as it does in *The Jewel of Seven Stars* (1903, revised 1912)) rather than enlighten. Decoding the dead in that instance involved looking at the wider political and religious context of modern and ancient Egypt. The femme fatale enabled an engagement with the past that generated epistemic considerations that were explored in quasi-scientific contexts in the final chapter.

We have seen how death and creativity were culturally linked in the instance of the Gothic of the long nineteenth century, and how death became subject to various forms of figuration. Death might seem to be an ultimately ineffable state, but the discourse of death as it progresses from eighteenth-century empathy to late-nineteenth-century science suggests that death is potentially knowable.

Finally, I want to briefly sketch some issues that lie beyond the historical scope of this enquiry in order to suggest areas for future research. This study stops before the First World War, when the mass deaths it occasioned intensified a popular interest in spiritualism. The issues about writers and readers addressed in this study did not go away, however, as witnessed by Oliver Lodge's best-selling *Raymond* (1916), which evidenced a concern with decoding spirit messages relating to Lodge's son, who was killed on the Western Front in 1915. Lodge claims that the spirit of F. W. H. Myers appeared at a number of seances and was helping Raymond's spirit to communicate. The spirit world of *Raymond* reworks Myers's idea of a subliminal realm that can be occupied by spirits who commune with our inner world, leading Raymond to claim that in the spiritual realm, 'There are books ... not yet published on the earth plane ... these books will be produced ... the matter in them will be impressed on the brain of some man, he supposes an author'.[1] These ideas are not necessarily specific to the war (although there is some discussion on whether the spirit, like the body, can be blown apart), and draw upon Edwardian spiritualist contexts that would influence a later culture of Modernism.

As discussed in Chapter 6, Charles Ko has noted that Myers's model of inter-psychic communication was reflected in the multi-vocal intertextual Modernist writings of James Joyce.[2] Helen Sword has also claimed that ideas about automatic writing, through which the dead communicate via a medium, had an influence on T. S. Eliot, Ezra Pound and W. B. Yeats and H. D. Sword notes that automatic texts:

> engage with many of the dominant tropes of literary modernism – linguistic playfulness, decenterings of consciousness, fracturing of conventional gender roles – and betray a characteristically modernist obsession with all

things textual: reading, writing, literature, authorship, publication, libraries, and even the discourses and methodologies of literary criticism.[3]

Sword's account of the Modernist text could equally stand as an account of the textual complexities we witnessed in Arthur Machen. This type of 'fracturing' is a feature of the Gothic as much as it is of the Modernist text. The Gothic subject mapped here is one that is embedded in narratives about death, and this becomes re-routed into Modernism by the implicit Gothic images that so often underpin Modernist writings.[4] This is another way of acknowledging that the Modernist self is constructed out of discourses that, like Myers's, suggest that the subject gains a superior understanding of the world through predominantly literary encounters. How to read and how to write are therefore given a particular intensity in Modernism.

How a Gothic aesthetic of death becomes reframed through a Modernist inheritance of the traumas generated by the First World War would broaden our understanding of the Gothic. Images of the dead and the dying culturally persist and how they appear in a post-war Gothic *and* shape the Gothic presence that lurks within Modernism would be one way in which to advance this literary history of death.

Notes

1 Sir Oliver Lodge, *Raymond* (London: Methuen, 1917 [1916]), p. 209.
2 Charles Ko, 'Subliminal Consciousness', *The Review of English Studies*, 59:242 (2007), 740–65.
3 Helen Sword, *Ghostwriting Modernism* (Ithaca, NY and London: Cornell University Press, 2002), p. 11. Although Sword acknowledges that spirit writing lacks the adventurous experimental qualities of the Modernist text, she does see a shared in interest in radical ideas about literary production.
4 See Andrew Smith and Jeff Wallace (eds), *Gothic Modernism*, (Basingstoke: Palgrave, 2001), for a fuller account of these engagements.

Bibliography

Abraham, Nicholas and Maria Torok, *The Wolf Man's Magic Word: A Cryptonymy* (Minneapolis: University of Minneapolis Press, 1986 [1976]).

Albrecht, Thomas, 'Sympathy and Telepathy: The Problem of Ethics in George Eliot's *The Lifted Veil*', *ELH*, 73:2 (Summer 2006), 437–63.

Ariès, Philippe, *The Hour of Our Death*, trans. Helen Weaver (New York: Random House, 2008).

Arnold, Matthew, 'Dover Beach', in *The Norton Anthology of English Literature: The Victorian Age*, ed. Catherine Robson and Carol T. Christ (New York and London: W. W. Norton, 2012), pp. 1,387–8.

Baldridge, Cates, 'Voyeuristic Rebellion: Lockwood's Dream and the Reader of "Wuthering Heights"', *Studies in the Novel*, 20:3 (Fall 1988), 274–87.

Bernard, Catherine A., 'Dickens and Victorian Dream Theory', *Annals of the New York Academy of Sciences*, 360 (April 1981), special issue on 'Victorian Science and Victorian Values: Literary Perspectives', 197–216.

Bernstein, Susan David, 'Transatlantic Magnetism: Eliot's "The Lifted Veil" and Alcott's Sensation Stories', in Jennifer Phegley, John Cyril Barton and Kristin N. Huston (eds), *Transatlantic Sensations* (Ashgate: Aldershot, 2012), pp. 183–206.

Blair, Robert, 'The Grave', in *Roach's Beauties of the Poets of Great Britain* (London: J. Roach, 1794), pp. 25–53.

Bloom, Clive, *Reading Poe, Reading Freud: The Romantic Imagination in Crisis* (Basingstoke: Macmillan, 1988).

Boaden, James, *The Man of Two Lives: A Narrative Written by Himself* (London: Henry Colburn, 1828).

Bronfen, Elisabeth, *Over Her Dead Body: Death, Femininity and the Aesthetic* (Manchester: Manchester University Press, 1992).

Brontë, Emily, *Wuthering Heights*, ed. and Introd. Pauline Nestor (Penguin: Harmondsworth, 2003).

Bulfin, Ailise, 'The Fiction of Gothic Egypt and British Imperial Paranoia: The Curse of the Suez Canal', *English Literature in Transition, 1880–1920*, 54:4 (2011), 411–43.

Burke, Edmund, *A Philosophical Enquiry into the Origins of Our Ideas of the Sublime and the Beautiful*, ed. Adam Phillips (Oxford: Oxford University Press, 1998 [1757]).

Burton, Robert, *The Anatomy of Melancholy* (1621), in *The Nature of Melancholy: From Aristotle to Kristeva*, ed. Jennifer Radden (Oxford: Oxford University Press, 2000).

Castle, Terry, 'The Spectralization of the Other in *The Mysteries of Udolpho*', in *The Female Thermometer: Eighteenth-Century Culture and the Invention of the Unconscious* (Oxford: Oxford University Press, 1995), pp. 120–39.

Chadwick, Edwin, *A Supplementary Report on the Results of a Special Inquiry into the Practice of Interment in Towns* (London: Clowes and Sons, 1843).

Crookes, William, 'Address', in *Report of the Sixty-Eighth Meeting of the British Association for the Advancement of Science, Held in Bristol in September 1898* (London: John Murray, 1899), pp. 3–33.

Csengei, Ildiko, *Sympathy, Sensibility and the Literature of Feeling in the Eighteenth Century* (Basingstoke: Palgrave, 2012).

Cunningham, Valentine, 'Dickens and Christianity', in David Paroissien (ed.), *A Companion to Dickens* (Oxford: Blackwell, 2008), pp. 255–76.

Curran, Stuart, 'Romantic Elegiac Hybridity', in Karen Weisman (ed.), *The Oxford Handbook of the Elegy* (Oxford: Oxford University Press, 2010), pp. 238–50.

Davis, Michael, 'Mind and Matter in *The Picture of Dorian Gray*', *Victorian Literature and Culture*, 41 (2013), 547–60.

Davison, Carol Margaret, 'The Brontës and the Death Question', unpublished article.

Deane, Bradley, 'Mummy Fiction and the Occupation of Egypt: Imperial Striptease', *English Literature in Transition, 1880–1920*, 51:4 (2008), 381–410.

Derbyshire, Val, '"Holmes and the Adventure of the London Burial Grounds": Discourses of Death in the Fin-de-Siècle' (MA essay, University of Sheffield, 2014).

Derrida, Jacques, *The Death Penalty*, ed. Geoffrey Bennington, Marc Crépon and Thomas Dutoit, trans. Peggy Kamuf (Chicago and London: University of Chicago Press, 2014), vol. I.

Dickens, Charles, *American Notes for General Circulation*, ed. John S. Whitley and Arnold Goldman (Harmondsworth: Penguin, 1985).

—— 'Capital Punishment', *The Daily News* (28 February 1846).

—— 'Capital Punishment', *The Daily News* (9 March 1846).

—— 'Capital Punishment', *The Daily News* (13 March 1846).

—— 'Capital Punishment', *The Daily News* (16 March 1846).

—— Letter titled 'Mr Charles Dickens and the Execution of the Mannings', *The Times* (13 November 1849).

—— Letter to *The Times* (19 November 1849).

—— *Dombey and Son*, ed. Peter Fairclough (Harmondsworth: Penguin, 1975).

—— 'Dreams', *Household Words* (8 March 1851), pp. 566–72.

—— *Great Expectations*, ed. Angus Calder (Harmondsworth: Penguin, 1986).

—— 'Lying Awake', *Household Words* (30 October 1852), in *'Gone Astray' and Other Papers from* Household Words, ed. Michael Slater (London: J. M. Dent, 1998), pp. 88–95.

—— *The Mystery of Edwin Drood*, ed. Arthur J. Cox (Harmondsworth: Penguin, 1974).

—— *Oliver Twist* (Harmondsworth: Penguin, 1985).

—— *Pictures from Italy*, ed. Kate Flint (Harmondsworth: Penguin, 1998).

—— 'Review: The Night Side of Nature', in *The Examiner* (26 February 1848), in *Dickens' Journalism*, ed. Michael Slater (London: J. M. Dent, 1996), pp. 80–9.

—— 'A Sleep to Startle Us', *Household Words* (13 March 1852), pp. 577–80.

—— *A Tale of Two Cities*, ed. George Woodcock (Harmondsworth: Penguin, 1989).

Doyle, Arthur Conan, *The History of Spiritualism*, 2 vols (Teddington: The Echo Library, 2006 [1926]), vol. II.

Drake, Nathan, 'On Gothic Superstition', in *Literary Hours, or Sketches Critical and Narrative*, 2 vols (New York: Garland, 1800), vol. I, pp. 137–49.

Drummond, Henry, *Natural Law in the Spiritual World* (London: Hodder & Stoughton, 1884).

Duff, William, *An Essay on Original Genius and Its Various Modes of Exertion in Philosophy and the Fine Arts, Particularly in Poetry* (London: Dilley, 1767).

Eliot, George, 'The Lifted Veil', in *The Lifted Veil; Brother Jacob*, ed. and Introd. Helen Small (Oxford: Oxford University Press, 1999), pp. 3–43.

—— 'The Natural History of German Life', in *Essays of George Eliot*, ed. Thomas Pinney (New York: Columbia University Press, 1963), pp. 266–99.

Empson, William, *Some Versions of Pastoral* (London: Chatto & Windus, 1935).

Evans, Anthony, 'Mesmerism and the Electric Age: From Poe to Edison', in Martin Willis and Catherine Wynne (eds), *Victorian Literary Mesmerism* (Amsterdam and New York: Rodopi, 2006), pp. 61–82.

Falk, Doris V., 'Poe and the Power of Animal Magnetism', *PMLA*, 84:3 (1969), 536–46.

Ferguson, Christine, 'Decadence as Scientific Fulfilment', *PMLA*, 117:3 (2002), 465–78.

Ferguson, Frances, 'Romantic Memory', *Studies in Romanticism*, 35:4 (Winter 1996), 509–33.

Flint, Kate, 'Blood, Bodies, and *The Lifted Veil*', *Nineteenth-Century Literature*, 51:4 (March 1977), 455–73.

Forlini, Stefania, 'Modern Narratives and Decadent Things in Arthur Machen's *The Three Impostors*', *English Literature in Transition, 1880–1920*, 55:4 (2012), 479–98.

Franklin, J. Jeffrey, 'The Counter-Invasion of Britain by Buddhism in Marie Corelli's *A Romance of Two Worlds* and H. Rider Haggard's *Ayesha: The Return of She*', *Victorian Literature and Culture*, 31:1 (2003), 19–42.

Freeman, Nicholas, 'Arthur Machen: Ecstasy and Epiphany', *Literature & Theology*, 24:3 (September 2010), 242–55.

Freud, Sigmund, *The Interpretation of Dreams*, The Penguin Freud Library, vol. IV, ed. James Strachey (Harmondsworth: Penguin, 1991).

—— 'Mourning and Melancholia' (1917), in *On Metapsychology: The Theory of Psychoanalysis*, The Penguin Freud Library, vol. XI, trans. James Strachey, ed. Angela Richards (Harmondsworth: Penguin, 1991), pp. 251–72.

—— 'A Special Type of Choice of Object Made by Men (Contributions to the Psychology of Love I)', in *On Sexuality*, The Penguin Freud Library, vol. VII, ed. Angela Richards and Albert Dickson (Harmondsworth: Penguin, 1991), pp. 227–42.

—— 'The Uncanny', in *Art and Literature: Jensen's 'Gradiva', Leonardo da Vinci and Other Works*, The Penguin Freud Library, vol. XIV, ed. Albert Dickson (Harmondsworth: Penguin, 1990), pp. 335–76.

Galvan, Jill, 'The Narrator as Medium in George Eliot's "The Lifted Veil"', *Victorian Studies*, 48:2 (Winter 2006), 240–8.

Gange, David, 'Religion and Science in late Nineteenth-Century British Egyptology', *The Historical Journal*, 49:4 (December 2006), 1083–103.

Geerken, Ingrid, '"The Dead Are Not Annihilated": Mortal Regret in "Wuthering Heights"', *Journal of Narrative Theory*, 34:3 (Fall 2004), 373–406.

Gifford, Terry, *Pastoral* (London and New York: Routledge, 1999).

Gilbert, Sandra M. and Susan Gubar, *The Madwoman in the Attic* (New Haven, CT and London: Yale University Press, 2000).

Gillman, Susan K. and Robert L. Patten, 'Dickens: Doubles: Twain: Twins', *Nineteenth-Century Fiction*, 39:4 (March 1985), 441–58.

Godwin, William, 'Essay on Sepulchres', in *Political and Philosophical Writings of William Godwin*, 7 vols, ed. Mark Philip (London: Pickering & Chatto, 1993), vol. VI, pp. 1–30.

Gold, Barri J., 'Embracing the Corpse: Discursive Recycling in H. Rider Haggard's *She*', *English Literature in Transition, 1880–1920*, 38:3 (January 1995), 305–27.

Gomel, Elana, 'Oscar Wilde, *The Picture of Dorian Gray*, and the (Un)death of the Author', *Narrative*, 12:1 (January 2004), 74–92.

Gray, Thomas, 'Elegy Written in a Country Church-Yard', in *Gray and Collins: Poetical Works*, ed. Roger Lonsdale (Oxford: Oxford University Press, 1977), pp. 34–9.

—— 'Lines on Dr Robert Smith', in *Gray and Collins: Poetical Works*, ed. Roger Lonsdale (Oxford: Oxford University Press, 1977), p. 83.

Grimes, Hilary, *The Late Victorian Gothic: Mental Science, the Uncanny and Scenes of Writing* (Farnham: Ashgate, 2010).

Gurney, Edmund, 'The Nature of Evidence in Matters Extraordinary', *National Review*, 22 (1884), 472–91.

Haggard, Henry Rider, *Ayesha: The Return of She* (Polegate: Pulp Publications, 1998).

—— *She* (Ware: Wordsworth Editions, 1995).

Bibliography

Harrison, Mary-Catherine, 'The Paradox of Fiction and the Ethics of Empathy: Reconceiving Dickens's Realism', *Narrative*, 16:3 (October 2008), 256–78.

Hazlitt, William, 'Byron', in *The Spirit of the Age* (London: Henry Colburn, 1825), pp. 160–85.

—— 'On the Fear of Death', in *Table-Talk* (London: Dent, 1942), pp. 321–30.

—— 'On Will-Making', in *Table-Talk* (London: Dent, 1942), pp. 113–21.

Herbert, Christopher, 'Vampire Religion', *Representations*, 79:1 (Summer 2002), 100–21.

Hervey, James, *Meditations and Contemplations* (Bungay: Brightly and Child, 1816).

Hoeveler, Diane Long, *Gothic Riffs: Secularizing the Uncanny in the European Imaginary, 1780–1820* (Columbus: Ohio State University Press, 2010).

Hogle, Jerrold E., 'Elegy and the Gothic: The Common Grounds', in Karen Weisman (ed.), *The Oxford Handbook of the Elegy* (Oxford: Oxford University Press, 2010), pp. 565–84.

Holden, Philip, 'Castle, Coffin, Stomach: *Dracula* and the Banality of the Occult', *Victorian Literature and Culture*, 29:2 (2001), 469–85.

Hole, Stephen, 'Ode to Terror', in *Gothic Documents: A Sourcebook 1700–1820*, ed. E. J. Clery and Robert Miles (Manchester: Manchester University Press, 2000), p. 139.

Hotz, Mary Elizabeth, *Literary Remains: Representations of Death and Burial in Victorian England* (Albany: State University of New York, 2009).

Hughes, William, *The Devil's Trick: Hypnotism and the Victorian Popular Imagination* (Manchester: Manchester University Press, 2015).

Hume, David, *A Treatise of Human Nature*, ed. L. A. Selby-Bigge and P. H. Nidditch (Oxford: Oxford University Press, 1978).

James, Simon J., 'The Mystery of Edwin Drood', in David Paroissien (ed.), *A Companion to Dickens* (Oxford: Blackwell, 2008), pp. 444–51.

John, Juliet, *Dickens's Villains: Melodrama, Character, Popular Culture* (Oxford: Oxford University Press, 2003).

Jones, Darryl, 'Borderlands: Spiritualism and the Occult in Fin de Siècle and Edwardian Welsh and Irish Horror', *Irish Studies Review*, 17:1 (2009), 31–44.

Kennedy, J. Gerald, *Poe, Death and the Life of Writing* (New Haven, CT and London: Yale University Press, 1987).

King, Thomas A., 'Performing "Akimbo": Queer Pride and Epistemological Prejudice', in Moe Meyer (ed.), *The Politics and Poetics of Camp* (London: Routledge, 1994), pp. 23–50.

Kipling, Rudyard, 'Wireless', in *Traffics and Discoveries* (London: Pocket Macmillan Edition, 1904), pp. 213–39.

Ko, Charles, 'Subliminal Consciousness', *The Review of English Studies*, 59:242 (2007), 740–65.

Lankester, Edwin, *Degeneration: A Chapter in Darwinism* (London: Macmillan, 1880).

Laycock, Thomas, *A Chapter on Some Organic Laws of Personal and Ancestral Memory* (Lewes: George P. Bacon, Steam Printing Offices, 1875).

Lee, Vernon, 'Faustus and Helena: Notes on the Supernatural in Art' (1880), in *Hauntings and Other Fantastic Tales*, ed. Catherine Maxwell and Patricia Pulham (Peterborough: Broadview Press, 2006), pp. 291–319.

Lewes, George Henry, *The Physiology of Common Life*, 2 vols (Edinburgh and London: Blackwood, 1860).

Litvack, Leon, '*Dickens's Dream* and the Conception of Character', *The Dickensian*, 103:1 (Spring 2007), 5–36.

Lloyd Smith, Allan, 'The Phantoms of *Drood* and *Rebecca*: The Uncanny Reencountered through Abraham and Torok's "Cryptonymy"', *Poetics Today*, 13:2 (Summer 1992), 285–308.

Lodge, Sir Oliver, *Raymond* (London: Methuen, 1917).

Lootens, Tricia, 'Fear of Furniture: Commodity Gothicism and the Teaching of Victorian Literature', in Diane Long Hoeveler and Tamar Heller (eds), *Gothic Fiction: The British and American Traditions* (New York: MLA, 2003), pp. 148–53.

Lowe, Bridgid, 'Dombey and Son', in David Paroissien (ed.), *A Companion to Dickens* (Oxford: Blackwell, 2008), pp. 358–68.

Luckhurst, Roger, *The Invention of Telepathy 1870–1901* (Oxford: Oxford University Press, 2002).

Machen, Arthur, 'A Fragment of Life', in *The White People and Other Stories*, ed. S. T. Joshi (Hayward: Chaosium, 2003), pp. 99–174.

—— *The Great God Pan* in *The Great God Pan, The Shining Pyramid, The White People* (Cardigan: Parthian, 2010), pp. 1–76.

—— *Hieroglyphics: A Note upon Ecstasy in Literature* (London: Martin Secker, 1902).

—— *The Hill of Dreams* (Cardigan: Parthian, 2010).

—— *The Three Impostors* (New York: Dover, 2007).

Mansel, H. L., 'Sensation Novels', *Quarterly Review* (April 1863), 481–514.

Marsh, Richard, *The Beetle*, ed. Julian Wolfreys (Peterborough: Broadview, 2004).

Matthews, Samantha, *Poetical Remains: Poets' Graves, Bodies, and Books in the Nineteenth Century* (Oxford: Oxford University Press, 2004).

Mellor, Anne K., '"Anguish No Cessation Knows": Elegy and the British Woman Poet', in Karen Weisman (ed.), *The Oxford Handbook of the Elegy* (Oxford: Oxford University Press, 2010), pp. 442–62.

—— *Mary Shelley: Her Life, Her Fiction, Her Monsters* (London: Routledge: 1990).

—— *Romanticism and Gender* (London: Routledge, 1993).

Meyer, Moe, 'Under the Sign of Wilde: An Archaeology of Posing', in Moe Meyer (ed.), *The Politics and Poetics of Camp* (London: Routledge, 1994), pp. 75–109.

Mighall, Robert, 'Dickens and the Gothic', in David Paroissien (ed.), *A Companion to Dickens* (Oxford: Blackwell, 2008), pp. 81–96.
—— *A Geography of Victorian Gothic: Mapping History's Nightmares* (Oxford: Oxford University Press, 1999).
Mitchell, Charles, '*The Mystery of Edwin Drood*: The Interior and Exterior of Self', *ELH*, 33:2 (June 1966), 228–46.
Morton, Timothy, 'Mary Shelley as Cultural Critic', in Esther Schor (ed.), *The Cambridge Companion to Mary Shelley* (Cambridge: Cambridge University Press, 2003), pp. 259–73.
Myers, Frederic W. H., *Human Personality and Its Survival of Bodily Death* (London: Longmans, 1907).
Noakes, Richard, 'Haunted Thoughts of the Careful Experimentalist: Psychical Research and the Troubles of Experimental Physics', *Studies in History and Philosophy of Biological and Biomedical Sciences*, 48 (2014), 46–56.
—— 'Spiritualism, Science and the Supernatural in Mid-Victorian Britain', in Nicola Brown, Carolyn Burdett and Pamela Thurschwell (eds), *The Victorian Supernatural* (Cambridge: Cambridge University Press, 2004), pp. 23–43.
O'Leary, Joanna Shawn Brigid, 'Two for the Price of One?: Twins and the Anxieties of (Re)production in Dickens', *English: Journal of the English Association*, 62:238 (2013), 275–93.
Owen, Alex, *The Place of Enchantment: British Occultism and the Culture of the Modern* (Chicago: University of Chicago Press, 2004).
Parisot, Eric, *Graveyard Poetry: Religion, Aesthetics and the Mid-Eighteenth-Century Poetic Condition* (Farnham: Ashgate, 2013).
Pfau, Thomas, 'Mourning Modernity: Classical Antiquity, Romantic Theory, and Elegiac Form', in Karen Weisman (ed.), *The Oxford Handbook of the Elegy* (Oxford: Oxford University Press, 2010), pp. 546–64.
—— *Romantic Moods: Paranoia, Trauma, and Melancholy, 1790–1840* (Baltimore, MD: Johns Hopkins University Press, 2005).
Pinch, Adela, *Strange Fits of Passion: Epistemologies of Emotion, Hume to Austen* (Stanford, CA: Stanford University Press, 1996).
Poe, Edgar Allan, 'Editorial Miscellany', *Broadway Journal*, 2:23 (13 December 1845).
—— *Eureka: An Essay on the Material and Spiritual Universe*, in *The Science Fiction of Edgar Allan Poe*, ed. and Introd. Howard Beaver (Harmondsworth: Penguin, 1979), pp. 205–309.
—— 'The Facts in the Case of M. Valdemar', in *Edgar Allan Poe: Selected Writings*, ed. and Introd. David Galloway (Harmondsworth: Penguin, 1982), pp. 350–9.
—— 'Ligeia', in *The Complete Tales and Poems of Edgar Allan Poe* (Harmondsworth: Penguin, 1982), pp. 654–66.
—— 'Mesmeric Revelation', in *The Complete Tales and Poems of Edgar Allan Poe* (Harmondsworth: Penguin, 1982), pp. 88–95.

—— 'Morella', in *The Complete Tales and Poems of Edgar Allan Poe* (Harmondsworth: Penguin, 1982), pp. 667-71.
—— 'The Murders in the Rue Morgue', in *The Complete Tales and Poems of Edgar Allan Poe* (Harmondsworth: Penguin, 1982), pp. 141-68.
—— 'The Philosophy of Composition', in *Edgar Allan Poe: Selected Writings*, ed. and Introd. David Galloway (Harmondsworth: Penguin, 1982), pp. 480-92.
—— 'A Tale of the Ragged Mountains', in *The Complete Tales and Poems of Edgar Allan Poe* (Harmondsworth: Penguin, 1982), pp. 679-87.
—— '*Twice-Told Tales*, a Review', *Graham's Magazine*, 20 (May 1842), 298.
Punter, David, *Rapture: Literature, Addiction, Secrecy* (Brighton: Sussex Academic Press, 2009).
Radcliffe, Ann, *The Mysteries of Udolpho*, Introd. Terry Castle, ed. Bonamy Dobrée (Oxford: Oxford University Press, 1998 [1794]).
—— 'On the Supernatural in Poetry', in *Gothic Documents: A Sourcebook 1700-1820*, ed. E. J. Clery and Robert Miles (Manchester: Manchester University Press, 2000), pp. 163-71.
Rogers, Samuel, 'Ode to Superstition', in *The Pleasures of Memory* (Boston: Manning and Loring, 1795), pp. 93-104.
—— *The Pleasures of Memory* (Boston: Manning and Loring, 1795).
Rugg, Julie, 'Constructing the Grave: Competing Burial Ideals in Nineteenth-Century England', *Social History*, 38:3 (2013), 328-45.
—— 'Lawn Cemeteries: The Emergence of a New Landscape of Death', *Urban History*, 33:2 (August 2006), 213-33.
Sacks, Peter M., *The English Elegy: Studies in the Genre from Spenser to Yeats* (Baltimore, MD: Johns Hopkins University Press, 1985).
Sandy, Mark, *Romanticism, Memory, and Mourning* (Aldershot: Ashgate, 2013).
Schoene-Harwood, Berthold, *Writing Men: Literary Masculinities from 'Frankenstein' to the New Man* (Edinburgh: Edinburgh University Press, 1999).
Schor, Esther, *Bearing the Dead: The British Culture of Mourning from the Enlightenment to Victoria* (Princeton, NJ: Princeton University Press, 1994).
Scott, Anne, '"Visible Incarnations of the Unseen": Henry Drummond and the Practice of Typological Exegesis', *The British Journal for the History of Science*, 37:4 (December 2004), 435-54.
Shelley, Mary, *Frankenstein; or, the Modern Prometheus*, ed. and Introd. Maurice Hindle (Harmondsworth: Penguin, 1985 [1831]).
—— 'On Ghosts', in *Gothic Documents: A Sourcebook 1700-1820*, ed. E. J. Clery and Robert Miles (Manchester: Manchester University Press, 2000), pp. 280-5.
Shortt, S. E. D., 'Physicians and Psychics: The Anglo-American Medical Response to Spiritualism, 1870-1890', *Journal of the History of Medicine*, 39 (July 1984), 339-55.
Small, Helen, 'Introduction', in *The Lifted Veil; Brother Jacob*, ed. and Intro. Helen Small (Oxford: Oxford University Press, 1999), pp. ix-xxxviii.
Smith, Adam, *Theory of Moral Sentiments* (Edinburgh: W. Creech, 1813).

Smith, Andrew, 'Beyond Colonialism: Death and the Body in H. Rider Haggard', in Andrew Smith and William Hughes (eds), *Empire and the Gothic: The Politics of Genre* (Basingstoke: Palgrave, 2003), pp. 103–17.

Smith, Andrew, 'Colonial Ghosts: Mimicking Dickens in America', in Avril Horner and Sue Zlosnik (eds), *Le Gothic* (Basingstoke: Palgrave, 2008), pp. 185–200.

—— *The Ghost Story 1840–1920: A Cultural History* (Manchester: Manchester University Press, 2010).

—— *Gothic Radicalism: Literature, Philosophy and Psychoanalysis in the Nineteenth Century* (Basingstoke: Macmillan, 2000).

——'Love, Freud, and the Female Gothic: Bram Stoker's *The Jewel of Seven Stars*', *Gothic Studies*, 6:1 (May 2004), special issue on 'Female Gothic', ed. Andrew Smith and Diana Wallace, 80–9.

—— *Victorian Demons: Medicine, Masculinity and the Gothic at the Fin de Siècle* (Manchester: Manchester University Press, 2004).

—— 'Victorian Gothic Death', in Andrew Smith and William Hughes (eds), *The Victorian Gothic: An Edinburgh Companion* (Edinburgh: Edinburgh University Press, 2010), pp. 156–69.

Smith, Andrew and Jeff Wallace (eds), *Gothic Modernisms* (Basingstoke: Palgrave, 2001).

Smith, Charlotte, *Elegiac Sonnets* (London: T. Cadell, 1789).

Stewart, Garrett, *Death Sentences: Styles of Dying in British Fiction* (London: Harvard University Press, 1984).

Stoker, Bram, *Dracula*, ed. and Introd. Roger Luckhurst (Oxford: Oxford University Press, 2011).

—— *The Jewel of Seven Stars*, Introd. David Glover (Oxford: Oxford University Press, 1996).

—— *The Lady of the Shroud*, Introd. Ruth Robbins (Stroud: Sutton, 1994).

Sword, Helen, *Ghostwriting Modernism* (Ithaca, NY and London: Cornell University Press, 2002).

Thackeray, William M., 'On Going to See a Man Hanged', *Fraser's Magazine*, 22 (August 1840), 150–8.

Thompson, G. R., 'Unity, Death, and Nothingness: Poe's "Romantic Skepticism"', *PMLA*, 85:2 (March 1970), 297–300.

Warton, Thomas, *The Pleasures of Melancholy* (London: R. Dodsley, 1747).

Wells, H. G., 'Zoological Retrogression', *Gentleman's Magazine*, 271 (1891), 246–53.

Westover, Paul, *Necromanticism: Traveling to Meet the Dead, 1750–1860* (Basingstoke: Palgrave Macmillan, 2012).

White, Henry Kirke, 'Ode to H. Fuseli, Esq., R.A., on Seeing Engravings from His Designs', in *Gothic Documents: A Sourcebook 1700–1820*, ed. E. J. Clery and Robert Miles (Manchester: Manchester University Press, 2000), p. 144.

Wilde, Oscar, *The Picture of Dorian Gray*, ed. Peter Ackroyd (Penguin: Harmondsworth, 1985).

Wolfreys, Julian, *Victorian Hauntings: Spectrality, Gothic, the Uncanny and Literature* (Basingstoke: Palgrave, 2001).

Wood, Claire, *Dickens and the Business of Death* (Cambridge: Cambridge University Press, 2015).

Wordsworth, William, 'Lines Written a Few Miles above Tintern Abbey', in *William Wordsworth: Selected Poetry*, ed. and Introd. Stephen Gill and Duncan Wu (Oxford: Oxford University Press, 2008), pp. 57-61.

Wynne, Catherine, 'Bram Stoker, Geneviève Ward and *The Lady of the Shroud*: Gothic Weddings and Performing Vampires', *English Literature in Transition, 1880-1920*, 49:3 (2006), 251-71.

Young, Edward, 'Conjectures on Original Composition', in *Critical Theory since Plato*, ed. Hazard Adams and Leroy Searle (Andover: Cengage, 2005), pp. 338-47.

Young, Edward, *Night Thoughts on Life, Death and Immortality* (London: Baynes and Son, 1824).

Index

Note: 'n' after a page reference indicates the number of the note on that page.

Abraham, Nicholas 54, 131
Albrecht, Thomas 94–5
Ariès, Phillippe 78, 79
Arnold, Matthew
   'Dover Beach' 151

Baldridge, Cates 90
Bentley, Richard 13, 14
   see also Gray, Thomas
Bernard, Catherine A. 129, 130
Bernstein, Susan David 96
Blair, Robert
   'The Grave' 6, 22–4, 27, 29, 31, 33, 35, 37
Blake, William 171
Bloom, Clive 104n15
Boaden, James 64
   The Man of Two Lives 6–7, 44–5, 64–71, 76, 81
Breuer, Josef 171
Bronfen, Elizabeth 83, 84, 85, 87
Brontë, Emily 89
   Wuthering Heights 3, 7, 59, 75, 89–94, 95, 97, 98, 99, 101, 102
Bulfin, Ailise 142
Burke, Edmund 6
   Philosophical Enquiry 17–18, 19, 26, 27, 36, 38, 45, 48, 70, 71, 86, 95, 107, 108–9, 110, 111, 119, 180, 193
Burton, Richard
   Anatomy of Melancholy 54
Byron, George Gordon 70

capital punishment 106, 108–13, 125, 126, 133
Castle, Terry 4, 44, 52–4, 61
Chadwick, Edwin 120–3
Clifford, W.K. 160
Coleridge, Samuel Taylor 172
   'Kubla Khan' 128
Crookes, William 169–70
Csengei, Ildiko 19
Cunningham, Valentine 115
Curran, Stuart 52

Dante 39, 40
Darwin, Charles 166, 167
Davis, Michael 159–60
De Man, Paul 15
Deane, Bradley 142, 143
decadence 179
Derrida, Jacques 110–1, 115, 166, 155
Dickens, Charles 3, 7–8, 106–37
   American Notes 124–5, 126
   Bleak House 107, 115
   A Christmas Carol 107, 123
   Dombey and Son 123–4
   Great Expectations 119, 120, 126, 130
   The Mystery of Edwin Drood 8, 107, 130–3, 138, 194
   Oliver Twist 7, 113–9, 120, 121–2
   A Tale of Two Cities 8, 115, 118–9, 125
Doyle, Arthur Conan 164–5
Drake, Nathan 2, 3, 6, 26
   'On Gothic Superstition' 2, 16, 34

Index

dreams 127–30
Drummond, Henry
   Natural Law in the Spiritual World 21, 164, 165–8, 172, 176, 178, 185
Duff, William 2, 6
   An Essay on Original Genius 34, 35

elegy 6, 11–43, 49, 50, 93, 193
Eliot, George 71, 76, 107
   'The Lifted Veil' 3, 7, 75, 94–9, 101, 102, 126, 194
   'The Natural History of German Life' 94, 95, 99, 107–8
Eliot, T.S. 195
Empson, William 30
Evans, Anthony 99

Falk, Doris V. 76, 77, 82
Ferguson, Christine 176, 178, 179
Fergusson, Frances 45–6, 48
Flint, Kate 97–8
Forlini, Stefania 182–3, 184, 185
Franklin, J. Jeffrey 148–9
Freeman, Nicholas 180
Freud, Sigmund 5, 12, 14, 15, 52, 123, 144, 170, 171
   The Interpretation of Dreams 144
   'Mourning and Melancholia' 72n15
   'The Uncanny' 4, 85–6, 126, 194
   see also uncanniness
Fuseli, Henry 39–40, 66, 69

Galvan, Jill 97
Gange, David 143
Genet, Jean
   Our Lady of the Flowers 116, 155
Geerken, Ingrid 91, 92, 93
Gifford, Terry 30, 31, 36
Gillman, Susan K. 125, 126
Goethe, Johann Wolfgang Von
   The Sorrows of Young Werther 52, 55, 57–8, 62
Gold, Barri J. 141, 142, 143
Gomel, Elana 158–9
graveyard poetry 11–43, 187
graveyards 119–23, 132, 187
Gray, Thomas 30, 43n28

'Elegy Written in a Country Church-Yard' 6, 13, 14, 29, 30–1, 36, 37, 44
Grimes, Hilary 191n12
Gurney, Edmund 170

Haggard, Henry Rider 3, 9, 160, 195
   Ayesha: The Return of She 8, 146, 148–52, 160–1
   She 8, 139–44, 147, 149, 150, 151, 155
Harrison, Mary-Catherine 107
Hazlitt, William 70–1
Hegel, Georg Wilhelm Friedrich 56–7
Herbert, Christopher 154
Hervey, James 29, 30, 31, 37, 77
   'Contemplations on the Night' 26–7
   'Meditations among the Tombs' 6, 24–6
Hoeveler, Diane Long 4, 45, 48, 102
Hogg, James
   Confessions of a Justified Sinner, 46
Hogle, Jerrold E. 12–14, 19, 30
Hole, Stephen
   'Ode to Terror' 37–9, 40
Hotz, Mary Elizabeth 121, 122
Hughes, William 73n30
Hume, David 17, 18–19

James, Simon J. 130–1
John, Juliet 113, 126
Jones, Darryl 175
Joyce, James 180, 195

Kant, Immanuel 32, 110–1
Keats, John 30, 189–90
Kennedy, J. Gerald 76, 83, 84–5
King, Thomas A. 157–8
Kipling, Rudyard
   'Wireless' 189–90
Ko, Charles 180, 195

Laycock, Thomas 129–30
Lee, Vernon 138–9
Lewes, G.H.
   The Physiology of Common Life 97, 98
Litvack, Leon 130, 132
Locke, John 62

Index

Lodge, Oliver 182
  Raymond 195
Lootens, Tricia 136n42
Lowe, Brigid 123
Luckhurst, Roger 170, 173

Machen, Arthur 4, 196
  'A Fragment of Life' 175
  The Great God Pan 9, 164, 171, 175–8, 188
  Hieroglyphics 173–5, 178
  The Hill of Dreams 180
  The Three Imposters 5, 9, 164, 180–5
Mansel, H.L. 96
Marsh, Richard
  The Beetle 189
melancholy 11, 13, 16, 17, 20, 27–30, 35, 36, 44–74, 83, 86–7, 88
Mellor, Anne K. 52, 59, 63–4
memory 44–74
Mesmer, Franz 6, 65, 94, 168, 195
Meyer, Moe 158
Mighall, Robert 106
Milton, John
  Comus 28, 37
  Lycidas 174
  Paradise Lost 55, 62
Mitchell, Charles 132
modernism 180, 195–6
Morton, Timothy 60, 61
Myers, F.W.H.
  Human Personality and Its Survival of Bodily Death 164, 170–3, 174, 176, 178, 179, 180, 185, 189, 191n11, 196

Nietzsche, Friedrich 110–1, 112
Noakes, Richard 169, 191n6

O'Leary, Joanna Shawn Brigid 125–6
Owen, Alex 168–9, 170

Pattern, Robert L. 125–6
Pfau, Thomas 14–15, 19, 24, 26, 32, 34, 41n4, 54–5, 56–7, 60
Pinch, Adela 18–19, 52–3
Poe, Edgar Allan 1–2, 3, 7, 71, 75, 76, 83, 89, 94, 95, 101, 102, 173–4
  Eureka 7, 78–81, 82, 83, 85, 86, 87, 89, 97, 99, 101
  'The Facts in the Case of M. Valdemar' 1, 7, 76, 77–8, 80, 94, 194
  'Ligeia' 7, 82, 83–5, 87
  'Mesmeric Revelation' 7, 76–7, 78, 79, 80, 81, 82, 89, 97, 189, 194
  'Morella' 7, 82, 83
  'The Murders in the Rue Morgue' 100
  'The Philosophy of Composition' 4, 82–3, 86–7, 88, 89, 99
  'The Purloined Letter' 101
  'A Tale of the Ragged Mountains' 7
  'William Wilson' 76, 86
Pound, Ezra 195
Punter, David 154, 155

Radcliffe, Ann 6, 11, 44, 50, 52, 60, 71, 193
  The Mysteries of Udolpho 6, 45, 52–4, 61, 64
  'On the Supernatural in Poetry' 36–7, 40
Rogers, Samuel
  'Ode to Superstition' 49–50
  The Pleasures of Memory 6, 46–9, 50, 51, 60, 71, 83
Rugg, Julia 120, 122

Sacks, Peter M. 12, 13, 14, 15, 49
Schiller, Friedrich 15, 32
Schoene-Harwood, Berthold 64
Schor, Esther 16–17
sensibility 11, 16–19, 39
Shakespeare, William
  Hamlet 36–7, 39
  The Merchant of Venice 187
Shelley, Mary 11, 71, 193
  Frankenstein 3, 6–7, 15, 24, 33, 40, 44, 50, 52, 54–64, 65–7, 68–9, 70, 91
  'On Ghosts' 60, 64, 66–7
Shelley, Percy 56
Shortt, S.E.D 169
Small, Helen 96
Smith, Adam 6, 18, 20, 23, 29, 36, 38, 45, 95, 107, 180, 193
  Theory of Moral Sentiments 16, 70, 86
Smith, Allan Lloyd 131–2
Smith, Andrew 10n8, 104n17

Index

Smith, Charlotte 11
  Elegaic Sonnets 6, 44, 50–2, 193
Spencer, Herbert 166, 167
Spenser, Edmund
  The Faerie Queene 28, 42n17
Stevenson, Robert Louis
  Strange Case of Dr Jekyll and My Hyde 173, 175
Stewart, Garrett 9–10n3
Stoker, Bram 3, 9
  Dracula 4, 5, 9, 24, 154, 164, 186–90
  The Jewel of Seven Stars 8, 144–8, 151, 152, 154, 155, 156, 160
  The Lady of the Shroud 8, 152–7, 163n30, 192n30
Sword, Helen 195

Tennyson, Alfred Lord
  In Memoriam 102
Thackeray, William Makepeace
  'On Going to See a Man Hanged' 108
Thompson, G.R. 79, 80
Torok, Maria 54, 131

uncanniness 45, 46, 69, 85–6, 87, 106, 125, 133
  see also Freud; Castle

Walpole, Horace
  The Castle of Otranto 12, 13, 14
Warton, Thomas
  The Pleasures of Melancholy 6, 27–30, 31, 36
Weidmann, Eugen 116
Wells, H.G. 167
West, Benjamin 66
White, Henry Kirke
  'Ode to H, Fuseli' 39–40
Wilde, Oscar 160
  The Picture of Dorian Gray 9, 157–60
Wolfreys, Julian 105n37
Wood, Claire 134n15
Wordsworth, William 172, 174
  'Tintern Abbey' 48, 59
Wynne, Catherine 157

Yeats, W.B. 195
Young, Edward 2, 47, 77, 193
  'Conjectures on Original Composition' 32–4, 40, 172
  Night Thoughts 2, 6, 19–22, 23, 24, 25, 26, 27, 29, 31, 32, 34, 35, 37, 38–9, 48, 49, 79, 92, 94, 133, 139

EU authorised representative for GPSR:
Easy Access System Europe, Mustamäe tee 50,
10621 Tallinn, Estonia
gpsr.requests@easproject.com

www.ingramcontent.com/pod-product-compliance
Lightning Source LLC
Chambersburg PA
CBHW070354240426
43671CB00013BA/2496